B+T ~3/66

Tsars, Mandarins, and Commissars

ALSO BY HARRY SCHWARTZ

The Red Phoenix
Russia's Soviet Economy
The Many Faces of Communism
Migratory Agricultural Labor in the United States
Russia Enters the 1960s (Editor)
Russia's Postwar Economy
Communist Economic Power

TSARS, MANDARINS, AND COMMISSARS

A History of Chinese-Russian Relations

by Harry Schwartz

J. B. LIPPINCOTT COMPANY

PHILADELPHIA AND NEW YORK

For Ruth

Preface

THIS VOLUME is an attempt to present the facts about the long history of Russian-Chinese relations in as brief and interesting a compass as possible. The effort is motivated by the belief that, for much of the period since World War II, the West in general and the United States in particular have made major mistakes in their conduct of foreign policy because of needless public ignorance about the long heritage of hate and conflict which weighs so heavily on Soviet-Chinese relations, and weighed upon it even at the height of seeming friendship and cooperation during the 1950's. The author's conviction is that this history teaches that the Sino-Soviet struggle which has so altered the political outlook of the 1960's is only secondarily an ideological struggle. Its primary components are much more nationalistic and racial distrust between Russians and Chinese, as well as competitive striving for power between the leaderships of the two countries, notably between Nikita S. Khrushchev and Mao Tse-tung. But the writer has striven—with what success only the reader can judge—to prevent his interpretation of this history from distorting his presentation of the facts of that history.

In recounting the history told here, the author has sought to give a bird's eye view of more distant periods, emphasizing general trends and key events. As the chronicle has come closer to the present, there has been more detail added to the picture. The greatest detail and the fullest account have been given about the politically shattering events of 1962 and 1963 which have ended the myth of Soviet-Chinese friendship and revealed the antagonism that was only briefly hidden by the alliance born of common dogma. This writer has sought to take into account the many major—and previously secret—revelations about Soviet-Chinese relations in the 1950's and early 1960's which were made public

7

in the exchange of verbal broadsides Peking and Moscow hurled at each other in the summer and fall of 1963.

The writer of a volume such as this has many debts, primarily to the researchers and historians who did the spade work in earlier years to produce much of the material employed here. It is the author's regret that the need to remain within a fixed size of book and the importance of recounting the Soviet-Chinese verbal duels which continued even while this book was being set in type forced the elimination of the extensive bibliography which had been prepared. However the notes indicate some of the major sources used and name some of the key earlier writers upon whom this book has drawn.

George Stevens of J. B. Lippincott Company made possible the writing of this volume, for which the author is grateful indeed. Stewart Richardson and Lavinia Russell of the same organization helped in many ways during the writing and printing. Dr. Allen Whiting was good enough to read most of the manuscript and made helpful suggestions, though he should not be blamed for errors or for this volume's interpretations. The author's wife, Ruth B. Schwartz, did yeoman service far above and beyond the call of duty in bearing with a writer in the agonies of composition and then copy-editing this volume and preparing the index. Thanks are due to the owners of copyrighted materials quoted in this volume for giving permission to reprint these materials. All errors in this volume are the author's sole responsibility, and the *New York Times*, the author's employer, is in no way responsible for the opinions expressed here.

HARRY SCHWARTZ

Scarsdale, N. Y.
November 3, 1963

Contents

Preface 7

I The Unnatural Alliance 11

II The Road to Nerchinsk 24

III From Kyakhta to St. Petersburg 37

IV Russian Imperialism in Victory and Defeat 62

V Tsarist Russia's Last Gains 80

VI Soviet Power vs. Chinese Nationalism in the 1920's 92

VII Russia, China and Japan in the 1930's 112

VIII World War II and Its Aftermath 129

IX The Two Communist Flowers 143

X The War of Words 197

XI The Past as Prologue 235

Notes 243

Appendix: Russian-Chinese Trade 248

Index 249

MAPS

following page 9
China, Siberia, and Soviet Central Asia
Territorial Changes along the Russo-Chinese Border since 1840

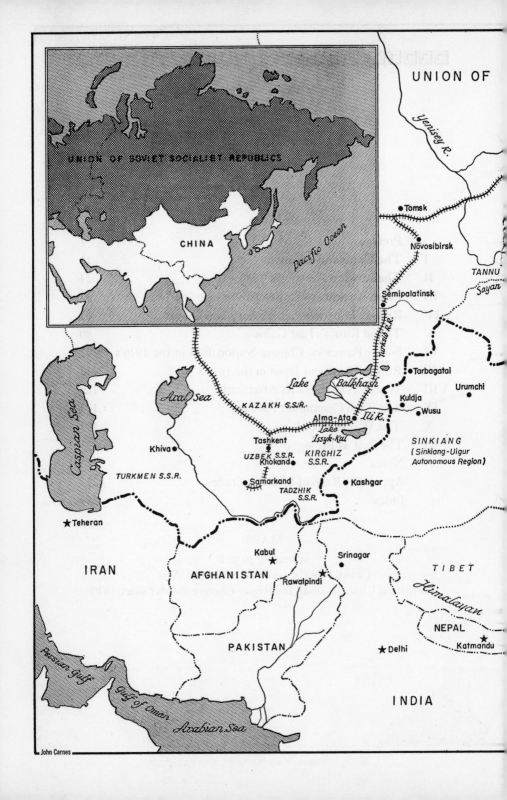

UNION OF

UNION OF SOVIET SOCIALIST REPUBLICS

CHINA

Pacific Ocean

Yenisey R.

Tomsk

Novosibirsk

Semipalatinsk

TANNU

Sayan

Tarbagatai

Urumchi

Lake Balkhash

Kuldja

Wusu

KAZAKH S.S.R.

Alma-Ata

Ili R.

Tashkent

Lake
Issyk-Kul

SINKIANG
(Sinkiang-Uigur
Autonomous Region)

Aral Sea

Khiva

UZBEK S.S.R.

KIRGHIZ
S.S.R.

Khokand

Caspian Sea

TURKMEN S.S.R.

Samarkand

TADZHIK
S.S.R.

Kashgar

Teheran

Kabul

Srinagar

TIBET

IRAN

AFGHANISTAN

Rawalpindi

Himalayan

NEPAL

Katmandu

Persian Gulf

PAKISTAN

Delhi

Gulf of Oman

Arabian Sea

INDIA

John Carnes

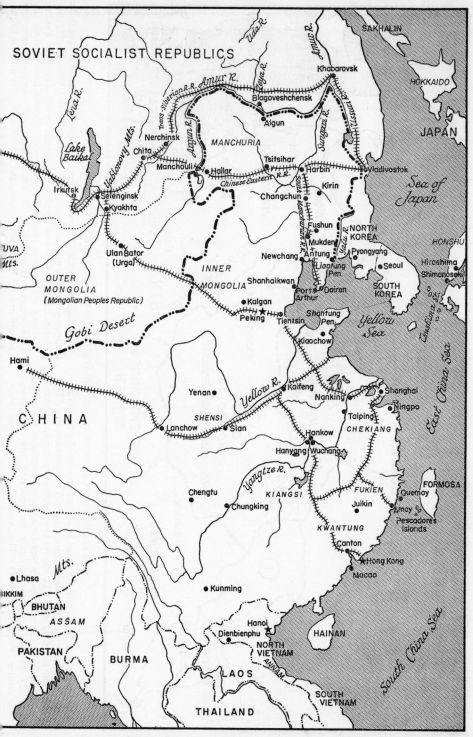

CHINA, SIBERIA, AND SOVIET CENTRAL ASIA

TERRITORIAL CHANGES ALONG THE RUSSO-CHINESE BORDER SINCE 1840

The map above shows border areas in or near the Soviet Union to which China may possibly assert future claims. The areas indicated by numbers on the map are: (1) the eastern section of Soviet Central Asia, whose inclusion in Russia is based mainly on treaties of the early 1860's; (2) Tannu Tuva was formally incorporated into the Soviet Union during World War II; (3) The Amur River Basin was taken by Russia under the Treaty of Aigun in 1858; (4) Sakhalin was fully reincorporated into the Soviet Union after World War II; (5) the Ussuri River Valley was obtained by Russia in the Treaty of Peking of 1860; (6) Korea's present divided political status derives from the 1953 Korean War truce; (7) Outer Mongolia's independence was recognized by Nationalist China, and later also by Communist China.

John Carnes

Tsars, Mandarins, and Commissars

CHAPTER I

The Unnatural Alliance

Surprise and incredulity dominated the Western world in the summer of 1963 as a furious battle of words raged between the planet's two great Communist-ruled nations. On July 31, 1963, for example, the government of Communist China declared in an official statement: "The indisputable facts prove that the policy pursued by the Soviet government is one of allying with the forces of war to oppose the forces of peace, allying with imperialism to oppose Socialism, allying with the United States to oppose China, and allying with the reactionaries of all countries to oppose the people of the world." In Moscow three days later the Soviet government asserted: "The leaders of China have shown to the whole world that their policy leads to the aggravation of international tensions, to further stepping up of the arms race, to still further expansion of its scope and scale. This position is tantamount to actual connivance with those who advocate world thermonuclear war, who are against the settlement of disputable international problems at a conference table."[1]*

The shock produced by this and other bitter Sino-Soviet exchanges that summer arose because this evidence contradicted what had for many years been the most basic assumption of American policy and American public opinion about the Cold War which had raged for almost two decades since the end of World War II. This assumption was the belief that the key fact of international politics was the struggle between the united forces of good against the unholy forces of evil, the former represented by the Western democracies and the latter by the Communist bloc under the leadership of the Sino-Soviet alliance. Only a few months before the public explosion of Moscow-Peking

* Superior figures refer to Notes at end of text.

11

enmity, the President of the United States had warned his people against attaching any great importance to earlier signs of discord between the two great Communist giants. To President Kennedy in early 1963, the dispute had seemed merely a quarrel over tactics, a dispute over the best means of burying the free world. This view was to be proved highly erroneous by the swift march of events which followed, but it flowed naturally from the belief—nurtured by the long Cold War—that the primary world struggle was essentially a kind of religious war, a contest to determine which of two competing ideologies would rule the world. Even after the United States, Great Britain and the Soviet Union had signed a limited nuclear test ban treaty in August 1963 and reciprocal Sino-Soviet denunciations over this action had become a daily event, American officials were still warning against exaggerating the importance of the break between Moscow and Peking. It was left to French President Charles de Gaulle, representative and leader of a far older and more sophisticated civilization, to express some essential truths which had long eluded American leaders and American public opinion alike:

> I will speak first on the ideological rupture, then about reality, that is the Moscow agreement [for a limited nuclear test ban]. The break? Over what ideology? During my lifetime, communist ideology has been personified by many people. There have been the eras of Lenin and Trotsky and Stalin—whom I knew personally—and of Beria and Malenkov and Khrushchev and Tito and Nagy and Mao Tse-tung. I know as many holders of the communist ideology as there are fathers of Europe. And that makes it quite a few. Each of these holders in his turn condemns, excommunicates, crushes and at times kills the others. In any event, he firmly fights against the personality cult of the others. I refuse to enter into a valid discussion of the ideological quarrel between Peking and Moscow. What I want to consider are the deep-rooted realities which are human, national and consequently international. The banner of ideology in reality covers only ambitions. And I believe that it has been thus since the world was born.[2]

It is the central thesis of this volume—a belief held by the author long before the climactic events of mid-1963—that President de Gaulle was more nearly right in July 1963 than President Kennedy had been six months earlier. The Sino-Soviet alliance was an unnatural one because the fundamental interests of those two nations were and are far more opposed than coincident. The long history of Chinese-Russian relations explored in this book provides abundant evidence of how conflicting the national interests of these two great nations have been and are. Only a widespread and needless ignorance of this history made possible the stereotyped views of the Sino-Soviet relationship which dominated United States thinking and policy during the 1950's and early 1960's.

Greater historical perspective might have enabled United States leaders and public opinion alike to understand at that time the full significance of the fateful event which occurred in Moscow on October 19, 1961. On that day a Chinese statesman, the scion of a great mandarin family, took a historic step. Rising to speak in the Kremlin before the Twenty-second Congress of the Soviet Communist party, the Premier of Communist China, Chou En-lai, declared:

> We hold that if a dispute or difference unfortunately arises between fraternal parties or fraternal countries, it should be resolved patiently in the spirit of proletarian internationalism and on the principles of equality and unanimity through consultations. Any public, one-sided censure of any fraternal party does not help unity, and is not helpful in resolving problems. To lay bare a dispute between fraternal parties or fraternal countries openly in the face of the enemy cannot be regarded as a serious Marxist-Leninist attitude. Such an attitude will only grieve those near and dear to us and gladden our enemies.[3]

At first glance these words seem mild, almost platitudinous. Actually they were a public declaration by China of political war against the rulers of the Soviet Union headed by Stalin's successor, Nikita Sergeyevich Khrushchev. Chou En-lai's words were a specific, direct and open refusal to accept the public denunciation of Albania, China's first modern European satellite, which Premier Khrushchev had delivered in that same hall before that same audience two days earlier. The immediate issue was Sino-Soviet rivalry over command of Albania, but Chou En-lai chose to ignore the difference of national interests and to phrase his criticism in ideological terms. His assertion that what Khrushchev had done "cannot be regarded as a serious Marxist-Leninist attitude" was a charge that the Moscow ruler had strayed from the true faith and was now a heretic.

The most perceptive observers of the Sino-Soviet relationship recognized the historic significance of this step at the time. They realized that the Red mandarin from China had boldly challenged the Communist Tsar of Muscovy in the very center of his realm. Their minds swept back to another October some 444 years earlier, to the day that Martin Luther chose to defy the Pope of Rome by posting his 95 Theses on the door of the castle church in Wittenberg. The analogy was intriguing. The fission of Christendom initiated by Luther had powerfully shaped the history of the West for almost half a millennium. Would the fission of the Communist world revealed by Chou En-lai in the Kremlin have comparable consequences? The potentials were certainly there.

But the full significance of this event was not realized at the time by either American policy makers or American public opinion. This failure of understanding occurred because a simple syllogism, derived from the logic of the Cold War, had been at the base of most United States thinking in this area since Mao Tse-tung conquered China's mainland in the late 1940's. Here are the premises and the conclusion drawn from them:

1. All Communists want to destroy the free world and establish world Communism.

2. The Soviet Union and Communist China are Communist-ruled nations.

3. Therefore, the Soviet Union and Communist China must be united in working to destroy the free world and to establish world Communism.

We can imagine Moslem thinkers of the Middle Ages arguing in a similar vein: all Christians want to destroy Islam and establish world Christianity. The nations of Western Europe are ruled by Christians. Therefore Western Europe must be united to destroy Islam and establish world Christianity.

From our vantage point in time we know how false any such Moslem reasoning turned out to be. In reality the history of Western Europe these past several centuries is one of frequent and bloody fratricidal strife, sometimes based on religious differences within Christianity, as during the Thirty Years' War, but more often derived from differences of national interest and ambition, as in the last two world wars. Anti-Moslem crusades have been unfashionable for centuries.

The essence of the matter is that normally neither men nor nations live exclusively on the basis of religion or its modern secular analogue, ideology. And even where religion has tended to be dominant in the past, that dominion has been no guarantee of unity. Each of the world's great religions has been split time and again as the many existing varieties of Christianity, Mohammedanism, Buddhism and Judaism testify. The relationship between two nations cannot be predicted in any simple manner for very long solely on the basis of the dominant religion or ideology. Along with religion or ideology, we must look at considerations of relative power, of national interest, of historic and cultural background, of level of economic development and—not least— the attitudes and ambitions of the national leaders of a given time. Let us try to look at the Soviet Union and China today from a broader perspective than that adopted in the simplistic syllogism recited above.

The Chinese possess one of the oldest and proudest civilizations of all history, a society which was accustomed to regarding foreigners—often with justice—as barbarians. Writing in 1939, Mao Tse-tung showed that he found national pride entirely compatible with his Communist beliefs:

In the history of Chinese civilization, agriculture and handicrafts have always been known as highly developed; many great thinkers, scientists, inventors, statesmen, military experts, men of letters, and artists have flourished, and there is a rich store of classical works. The compass was invented in China very long ago. The art of paper-making was discovered as early as 1,800 years ago. Block printing was invented 1,300 years ago. In addition, movable types were invented 800 years ago. Gunpowder was used in China earlier than in Europe. China, with a recorded history of almost 4,000 years, is therefore one of the oldest civilized countries in the world. . . .

All the nationalities of China have always rebelled against the foreign yoke and striven to shake it off by means of resistance. They accept a union on the basis of equality, not the oppression of one nationality by another. In thousands of years of history of the Chinese nation many national heroes and revolutionary leaders have emerged. So the Chinese nation is also a nation with a glorious revolutionary tradition and a splendid historical heritage.[4]

Until the middle of the nineteenth century, the Chinese felt they had every reason to be satisfied with their society and its culture, both of which they thought immeasurably superior to any others. For thousands of years the dominant Han people had survived through all vicissitudes, overcoming and absorbing conqueror after conqueror through their biological vitality and the attractiveness of their civilization. That civilization had been formed on the basis of ideas quite foreign to the West. In Confucius, Mo Tzu, Lao Tzu and other great shapers of their tradition, the Chinese felt they had great thinkers and exemplars without rival elsewhere. When Buddhism penetrated China almost 2,000 years ago, it was quickly absorbed and transformed, adding to and modifying the traditional Chinese philosophy and world outlook rather than ousting them. Christianity has had only peripheral and most superficial effects upon Chinese thinking, far less even than the minor impact of the Moslem religion which was adopted by some relatively small groups of Chinese subjects. China's self-satisfaction and high appreciation of its culture are best attested by the fact that for centuries the country was ruled under the Emperor by the mandarin bureaucracy whose members were selected and promoted on the basis of their performance on examinations testing their knowledge of the classical Chinese writings.

To the Chinese, their country traditionally was the Middle Kingdom, the head of a family of nations that included Japan, Siam, Korea, Annam and Burma. China, as the senior, had the responsibility for maintaining order within this family and coming to the aid of members when trouble struck. The other states were tributaries whose submission was shown by the periodic sending of envoys who performed the traditional *kowtow* before the Emperor, kneeling three times and knocking the head on the floor nine times. An envoy brought tribute to the Emperor and was allowed to sell goods from his own country which he had been permitted to bring with him duty-free. In turn, the Emperor gave the envoy, his retainers and the vassal king he rep-

resented rich gifts, presents often more valuable than those he
had brought. All this was a far cry from the Western concept of
equality between states.

The Chinese Emperor claimed to be the Son of Heaven and
ruler of all the world. The Book of Odes declared: "Under the
wide heaven, there is no land that is not the Emperor's, and
within the sea boundary of the land, there is none who is not a
subject of the Emperor." The Emperor and his people regarded as
barbarians all who did not accept Chinese civilization and culture.
As Professor Hsü has put it: "In their utter ignorance of the
beauty of the Chinese way of life and in their lack of sufficient
intellect to appreciate reason and ethics, the barbarians were considered no different from the lower animals." The duty of the
Emperor was to help civilize the barbarians, to chastise them if
need be and to guard the Empire against possible attack by the
barbarians. When Russia and China first met, therefore, and for
many decades afterward, it seemed to the men in Peking that
they had encountered a new tribe of barbarians, one to which the
precedents of the past could properly be applied.[5] Similar thinking was applied to the other Western nations, as well, in the early
phases of China's contacts with them. Perhaps the most generous
Chinese comment about Europeans before the nineteenth century was the assertion that while the Chinese alone had two eyes,
the Franks (that is, the Western Europeans) were one-eyed and
all of the earth's other peoples were blind.[6]

The rude and successful intrusion of the West into China in
the nineteenth century shattered this complacency as it quickly
became evident that neither Chinese philosophy nor its ancient
military lore were adequate to stand up to the military technology these new "barbarian" invaders possessed. But the ancient
pride was still strong, expressed even in this typical reform program presented by a high official, Feng Kuei-fen, in the mid-
nineteenth century:

> We have only one thing to learn from the barbarians, and that
> is strong ships and effective guns. . . . Funds should be al-
> lotted to establish a shipyard and arsenal in each trading port.
> A few barbarians should be employed and Chinese who are
> good in using their minds should be selected to receive instruc-
> tion so that in turn they may teach many craftsmen. . . .
> The intelligence and ingenuity of the Chinese are certainly

superior to those of the various barbarians; it is only that hitherto we have not made use of them. . . . There ought to be some people of extraordinary intelligence who can have new ideas and improve on Western methods. At first they may take the foreigners as their teachers and models; then they may come to the same level and be their equals; finally they may move ahead and surpass them. Herein lies the way to self-strengthening.[7]

Feng concluded his prescription with the exhortation that "the way to avoid trouble is to manufacture, repair, and use weapons by ourselves. Only thus can we pacify the empire; only thus can we become the leading power in the world; only thus can we restore our original strength, redeem ourselves from former humiliations, and maintain the integrity of our vast territory so as to remain the greatest country on earth." The words are worth remembering now, a century later.

From the point of view of China's present Communist rulers, Feng's advice was wrong because it overlooked the need to import a Western ideology, Marxism-Leninism, to revitalize the nation. The break with the older tradition implied thereby is clear, but it should not be overemphasized. The Chinese ability to modify and absorb imported doctrines has been shown before, and the ideological debates of the early 1960's have already demonstrated that Peking's understanding of Marxism-Leninism is by no means identical with the concept of that doctrine held further west.

It has been fashionable at times in the past to emphasize Russia's Asiatic heritage. The two centuries of Mongol domination and their aftereffects, both biological and cultural, are most often cited in this connection, along with the fact that Russia experienced neither the Reformation nor the Renaissance, which so powerfully molded Western and Central Europe.

But in comparison with China can there be any doubt that Russia belongs to the West biologically, culturally and historically? Russians, Ukrainians and Belorussians, who together make up some three-quarters of the Soviet population, are white men, the eastern representatives of the great Slavic linguistic branch of humanity whose western cousins are such unquestionably

European peoples as the Poles, the Czechs and the Serbs. It was almost a thousand years ago, in 988, that Vladimir, ruler of Kievan Rus, abandoned paganism for Christianity and made the Orthodox variety of this creed the dominant religion of Russia. Vladimir Monomakh, Grand Prince of Kiev from 1113 to 1125, had an Englishman's daughter as his wife. A century earlier his great predecessor Yaroslav had sired daughters who became queens of France, Hungary and Norway.

When Russia reformed under Muscovite leadership, ended Mongol dominion and began the expansion which brought it to its present borders, it was to the West that its rulers looked for ideas and technology. Peter the Great's services in reknitting the weakened ties with the West at the end of the seventeenth century and the first quarter of the eighteenth are too well known to need repetition. The intellectual giants of Western Europe were frequent and welcome guests at the court of Catherine the Great. Many a nineteenth century Russian nobleman spoke French more fluently than his native language. Napoleon was defeated by General Winter in Russia but the ideas of the French Revolution contributed much to the ferment in Russia during the last century of Romanov rule. And has anyone ever questioned that Pushkin, Tolstoy, Tschaikovsky, Glinka, Lobachevsky and Mechnikov belong to the main stream of western culture and science?

Most important for our present purpose is the strain of imperialism and expansionism which has been present in much Russian thinking these past 500 years. One aspect of this was enunciated by the monk Filofei a few decades after the fall of Constantinople. The original Rome had fallen to the barbarians, he declared, because it had lapsed into heresy. Constantinople had become the second Rome and had succumbed because of the same error. Now Moscow had become the third capital of the world, the third Rome. As subsequent developments were to show, many who came after Filofei shared his vision of Moscow's role in the world, even though they started from other assumptions. The great non-Communist Russian philosopher Nikolai Berdyayev wrote in the 1930's:

The Russian people have not realized their messianic idea of Moscow the Third Rome. . . . Instead of the Third Rome in

Russia, the Third International was achieved and many of the features of the Third Rome were transferred to the Third International. The fact that the Third International is not international but a Russian national idea is very poorly understood in the West. Here we have the transformation of Russian messianism. Western communists, when they join the Third International, do not understand that in joining the Third International they are joining the Russian people and helping to realize its messianic vocation.[8]

In China and Russia we have two very different peoples. One nation consists of men and women with what we call yellow skins; the other mainly of people whose skin colors we loosely lump together as white. Both are proud peoples and each has within its tradition ideas of racial and national superiority which are in their nature mutually incompatible. The Marxism-Leninism that united them during the 1950's and early 1960's was a recent accretion for both peoples, added to very different cultures, histories and world views. This was hardly the most auspicious background for a relationship of warm mutual confidence and trust. Perhaps what should surprise us is not that discord finally broke out into the open, but that the public façade of full unanimity and unmarred friendship could be kept up for as long as it was.

Adding to these differences of background is the vast gulf in economic development that now separates the Soviet Union and Communist China. Russia laid the foundation for modern industry and science more than half a century before the American Revolution. China did not begin to face up to the need for laying such foundations until about the time of the American Civil War. Tsarist Russia in 1913 was much more developed industrially and technically than was the China of 1950, while the average standard of living of the Russian peasant or worker in 1913 was well above anything which has yet been achieved in Communist China in the mid-1960's.

Today the Soviet Union, while probing the planets with its rockets, measures its economic and scientific strength boldly against that of the United States and dreams of achieving Utopian abundance by 1980. The China of today is a vast sink of poverty, dependent mainly upon the power of human muscles. And the

Chinese state is still not in a position to assure its people a ration of rice adequate for their strength and health. Russia today is relatively far richer in comparison to China than the United States is in comparison to the Soviet Union.

The rich man in his mansion does not usually see eye to eye with the beggar in his hovel, nor do the two usually feel any great common interest. This comparison may be helpful in understanding the relationship between Moscow's relatively affluent society and Peking's staggeringly poor society. The Chinese would be inhumanly virtuous if this obvious contrast did not excite their envy. Their resentment at what they consider Russia's miserliness in extending economic aid to China is suggested by more than a little evidence. The men in Moscow would be incredibly naive if they did not worry about the possibility of future threats to their relative prosperity from China. We know, of course, that the men in Moscow are not naive and have thought about these problems. In private conversations Premier Khrushchev and lower ranking Soviet officials have spoken openly of their concern. And concerned they may well be, for Russia has one-third China's population on a territory almost three times as large. May not a China of the future demand a more equitable sharing of *lebensraum* and natural resources between the "brotherly Soviet and Chinese peoples"? No more reassuring to Moscow are the population projections which forecast that the 700,000,-000 Chinese of today may increase to more than 1,500,000,000 souls by the year 2000. The year 2000, it should be added, is fewer years away than the years which have passed since Lenin's death in 1924.

The problem involved here, of course, is not Russia's alone. In the long run China's leaders—Communists or not—will surely demand a more equitable share of the entire world's resources, one giving their prolific people a "fairer portion" of the earth's land and other bounty than has been produced by the workings of history to date. From a Chinese point of view, the "injustice" of America's vast wealth spread among a people less than one-third as numerous as China's must seem even more flagrant than the Soviet good fortune. But the United States is a long way off on the other side of the vast Pacific Ocean. Russia with its long common border separating relatively empty and extremely rich Siberia from crowded China is literally next door.

What adds sharpness and urgency to these considerations, of course, is the long history of Soviet-Chinese disputes. As we shall see below, these stretch back at least to the middle of the seventeenth century, but the main discord to date has been concentrated in the period since 1850. Korea, Manchuria, Mongolia and Sinkiang have all been areas of bitter rivalry, while much of the present Soviet Far East was wrested from China by Russia only as recently as 1858–1860. A century is not long in the history of the Chinese nation, which prides itself on records stretching back four millennia. We need not wonder, therefore, that in early 1963 Communist China reminded Communist Russia that it had not forgotten the nineteenth century Muscovite imperialist forays against the hapless Manchu Empire. India has learned to its sorrow how seriously Communist China takes its border claims. Will the same lesson be taught Russia some day? The men in Moscow can only wonder, and prepare for the worst.

Before beginning our detailed discussion of the history of Russian-Chinese relations, a few words on the borderlands between the two nations may be helpful.

During the past several centuries, Russia and China have faced each other across a border stretching many thousands of miles, but breaking down naturally into three sectors. Proceeding from west to east, these three sectors are: the long boundary from the southwest to the northeast which separates Soviet Central Asia from Sinkiang (an area also known as Chinese Turkestan and, most recently, as the Sinkiang-Uigur Autonomous Region); then the long demarcation line drawn roughly due west to east separating Siberia from what used to be known as Outer Mongolia, now the independent Mongolian Peoples Republic; and finally the roughly crescent-shaped Far Eastern boundary—along the Amur River and its tributaries, the Argun and the Ussuri—which separates the Soviet Far East from Manchuria. The history of each of these boundaries —how it came into being, how it was altered and how its attempted alteration was frustrated at times—is a semi-separate story, since disputes and intrigues in one border area were often independent of developments elsewhere. This factor explains some of the complexity of the history recounted in this volume.

Much of the traditional Russian-Chinese boundary passes through difficult and unattractive country, often mountainous or desert-like in character and subject to extremes of heat and cold. On both sides of this vast boundary, comparatively few people lived in these borderlands before the twentieth century. Even as late as 1900 there were very few Han people—the basic group we call Chinese—among the inhabitants of China's border areas. In Sinkiang, the Moslem peoples had and have close historical, cultural and religious ties with the similar groups farther west in Soviet Central Asia. The political importance of that fact was underlined in September 1963 when the Peking regime revealed that tens of thousands of Sinkiang's inhabitants had fled across the border to Soviet territory in early 1962. The Mongols in Outer Mongolia were and are a comparatively small group spread over a vast area—much of it desert and poor pastureland. They are related historically and culturally both to the Mongols of China's Inner Mongolia and to some of the peoples of Siberia. The sensitivity of this division of the Mongols was vividly revealed in 1962 when the rulers of Outer Mongolia, with Soviet support, purged a high official on grounds he sought to glorify and exalt the memory of Genghis Khan. At the same time, in China's Inner Mongolia, Genghis Khan was being praised as a progressive figure in history, one whose conquests almost a millennium earlier had served the cause of mankind's advance. Finally we come to Manchuria—the original home of the last Chinese dynasty, that of the Manchu Emperors. During much of their rule over China, the Manchus sought to keep Manchuria sparsely settled and free of Chinese colonization.

On the Russian side of the border, as of 1900, the number of ethnic Russians living in Central Asia and Siberia was small. In many parts of these areas, Russians were greatly outnumbered by non-Russians. Siberia, we may recall, was for many decades a limbo to which political dissidents and criminals were exiled, though some bolder spirits among the peasantry came voluntarily, encouraged often by government subsidy and help. The conquered Moslem peoples of Central Asia—dreaming often of independence and of union with other Moslems—posed and still pose delicate political problems for the rulers of the Soviet Union. These geographic, political, ethnic and demographic factors have all played a role in determining the decisions taken by both sides in the numerous Russian-Chinese confrontations across the border, as well as in influencing the outcome of these confrontations.

CHAPTER II

The Road to Nerchinsk

IN THE MIDDLE of the sixteenth century, long after the discovery of America, the government of Ivan the Terrible had little knowledge of China. When the bold British adventurer Antony Jenkinson came to Moscow in the 1550's to begin his search for an overland route to China for the Muscovy Company, he got permission to traverse the Tsar's realm toward his goal, but little information. In the 1580's the Moscow regime sent emissaries to Siberia. They sought answers to questions that were put this way: "Where is the Chinese state? How rich is it? Is there anything we can get from it?"

But there had been earlier contacts between Russians and Chinese, many of them. Russia and China, after all, had been parts of the great Mongol empire at its height in the late thirteenth century. Russian princes such as Alexander Nevsky, who traveled to the Grand Khan's court in Karakorum to receive their *yarlik*, or patent of rule, must have met Chinese, many of whom played prominent roles at the court of the Mongol rulers. Kublai Khan—he whom Marco Polo observed and served—used thousands of drafted Russian soldiers when he began his major campaign to conquer South China in 1267. In the 1330's the Grand Khan's capital was in Peking and one of its military forces was a special Russian division stationed nearby. The Russians were settled on lands north of Peking and supplied with clothes, oxen, tools and seeds. Their obligation was to supply the imperial table with all the different kinds of game and fish which abounded in the area's forests, rivers and lakes. Thousands of Russian captives were enslaved and sent to Peking to serve the khan. Centuries later, when the first Russian envoys arrived in Peking to begin the modern history of Sino-Russian relations, they found much in the etiquette of the Chinese court which reminded them of the Tsar's court in Moscow, more evidence of the impact of the common Mongol rule.

Memories of the contacts with China during the Mongol era may have been dim or non-existent in sixteenth century Russia, but the memory of the Mongol rule itself has never been eradicated from Russian national memory. The belief grew in later centuries that Russia's backwardness compared to the West was the price of Russian heroism in protecting the ungrateful West from the warriors of the khans. The great Russian poet Aleksander Blok put it this way in his famous poem, *The Scythians:*[1]

> Centuries of your days are but an hour to us,
> Yet like obedient guards
> We've held a shield between two hostile races:
> Europe, and the Mongol hordes.

Blok calls on Europeans to join Russians as friends, putting the alternative in these graphic terms:

> But we, we will no longer shield you
> Nor fight at all,
> Content observing with our narrow eyes
> The death brew boil.

> Nor shall we flinch to see the ferocious Hun
> Pillage each corpse,
> Herd all his horses into church and burn
> Mounds of white flesh.

> Ah, Old World, before you have perished, join
> Our fraternal banquet. Hear
> Perhaps for the last time summoning you
> The barbaric lyre!

The argument Blok put forward in his poem is one that has been made in prose more than once these past few years by Russians conversing privately with Western friends. Now, of course, it is the Chinese hordes they have in mind.

China and Russia first faced each other as antagonists across a disputed border in the 1650's. The confrontation took place less than a decade after the Manchu dynasty had taken power in Peking. It was an inevitable byproduct of the remarkable burst

of energy which brought Russian dominion over much of northern Asia during the late sixteenth and early seventeenth centuries.
The secret of that remarkable expansion was stated succinctly
much later by Dostoyevsky when he declared: "In Europe we
were hangers-on and slaves, whereas we shall go to Asia as
masters. In Europe we were Asiatics, whereas in Asia we, too, are
Europeans."[2] The small, poor and primitive peoples who in-
habited Siberia were far more backward even than the subjects
of Ivan the Terrible and the early Romanovs. These weak and
disunited tribes had even less chance to stop the Russian conquest than had—thousands of miles away—the far more highly
civilized Aztecs and Incas of stopping the Spaniards under
Cortez and Pizarro. The Russian with the gun was the military
master of the dark-skinned native with primitive weapons and
inferior military organization.

It was a motley crew indeed that conquered Siberia for the
Russian Tsar, and only handfuls of men were involved in the
initial conquests. Vast areas were seized for Moscow by bands
of adventurers numbering only tens or hundreds of individuals.
The great Russian merchant family, the Stroganovs, provided
much of the initial impetus and financing for the great push eastward. The men who actually explored and conquered Siberia
were mainly Cossack freebooters, runaway serfs, vagrants and
other refugees from the ordered hierarchical society of the Tsar.
Their small groups traveled eastward, usually following the
great river systems of Siberia initially and then spreading out
along the tributary streams. They fought battles as the need
arose, withstood the rigors of Siberia's extreme cold and almost
as extreme heat, and overcame hunger and disease. To buttress
their power, they built rude forts at strategic points from which
they ruled the natives, forced them to swear allegiance to the
Tsar and collected tributes of furs and provisions. Greed, the
desire for adventure and fear of what would happen to them if
they returned to Old Russia drove these men on across the vast
distances. Rabble and cutthroats they may have seemed to the
Tsar and his court, but they brought Russia a vast domain whose
full potentials still remain to be realized in the future. The bulk
of this vast work of exploration and conquest took place between
1582 and 1639. By the latter year Russians had reached the
Pacific. A new era of history had been opened, but few men of
the time realized the enormous significance of the event.

This easy and rapid expansion into a power vacuum stopped only when the Russian force collided with another power of comparable strength, the Chinese under the direction of the Manchus. To the Chinese and their rulers the Russians were barbarians, fit only to be tribute-paying subjects of the Emperor if that could be accomplished. It took decades before the Chinese court was willing to treat with the Russians on an equal basis. To the crude but vigorous and expansion-minded Russians, the strength of the new antagonist came as an unwelcome shock, but the riches of the Chinese empire stimulated thoughts of gains from trade and even richer gains from future conquest. The strength of Russian imperialist aspirations and feelings of superiority is suggested by this extract from a poem by Gavrila Derzhavin, the eighteenth century predecessor of Pushkin, who praised the ideal reign of Catherine II and expressed the hope that

> Peoples savage and remote
> Covered still with wool and scales,
> Dressed only with leaf and bark,
> And adorned with wings of birds,
> Should all gather at her throne,
> Hear the gentle voice of Law,
> So that tears should run in torrents
> Down their swarthy sunburned faces.
> They should cry and understand
> The bliss of living in our time,
> Should abandon their equality
> And all subject be to Her.[3]

It was through Mongolia that the first modern direct contact between Moscow and Peking took place. As the Russians moved into this area in the early 1600's and communicated with the nomadic and semi-nomadic peoples there, they learned of a great and rich civilization far to the southeast. Here is the way *Voyevod* Volynsky put the astonishing news in a message to the Tsar in 1608:

Beyond the land of Altyn Khan of the Mongols, three months travel away, is the country of Kitai. Here there are towns built of stone, and dwellings such as are found in Moscow. The Tsar of Kitai is stronger and richer than the Altyn Khan. There are many churches in the town with bells that ring. But these churches are without crosses and we do not know of what religion they are. The people live like Russians, they possess

weapons, and they trade with different countries from which
they obtain precious objects from all parts of the world.[4]

The news was fascinating and intriguing; it raised rich perspectives for the future, though it may have brought forebodings
to some far-sighted men. But more information was needed. In
1618 the *voyevod* of Tomsk, Prince Kurakin, decided to send a
mission directly to Peking. He chose the Cossacks Ivan Petlin
and Peter Kozylov. They must have been brave and hardy men
for they reached their destination following a path that can be
approximately marked on a modern map through the cities
Tomsk-Kuznetsk-Ulan Bator-Kalgan-Peking. The envoys received a message from the Chinese Emperor indicating his willingness to trade with the Russians, and they brought it back to
the Siberian city of Tobolsk. But since no one in Tobolsk could
read the language of the message it lay in the archives there for
more than half a century before being translated into Russian.

The Petlin-Kozylov mission thus had no practical results. But
as the seventeenth century wore on, the two nations' knowledge
about each other increased. Moreover, their direct and indirect
contacts became more frequent. In Mongolia itself there was
sharp rivalry as the Russians and the Manchus intrigued to extend their sway over this vast area. In 1634 the Russians scored
a diplomatic *coup* when they induced the Mongol Altyn Khan
to sign a document acknowledging himself a vassal of the Tsar.
The Mongols became trade intermediaries between Russia and
China. Their caravans brought Chinese silks, silver and other
goods to Tomsk. It is a measure of the Russians' continued ignorance about China that the trade records for Tomsk for such years
as 1640, 1652 and 1653 give no indication of Chinese goods being
received there. A Russian chronicler explains that at the time
even silk cloth was not regarded as a Chinese product in Russia.[5]
But the real Russian-Chinese confrontation came in the second
half of the seventeenth century, when the Russians went far beyond Lake Baikal and began to settle along the Amur River in
what is now the Soviet Far East.

The Russians arrived in the Amur River Basin almost simul-
taneously with the Manchu conquest of China, in particular the
Manchu capture of Peking in 1644. An expedition headed by
Vasily Poyarkov left Yakutsk in 1643 and reached the Amur

Basin after crossing the Stanovoi Mountains. They went from the Zeya River to the Amur and explored the latter to its mouth in the Pacific. When Poyarkov finally managed to return to Yakutsk in 1646, he brought back many valuable furs and a detailed description and maps of the territories and rivers he had traversed. A Cossack *ataman*, Yerofei Pavlovich Khabarov (the modern city of Khabarovsk is named after him), began the job of Russian colonization in this new area, dreaming of a Russian peasant paradise in the fruitful land that had been discovered. He took 70 men from Yakutsk on his first expedition in 1649, and then brought several hundred more in 1651. They founded a number of small towns, notably Albazin, and Russian farmers and hunters began to spread along the Amur. The local Daur people were easily defeated when they tried to resist this colonization; their arrows were no match for Khabarov's muskets and cannon. But behind the Daurs, the Achans and other native peoples were the Manchus, who had noted the Russian arrival with great uneasiness and who were determined to defend what they regarded as their domain. And the Manchus had some guns and cannons comparable to those the Russian freebooters possessed.

The first battle between Russians and troops of the Chinese empire took place at the mouth of the Ussuri River in 1652. Some 2,000 Manchu troops attacked the Russian fort there and at first won the upper hand. But, according to the Russian account, a desperate Cossack counterattack sent the Manchus fleeing in disorder after hundreds of their troops had been killed. If the Russian account is true, the Russians won this first battle. But the Cossacks gave up the fort and retreated, apparently fearing further attacks.

This battle of Achansky Gorod and the date it began, March 24, 1652, do not loom large in military history. By modern standards it was a mere skirmish. But symbolically it was a major milestone in the history of Asia. The Russian effort to seize more territory had met its first Chinese resistance. The results of the clash itself were indecisive, but a pattern had been set for the centuries ahead.

The significance of this first clash was not lost on Moscow. It decided to send an envoy to China to try to negotiate the border disputes and also to get an agreement for trade between the two countries. His instructions also included the injunction "to learn

secretly the Chinese military strength, and all the routes into
the country; and to acquire information on the customs, population, financial condition and economic wealth of the country."[6]
The man chosen as envoy was a nobleman, Fyedor Isakovich
Baikov. He was given 50,000 rubles from the Tsar's treasury and
instructed to buy goods in Russia for resale in China. He left
Moscow in 1653 and reached Peking in March 1656, bringing
Russian leathers, furs and diamonds with him. Baikov had a hard
time in Peking. The Chinese, determined to have Russia's inferiority acknowledged, demanded that Baikov *kowtow* to the
Emperor and give the Tsar's message to a subordinate official
rather than to the Emperor directly. Baikov regarded these conditions as insulting and refused to accede to them. He did not see
the Emperor, as a result, but he did sell his goods at a profit before he departed in 1658. When he returned, he brought much
valuable information. Even before Baikov had returned to Moscow, a second mission headed by one Perfilyev departed from
Moscow in 1658 with instructions both to negotiate and trade.
Perfilyev was received more hospitably in Peking when he arrived in 1660, and an exchange of presents between the Tsar and
the Emperor took place. But the Chinese felt that the letter
Perfilyev brought was lacking in respect and refused to make
any diplomatic agreements with him.

Even while these diplomatic efforts were being made, however,
clashes between Russian and Chinese forces continued in the
Amur River Valley during the 1650's. Moscow sent out a regular
force of troops, several thousand in number, to this region. The
intention was to lay the basis for permanent occupation regardless of what the Chinese might do. But the plans to build forts
and gather provisions for an even larger force of troops to come
later miscarried. This Army of the Amur dwindled in size and
strength as its ranks were thinned by cold, desertion and disease,
and as much of its supplies and equipment was stolen. In 1654
what remained of this army went down the Sungari River under
the command of Onufrei Stepanov and fought a major engage-
ment with a Manchu fleet. Stepanov lost some of his boats and
much of his artillery and supplies as well as many of his men in
this battle. He decided to retreat and go into winter quarters at
the mouth of the Kamara River where a fort, Kamarskoy Os-
trog, was built. In March 1655 a large and well equipped Chinese

force assailed the fort. The Chinese attacked vigorously for three weeks and several times came close to breaking into the fort, but at last they withdrew, apparently for lack of provisions. His forces greatly depleted by battle losses and disease, Stepanov now settled down to several years of freebooting activity, forcing the natives to give him furs and such food as they had. The Manchus decided to try to expel the invaders by starving them out, instructing the natives to leave their homes and cease cultivating crops. Stepanov tried to go on the offensive in 1658 and sailed down the Sungari again. This time the Manchus were well prepared and waited for him with a warfleet of some 47 boats, far stronger than Stepanov's force. The battle was soon over and the Chinese gained a clear-cut victory. Two years later, in 1660, the Manchus under Bahai defeated another Russian force under *Voyevod* Pashkov at Kufatan village. For the time being at least, Russian expansion had been halted by Chinese military power.

But the Amur region remained free of Russians only briefly. In the 1660's new Russian settlers and troops arrived and built forts and towns. This led to sporadic but indecisive fighting. The irritation to Russian-Chinese relations this produced was intensified when the Russians gave refuge to a native noble, the Tungus prince Gantimur, and his tribe. Gantimur had occupied a high military post under the Manchus and helped them in their earlier battles against the Russians. The Manchus demanded repeatedly that he be returned and were embittered when the Russians stalled under one pretext after another.

In the course of the negotiations over Gantimur, an incident occurred which casts a revealing light on the psychology and aspirations of these early Russians on the Amur. This was the dispatch to Peking by the *voyevod* of Nerchinsk, Danilo Arshinsky, of a document demanding that the proud Chinese Emperor become a subject of the Tsar. Here is the text of this extraordinary demand:

> The Great Sovereign, Tsar and Grand Duke Alexei Mikhailovich, Autocrat of all of Great, Little, and White Russia, Master of numerous states, already retains under his supreme control several tsars and kings and their states, to whom His Majesty the Tsar grants favors and lends assistance. The Bogdoi Khan [Emperor of China] would do well likewise to beg for the

protection of His Majesty the Tsar . . . and to become a *protégé* under his supreme control. The Great Sovereign, Tsar, etc., then would lavish his favors on Bogdoi Khan, grant him his imperial protection, and defend him against all enemies. And the Bogdoi Khan, himself forever protected under the supreme control of His Majesty the Tsar, would pay a tribute to the Great Sovereign, while his subjects would trade freely with the Tsar's subjects to the profit of both states.[7]

The sheer insolence of the demand takes the breath away, especially when one remembers that it was addressed to the head of an empire which traditionally considered itself natural master of all nations. Presumably Ignaty Milovanov, the envoy who brought this message, had the good sense when in Peking to see that this demand did not reach Chinese eyes. His life would almost certainly have been forfeit had the Emperor known of this presumption.

The importance of the Gantimur incident—which disturbed Sino-Russian relations for two decades—arose from the competition between the two powers for the allegiance of the native peoples in the areas where the two empires were meeting. The ability of Gantimur and other refugees to escape Manchu vassalage by receiving Russian protection was a blow to the prestige and power of the Chinese rulers. The political and propaganda importance of this blow was fully appreciated by each side. In the end the Russians won; Gantimur, who became a convert to Christianity, was not returned.

Moscow in the mid-1670's was in no hurry to settle either the border or the refugee problems. It did not have the power in the area to impose settlements of its own. Moreover, there were differences of opinion among the Russians, some urging efforts to push forward rapidly against the Chinese and others urging a more cautious policy. Yuri Krizhanich, a representative of the latter school, warned against adventurism here, writing: "Only our enemies are interested in turning us away from realizable undertakings and to push us on to things impossible to carry out. Should the Russian people plunge into a stupid war with China, the Germans and the Turks will take advantage of the opportunity and seize the Russian state." The Russians therefore stalled on the question of Gantimur's return, pleading one pretext after another to explain why they could not return him. But finally

Nikolai Gavrilovich Spathari, a Greek by origin, was sent from Moscow to the Manchu court in 1675. A recent Russian writer has complained in these terms of Spathari's reception in Peking:

Spathari's negotiations with the Manchu mandarins met with great difficulties. The mandarins demanded the execution of degrading ceremonies, showed arrogance and disrespect to the envoy, and finally established a prison regimen for the members of the mission. Russian merchants arriving with the mission were forbidden to communicate with Chinese merchants and they were allowed to buy Chinese goods only in one specially set up store. The Manchus set up fixed, artificially low prices for the Russian goods brought along with the mission, and Chinese merchants violating this trading procedure were mercilessly punished.[8]

Other sources make it clear the matter was more complex. On the basic issue, Spathari won. This was the Russian demand that dealings between the two countries be on a basis of equality. The symbol of this victory was the fact that Spathari was not required to *kowtow* when he met the Emperor. The sensitivity of the issue is evidenced by the fact that the official court bulletin put out a version of the negotiations which was far from the actuality. According to this:

The White Khan of Russia sent his subject Nikolai Gambriolovich [sic] with tribute of local articles. His presentation was to the effect that Russia lay far away in remote obscurity; that from ancient times there had been no relations with China; that he [the Tsar] was ignorant of Chinese letters and unacquainted with the proper style of address, that he now inclined toward civilization, expressed his devotion, and was desirous to open tribute relations.[9]

Such limited success as Spathari achieved on his mission was due to his contact with the Jesuits who served the Chinese Emperor as mathematicians, astronomers and, in this case, as translators. One of these Jesuits, Father Verbiest, became a close confidant of Spathari and the two men planned together the Russian approach to the Emperor. As a result, at this key early diplomatic negotiation between Russia and China, Latin became the common language of communication. Spathari's note to the Emperor, in Latin, asked the Manchu ruler to send an envoy to Moscow, to permit free travel of merchants between the two countries, to permit an annual exchange of Russian goods for Chinese silver, to permit precious stones to be sent to Russia and to permit skilled Chinese craftsmen to migrate to Russia. Of the border questions and Gantimur there was no mention.

Not unnaturally, this communication displeased the Chinese court, which was not interested in mere matters of trade. The Chinese answer made three points. Complaining of the past futile attempts to regain Gantimur, the Chinese reply demanded the Tungus prince be sent to Peking with a Russian ambassador. It called for this ambassador to be a reasonable man who would perform the customary ritual at the Chinese court, and it demanded that peace be established on the border. These were the Chinese conditions for good relations with Russia. If they were not fulfilled, the mandarins threatened, Chinese armies would wipe out the Russian settlements and forts on the Amur. After three and a half months in Peking, Spathari was forced to leave.

In the early 1680's Peking moved to solve the problem of the border. It was anxious for a resolution because it was preparing for war against the Western Mongols and did not want to become involved in simultaneous conflict on two fronts against two foes. Two steps were therefore taken. One was the dispatch by the Emperor of a letter to the commander of the Russian base at Albazin demanding that he give up the city and leave the Amur. In what may have been a bit of psychological warfare, the Emperor promised to treat the Russians leniently and offered them the opportunity to serve in his forces if they wished. More important were the moves made to get ready for military action. High Chinese officials were sent to the Amur region to scout the situation and also to begin building ships and gathering supplies for a large, well trained army. Skirmishes were renewed; orders were given to destroy all food supplies in the area of operations in an effort to starve out the Russians, and the systematic destruction of the Russian forts on the Amur was begun. Finally the town of Albazin was isolated. In June 1685 the Chinese under General Peng Chen attacked. After a few days' resistance the defenders sued for peace. Most of the remaining Russians were allowed to leave with their arms for the Russian base at Nerchinsk; a few enlisted with the Chinese forces. Albazin itself was destroyed.

Later in 1685 the Russians returned to Albazin and built an

even stronger fort there. At about the same time the Manchu Emperor sent a letter to Moscow, using two Russians as messengers, demanding that the Tsar's forces leave the Amur region and thus remove the main hindrance to peace and friendship between Russia and China. Before a reply could be received from Moscow, the Chinese forces attacked Albazin again, in July 1686. The much smaller Cossack force fought well and bravely, and the Manchus had to retire from their siege at the onset of winter. In November 1686 Peking received word from Moscow that the Russians were willing to negotiate. The peace party in Peking persuaded the Emperor to accept the idea of negotiations, and a renewed Manchu attack on Albazin was ordered halted when the small remaining force of defenders was almost defeated. Thus, in the spring of 1687 the sporadic Russian-Chinese war on the Amur which had lasted for a quarter of a century came to an end.

Negotiations finally took place in 1689 at Nerchinsk. Russia was represented by Fyedor Alekseyevich Golovin, a former tutor of Peter the Great. He was esteemed by Peter as something of an expert on China, and he insisted that great time and expense be taken to assure that he had a properly colorful and impressive costume and trappings with which to meet the Chinese. When he finally arrived in the Amur region he was accompanied by some 2,000 soldiers, diplomats, scribes and serving people. But the Chinese delegation which arrived for the negotiations was far larger, grander, more impressive and—what was to prove decisive at key points in the negotiations—it had many more soldiers. The Chinese party headed by Prince San-go-tu is estimated to have numbered 15,000. The negotiations began with both sides presenting exaggerated demands. The Chinese delegation suggested the boundary between the two countries be set in the neighborhood of Lake Baikal and the Lena River, arguing that the area east of this had belonged to Mongols who were vassals of China. Golovin for his part called for the Amur River to be fixed as the boundary. As the negotiations proceeded, relations between the two sides grew very tense. The Jesuit Fathers Gerbillion and Pereira, who had come as translators, exerted themselves in the role of intermediaries seeking to bring the two sides together, but finally the Manchu prince threatened that if his concessions were not accepted his superior forces would attack both Nerchinsk and Albazin. Faced with this threat, Golovin moderated

his position and a compromise agreement, the Treaty of Nerchinsk, was signed on August 27, 1689. The first major chapter
in the history of Russian-Chinese relations thus came to an end
with a document which was the first treaty between China and
any European power. The official text of the treaty was in Latin
and this was the only copy signed by both plenipotentiaries.

The Treaty of Nerchinsk recognized Chinese rule over most
of the Amur Basin. It had six clauses. The first two defined the
common boundary, which was fixed at the Argun River and from
that along the Amur to south of the Kerbi River, a tributary of
the Amur. Then the boundary was set at the ridge of the
Yablonovy and Stanovoi Mountains whose southern slopes and
whose rivers running into the Amur were defined as Chinese
territory. No boundary was set in the Uda River Valley and
this was left for future delimitation. The third clause provided
for demolition of the Russian town of Albazin, and for all of its
people and property to be moved to Russian territory. All refugees who had fled from either side earlier were to be allowed to
remain where they were, but all future refugees would be
handed back to the authorities of the country they had come
from. Clause Five provided for free travel between the two countries by their citizens having proper passports and wishing to
carry on commerce and other private business. The final clause
declared that all previous quarrels between the two sides would
be forgotten, and no claims arising from such quarrels would be
entertained. If citizens of one country committed crimes in the
other they were to be handed over to their own nation's authorities for execution.[10]

A Soviet encyclopedia issued in 1954 hails the Treaty of Nerchinsk as a "great success of Russian diplomacy," pointing out
that it confirmed Russian possession of Eastern Siberia.[11] But
subsequent developments were to show that Russia was by no
means satisfied with the gains ratified in Nerchinsk. As we shall
see, Russia wanted not only the Amur Basin which had been
denied it at Nerchinsk but also much beyond. From the Chinese
point of view, however, the Nerchinsk Treaty was a victory in
that for 170 years it halted Russian imperialism's progress in the
Far East. Prince San-go-tu had drawn a line which was to last
almost two centuries. Few others who negotiated with Russia
in that era could make a comparable claim.

CHAPTER III

From Kyakhta to St. Petersburg

VOYEVAT ILI TORGOVAT (Fight or Trade), these were the two alternative Far Eastern policies for Russia which Peter the Great turned over in his mind at the beginning of the eighteenth century. Sometimes he dreamed of extending his dominion to the Great Wall of China itself. But the main line of his policy, and that of his successors until the middle of the nineteenth century, was more cautious. There was sympathy at the Romanov court for the adventurers who time and again suggested a bolder policy against China. But Russia's resources were limited; there were frequent wars and threats of wars on Russia's European frontiers; the Far East was many thousands of miles away from St. Petersburg and Moscow; and the account the Chinese forces had given of themselves in the fighting before Nerchinsk convinced the more sober heads in the Russian capital that the potential gains did not warrant the likely costs of an active aggressive policy. For roughly a century and a half after the Treaty of Nerchinsk, therefore, China was a secondary preoccupation of Russia's. Diplomacy, intrigue and trade were the instruments of Russian policy toward China during this period until it was climaxed at the end of the 1850's by a series of major gains at China's expense. Those gains proved that the expansionist dreams of earlier generations had not been forgotten.

The Treaty of Nerchinsk had defined the extreme eastern section of the Russian-Chinese border, but it had not solved all problems between the two nations. It left undefined the Russian border with Mongolia, an area in which there had been Russian-Chinese rivalry during much of the seventeenth century. Moreover, the Russians were interested in permanent and extensive trade arrangements. They knew their abundant supply of Sibe-

37

rian furs commanded an active and profitable demand in China. Peter the Great's advances in stimulating Russian industry substantially widened the list of goods Russia wanted to sell in China. And from China the Russians wanted silver, precious stones of various kinds and other more mundane but useful goods, notably tea.

Russia's first diplomatic move after Nerchinsk was to send a new envoy to Peking, the West European merchant Izbrand Ides. His mission had several objectives: to set up regular trade arrangements; to find out what Russian goods could be sold in China; to arrange for the return of Russian prisoners of war and refugees living in China; and to get permission to build a Russian Orthodox church in Peking, among others. When he got to Peking in 1693, Ides did not find a particularly good atmosphere for his negotiations. The Chinese rulers were not very interested in trade and they were suspicious of Russia's intentions and maneuvers in Mongolia. The mandarins were glad, therefore, to utilize a detail which they interpreted as a slight on the dignity of the Chinese Emperor, the fact that in the Tsar's letter Ides had brought, the titles of the Tsar were recited before those of the Emperor. Ides was humiliated at a public audience and his letter returned to him. But the envoy persisted and his stay was not without fruit after almost a year's negotiations. Russian trade caravans were to be permitted to arrive in Peking once every three years and to stay for 80 days, and Russia could trade without paying duties on the goods it exported and imported. But Ides could not get permission for a Russian church to be built in Peking. To his arguments that Russian *émigrés* there needed a church which could also serve the Russian merchants, the Manchus replied loftily: "It is impossible that churches for all neighboring and distant states be established in Peking." Behind this refusal was probably the Chinese fear that such a church would become a center for Russian intrigue and influence in the capital. The Jesuits, who at this time still commanded considerable influence in Peking, also could hardly have been favorable toward establishment of a rival Christian church in a capital whose rulers the Roman Catholic Church hoped to win over.

Peter the Great spurred the trade with China, seeing in it a source of the wealth he needed to finance his wars and his domestic industrialization program. The trade grew swiftly. The first trade expedition sent by his treasury in 1693 carried goods worth

41,900 rubles; by 1710 such expeditions were bringing goods worth 200,000 rubles. Peter was interested in maximizing his treasury's profits. Annoyed by the competition of private traders, he prohibited private commerce in 1706. But private enterprise was not to be stilled so easily; illegal Russian caravans arrived in Peking, apparently often posing as official missions, while the personnel of the treasury caravans continued to make sure that they personally profited from the long and arduous trips.

A growing shadow was cast over this thriving commerce, however, by Chinese suspicions of Russian intentions and activities in Mongolia. The Mongols had split into many rival groups and were very greatly weakened after the heyday of their empire had passed. One of the regional Mongol rulers, the Altyn Khan, had supposedly signed in 1634 a document recognizing he was a subject of the Tsar, and the Chinese feared Russian claims arising from that act of submission. Chinese suzerainty over Mongolia was established during 1688–1696, in part as the result of brilliant military victories by the forces of Emperor Kang-Hsi over the Western Mongol troops led by Prince Galdan who had good relations with Russia.

Chinese suspicions of Russia in Mongolia arose from several factors. One was the growing importance and activity of private Russian merchants in Urga (later Ulan Bator) in Outer, or Northern, Mongolia. A second cause was the series of attempts by Peter the Great's emissaries to convert the Mongol spiritual leader in Urga to the Russian Orthodox faith. But the most serious factor around 1720 was the increasing flight of Mongols to Russian territory, flight induced by their unwillingness to supply Chinese armies in Mongolia with the horses and other provisions they demanded. The Treaty of Nerchinsk had provided for the return of such deserters, but the Russians ignored it, much to Chinese annoyance. As a result of these suspicions, China made a series of efforts to isolate Mongolia from Russia. But for full success the Chinese needed a formal treaty clearly defining the border between Russia and China, and they pressed for one while the Russians stalled.

The Chinese began showing their displeasure increasingly after 1710. They tightened controls over Mongolia and sought to prevent contacts between local Mongol khans and the Russian government. A Russian caravan that arrived in Peking in 1717 found major difficulties put in the way of its sales activities, and the next year a Russian caravan was prohibited from passing through Chinese territory. These and other difficulties induced Peter the Great to send a new envoy to Peking, Lev Izmailov, who arrived there in November 1720. His instructions were to secure the removal of the Chinese restrictions on trade, to have his secretary, Lorents Langa, accepted as the first permanent Russian consul in Peking and to reassure the Chinese that Russian forts being built in Siberia were not intended for aggression southward. The Manchu Emperor soon made clear to Izmailov that he was un- interested in trade but very much interested in getting a final Russian-Mongolian border treaty and in having the Mongol refugees in Russia returned. Izmailov pleaded he was not em- powered to negotiate on these two matters. The result of the mission was therefore unsatisfactory from the Russian point of view. Izmailov did not get the new trade treaty he wanted nor permission to have a permanent Russian consulate in Peking. In- stead, he got oral permission for Langa to remain in Peking and for a new Russian caravan to come to that city. But when the caravan arrived in December 1721 its leader found that he was required to sell his best furs to the Manchu court at artificially low prices. General irritation on both sides reached a peak in the spring of 1722. The Chinese had captured several Russians fight- ing alongside their enemies, the Western Mongols or Dzungars. In retaliation they put a strict guard around Langa's residence, allegedly to protect him. Angered, Langa threatened that when Russia was through with its then current war against Sweden Russian armies would descend upon China. This was too much for the Manchu authorities and they ordered Langa and the caravan personnel out, complaining at the same time of the Rus- sian failure to return the refugees and of the absence of any progress on the boundary issue. About the same time all Russian traders were expelled from Mongolia and all Russian-Chinese trade in Peking halted for several years.

The resolution of these difficulties followed the death of Em- peror Kang-Hsi at the end of 1722 and of Peter the Great in early 1725. Kang-Hsi's successor, his son Yung Chen, seems to have decided to improve relations with Russia as a means of strengthening China's position in its continuing wars with the Western Mongols. In July 1724 his emissaries met at a border area near Selenginsk with Langa. They informed him that the Emperor wanted good relations with Russia and was displeased with the ministers who had prohibited Russian trade in Peking and ordered Langa's expulsion. They suggested Langa return to Peking and begin negotiations on a border treaty.

Count Savva Vladislavich Raguzinsky was the man selected by the Russian court to conduct the negotiations. His instructions were to get a trade treaty or other arrangement that would permit resumption of Russian-Chinese trade, to settle the problems of the Mongolian border and the deserters, to get land on which to build a Russian church in Peking and to gather all the intelligence he could on China's resources and strength. Arriving in Peking in October 1726 with a large party of 100 counselors and servants and 1,500 soldiers, he soon showed himself to be an excellent diplomat and intelligence officer. He established good relations with the influential Jesuits and bribed court officials to get secret information. The negotiations begun at Peking and later transferred to the border area were long, difficult and often filled with tension and threats of conflict. Finally two treaties were signed, at Bur (August 21, 1727) and Kyakhta (October 21, 1727). The Treaty of Kyakhta, the more important of the two, was a major compromise. The Chinese gave up some territory they had claimed, but in return Russia recognized Chinese sovereignty over Mongolia—a sovereignty Russia was to help destroy almost two centuries later.

The Treaty of Kyakhta defined the border between Russia and China in the area of Mongolia as running from the Sayan Mountains and Sapintabakha on the west to the Argun River in the east. It left the boundary in the Uda River Valley undefined, as it had been in the Treaty of Nerchinsk. Russian trade caravans were to be permitted to visit Peking once every three years, but Russian traders were prohibited from being active in Mongolia. Instead, border trade was to be concentrated at the towns of Nerchinsk and Kyakhta, and was to be under the joint control of authorities representing both countries. Once again, as at Nerchinsk almost four decades earlier, it was agreed that each side should hand back future deserters or criminals who crossed the border from the other side. Russia also received the right to send language students to China and to establish a diplomatic and ecclesiastical mission in Peking.

Count Raguzinsky feared that the authorities in Russia's capital would be displeased with the treaty. He had several of his assistants at the negotiations and several Mongol chiefs sign a

statement declaring "the newly established frontier is highly advantageous to Russia and . . . Russian possessions have been extended into Mongolia a distance of several days' march and in
certain sections of even several weeks."[1] But this defense proved
inadequate, and in 1731 he had to answer his critics at home in
other terms. At Kyakhta, he declared, he had had the alternative
of accepting the treaty or seeing war between Russia and China.
Then he stated the case against war in these terms:

> We may conceive of a war with China, but we must take into
> consideration that this would not be an easy undertaking. We
> would have to concentrate at the border at least ten regiments
> of the line and an equal number of regiments of irregulars,
> which would have to face all the Chinese forces and perhaps
> the Mongolian as well. The cost of such an undertaking, even
> assuming that it should be successful, will never be recovered,
> even in a hundred years. We would have to build fortresses,
> maintain strong garrisons there, supply them continuously
> with food and ammunition. Peace would be menaced for a
> long time, trade with China would be interrupted, and the
> Siberian population would become impoverished. Moreover,
> the Chinese would never acknowledge defeat, they would be-
> gin to arm themselves to an even greater extent and learn our
> military arts.[2]

But other opinions were being pressed in St. Petersburg, too.
Thus in 1733, on his way home from Peking, Langa made this
evaluation:

> At this moment the Chinese are in a critical position. Engaged
> in a terrible fight with the Dzungars, they are afraid of Russia
> and at the same time look to us to supply their armies with
> provisions and horses. The moment is most opportune to inter-
> vene in Peking and demand that all restrictions imposed upon
> our caravans be removed; that the Russian mission be freed
> of the insufferable surveillance of the Mandarins which hinders
> all trade; and that the dispute concerning frontiers be settled
> favorably. As long as the Dzungars keep the Chinese in check
> on the battlefields, the latter will not dare defy the Russian
> Court. We even believe that this is an excellent time to seek
> the extension of our frontier to the Amur River.[3]

A few words should be said at this point about the difference
in position relative to China between Russia and the other Euro-

pean powers. The Russians first came into overland contact with China, as we have seen. The basic problem in their relations during the late seventeenth and early eighteenth centuries was the definition of the frontier between the two countries. In the complex process of infiltration, fighting and negotiation that preceded the Nerchinsk and Kyakhta determinations, China was finally forced by the facts of geography and power to deal with Russia as an effective equal. The other European powers, however, were in a far more disadvantageous position in this initial stage of China's relations with the modern West. The English, the Dutch and the Portuguese came by sea in small numbers and weak force. The Dutch, it is true, conquered Formosa in 1642, but they lost it twenty years later to the forces of the Chinese pirate Koxinga. The basic pattern in these early years of western penetration was set in the ghetto-like enclaves at Macao (established by the Portuguese in 1557) and then at Canton where the British established a permanent building for trade in 1715, in the period between the Treaties of Nerchinsk and Kyakhta. What Canton was for the British and other Europeans, therefore, the town of Kyakhta was for the Russians, but in addition the Russians had the right to send caravans directly into Peking, though that, true enough, only once every three years. Early in the eighteenth century Peter the Great suggested that Russia, too, should establish maritime trade with China through Canton as a supplement to its long overland route, but that was not to happen until the nineteenth century.

The first Chinese diplomatic mission to Russia arrived in Moscow on January 14, 1731. It was greeted with an artillery salute of 31 rounds and by massed regiments and orchestras designed to show the majesty and might of the Russian state. The purpose of this mission was primarily to ask for Russian neutrality in the renewed Chinese warfare with the Western Mongols. The envoys told the Moscow authorities that they should not be suspicious of Chinese troop movements near the Russian border. They asked for permission to visit the khans of the Volga Kalmyks, subjects of Russia, hoping to enlist the support of the latter in the war against the Western Mongols. The Chinese also requested the Russians not to provide refuge in Russia for the Mongol troops and to imprison under guard any such troops that did get across the border. The Russians for their part thanked the envoys for the information on the troop movements. They permitted the visit to the Kalmyks, but warned that this was an exception and in the future the Chinese would have to make such contacts through the Russian envoy in Peking. For their part, the Russians complained about violations of the trade provision of the Kyakhta Treaty, charging that a treasury caravan which had arrived in Peking in 1727 had had to return home with part of its goods unsold. In 1732 another Chinese mission arrived in Russia. While it was in Moscow, the Russians showed its members factories and cultural places of interest. These were the first two Chinese embassies to foreign countries.

But matters did not improve for the Russian caravans. Government agents met strong competition in Peking from private Russian traders there. Moreover, Manchu officials put many obstacles in the way of sales. They demanded bribes and tried to have the Russian goods sold at low prices. Efforts to replace the government caravans with trade by a private company failed because Russian merchants found it more profitable to operate in company with an official caravan and—with the connivance of Tsarist officials—to shift any losses they suffered onto the government account. In 1756 the passage of the caravans was finally ended, though long before that the volume of goods brought by each caravan had fallen well below the peaks of 1711–1717. As a result, the border town of Kyakhta became essentially the main center of Russian-Chinese trade, a status it enjoyed well into the nineteenth century.

There was a good deal of friction between Russia and China in the Mongolian border area during the middle and late eighteenth century. At times this friction arose from trade disputes over tariffs, smuggling activities, incursions of tribesmen from Russia into China and the like. These factors lead to the closing of the Kyakhta market at Chinese insistence several times, during 1764–1768, 1779 and 1785–1792. Nevertheless trade at Kyakhta grew rapidly from the 1750's to 1800.

Potentially more serious were the complications of the Chinese clashes with their subject peoples. The Chinese were furious when the Russians gave refuge in the middle of the eighteenth century to the Western Mongol leader Amursana, and Chinese forces violated the Russian border in pursuit of this Dzungar

chief. In 1756 Outer Mongolia revolted against Chinese rule, and
five leading Mongol chiefs approached the Russian commander
of Selenginsk, Jacobi, asking him to arrange with the Russian
court to accept Mongolia as a protectorate and its people as
Russian subjects. This request came at a critical time, when the
main Chinese forces were far away in the west; Jacobi's superior,
Governor Myatlev, pointed out to St. Petersburg that acceptance
of the proposal would mean that "the Chinese force will be cut
off from its bases, and Russia will be able to dictate terms to
Peking." But by the time St. Petersburg had made up its mind on
this delicate issue, the revolt had been suppressed and the opportunity was gone. Great indeed was the bitterness of the Mongols,
the Russians in Siberia and their friends at the court who looked
with greedy eyes at the Chinese empire to the south. When the
Russian Senate sought to gain concessions from China for its
neutrality in the fighting, the Chinese sneered back that Russia
had failed to intervene only because it did not have the strength
to do so. If Russia had intervened, the Chinese continued, the
Russian troops would have been defeated as completely as the
Western Mongols. The Russians snapped back that their country
occupied almost half the world and was not to be treated like the
primitive Mongols or the small Tartar tribes. The Chinese replied that it was ridiculous to compare any sovereign with China's
omnipotent Emperor, especially if the sovereign were a mere
female—the latter gibe was directed, of course, at the then ruler
of Russia, Catherine the Great. This exchange, it is worth men-
tioning, took place when Russian troops had defeated Frederick
the Great and entered Berlin. But Mongolia and China proper
were much further from St. Petersburg than Berlin. Hence the
Russian court kept its temper and there was no war, though
advocates of such a war as the means of enlarging Russia's domain
were not absent from Catherine's entourage.

If some Russians dreamed of expansion at China's expense, the
Chinese wanted only to be left alone and to have as little as
possible to do with the Russians. Peking's policy, therefore,
sought to create a wide expanse of thinly populated buffer areas
along the full length of the Russian-Chinese border. Some peoples living near the border were evacuated; in the Amur River
area, settlement of Chinese and Manchus was forbidden. Chinese
emigration into Mongolia was largely barred during the nine-

teenth century, leaving that vast area the preserve of the relatively small number of Mongols. Between 1750 and 1850, the Manchu Emperors sought also to hinder Chinese migration into central and northern Manchuria, hoping thus to save their patrimony from Sinification. The effort was not entirely successful, but it was effective enough so that in the middle of the nineteenth century the Manchurian part of the border with Russia was still thinly populated.

Trade between China and Russia boomed at Kyakhta during this period. In 1769 the total value of this commerce was about 2,000,000 rubles; by 1781 it was valued at almost 7,500,000 rubles. It declined somewhat after that but then recovered again to reach a new peak of more than 13,000,000 rubles in 1810. The trade volume plunged more than 50 per cent in 1812, reflecting the impact of Napoleon's invasion of Russia, but by 1826 the commerce was back up to more than 12,000,000 rubles. However, in the early nineteenth century Kyakhta's future became more and more clouded as Western Europe's seaborne trade with China grew steadily. Merchants in Central and Western Europe no longer found it attractive to send their goods to China over the long land route to Kyakhta; it was far cheaper to send them by sea to Canton. Conversely, buyers in European Russia began to find it cheaper to buy Chinese goods coming by sea to Europe's Atlantic, Baltic and Mediterranean ports. And finally a new land route for Russian trade with China began to open up, this time in Central Asia where Russia met China in Sinkiang.

In its heyday, during the century after 1750, the trade at Kyakhta normally involved annually goods worth millions of dollars at current prices. It was a barter trade in which commodities were exchanged against commodities and sale for money was prohibited. The participants were private merchants, combined on the Russian side in various special companies authorized by the Tsar, and on the Chinese side into highly organized groups. The tight organization and strict discipline among the Chinese merchants excited the Russians' admiration, convincing them often that the Chinese had all the advantages in bargaining and made the more advantageous deals. A Russian account declares that each evening the Chinese official in charge of this trade convened the Chinese merchants in a meeting which decided what goods would be offered the next day in Kyakhta and what prices would be charged. Each Chinese merchant would be assigned certain goods for his participation in this trade. Any violation of the decisions regarding prices and goods was punished by penalties of varying severity. An offender could be barred from trading for periods of six days to two months, or he could be banished altogether from Maimachen, the Chinese border town where the merchants lived. When deemed necessary, corporal punishment of up to 50 blows with a bamboo cane was administered to offenders. On the Russian side, efforts were made to achieve similar organization. The Russian companies selected representatives who met to establish their own valuations for the goods being bought and sold. Before 1800 the value of all goods was set in units of Chinese cotton cloth, the so-called *kitaika;* beginning in 1800 the unit of common value was a given weight of Chinese tea. But all efforts on both sides to organize matters did not prevent disputes and hard feelings and, on the part of the Russians at least, the feeling that they were being out-traded.

The substantial growth of Kyakhta trade during the first decades of the nineteenth century was partly the result of the growing popularity of tea-drinking in Russia. Between the first and third decades of the century Russian purchases of tea at Kyakhta almost doubled. In 1825 tea purchases accounted for 87.3 per cent of all Chinese goods bought there. On the Russian side furs, and for a time cloth and textile products played the leading role. Many of the goods the Russians sold at Kyakhta came from Western Europe; Silesian cloth from Prussia was particularly important. But this trade in cloth declined after 1820 because of the competition of British cloth coming into China through Canton.

In 1800 the Russian government stepped in to regulate the trade at Kyakhta. The Russian traders were prohibited from changing the prices they bought and sold goods for. If demand conditions changed or traders wanted to get rid of goods they had held for an excessive time, merchants had to petition government officials for a changed price. The decision on such an appeal had to be made by the entire company of traders in formal session either the same day the petition was handed in, or the very next day.

A merchant who sold Russian goods for less than the established price or bought Chinese goods at a price above the established quotation was fined 15 per cent of the value of the goods involved. If he repeated the offense, he was expelled from Kyakhta and forbidden to engage in the trade. Any Russian merchant who attempted to use gold, silver or opium in his trade or traded for money had the goods or money confiscated and was expelled from that area of Siberia altogether. The proclaimed purpose of these regulations was to minimize the number of Russian-Chinese trade quarrels, but clearly the Russian government was also anxious to exercise as near a monopoly control over the prices in this trade as it could, and thus to duplicate what was believed to be the Chinese control. On the Chinese side, too, merchants were warned against acting out of individual greed and instructed that the advantage of the individual trader must play a secondary role to the common advantage.

Early in the nineteenth century, the Russians finally made efforts to begin a sea trade with China. The motives were in part economic. It was one-third to one-half cheaper to move tea by sea from China to England than to transport it overland from Kyakhta to Moscow, and the sea voyage took only half or a third as long a time. Adding to the economic pressure was the growth of the Russian fur catch in Alaska, Kamchatka, Sakhalin and other Russian areas in the North Pacific. It was clearly much more convenient and cheaper to move these furs to China by boat than to deliver them to the relatively inaccessible trade center at Kyakhta. Finally Russian interest in a sea route to the Pacific grew after the appearance of French and British naval expeditions in the North Pacific in the 1780's and 1790's. These expeditions aroused apprehensions about the future of Russian holdings in this area, and the search began for a way to supply and man these distant possessions by sea as an alternative to the long, slow and expensive land route across Siberia.

As a result, the Russian-American Company in 1803 sent out two ships, the *Nadezhda* and the *Neva*, to investigate sea routes to the Pacific and Indian Oceans. They were to bring food and other supplies to the Russian settlements on the American continent and then take furs from these settlements to Canton.

The ships accomplished their mission, arriving in Canton with their furs in December 1805. While they were trading, word came from Peking that Russians were forbidden to trade by sea since they already had land privileges, and Russian ships were ordered to leave immediately. A diplomatic effort to arrange for Russian ships to use Canton failed in 1805 when a mission headed by Count Y. A. Golovkin set out for Peking and got no further than the city of Urga, where it was refused permission to proceed and turned back. This first effort to trade by sea was not followed up significantly for the next half century.

In the 1840's the attention of Russian imperialists turned once again to the possibility of new territorial gains at the expense of China. One reason was China's glaring weakness so vividly exposed during the Opium War which Britain won at the beginning of the decade. A second reason was the fear that if Russia did not move to strengthen her position *vis-à-vis* China and make such gains as she could, the British would become dominant in China and would seize territories that might otherwise go to Russia. And if that happened, might not Britain and other Western powers move also against existing Russian possessions in the North Pacific? The powerful combination of opportunity, greed and fear was at work in a Russia still basking in the dimming glory of its successful defense against Napoleon. There were important and influential figures at the court in St. Petersburg, notably the chancellor, Count Nesselrode, who looked askance at the idea of adventure so far away. They could see little worthwhile gain and much grief from the enmity of China and Britain that might result. But these more cautious souls were overruled by the chief imperialist, Tsar Nicholas I.

The man Nicholas selected for the task of achieving territorial gains in the Far East was the governor of Tula Province in European Russia, the young (38), energetic, able and ambitious Nikolai Muraviev. At seven o'clock of a September morning in 1847, at a railroad station near Tula, the Tsar informed Muraviev he had been appointed governor general of Eastern Siberia. The Tsar emphasized to his appointee how vast this domain was—stretching from the Yenisei River to the Bering Strait—saying: "If any power seizes Kamchatka, you in Irkutsk will only find

out about it six months later." During conversation with Muraviev, the Tsar—after touching on relations with China—said: "As
for the Russian river Amur, you will hear from us later." The
Tsar ended his talk with the remark: "To one who knows how
to listen, even a few words are enough to understand." A far
stupider man than Muraviev would have known what was meant.

It is a sign of Soviet embarrassment over Muraviev's accom-
plishments that his biography in a recent (1959) encyclopedia is
summed up in 40 words. Actually this mid-nineteenth century
Russian empire builder is one of the most interesting characters
in the whole long history of Russian-Chinese relations. A loyal
and effective servant of the Tsar, he yet had advanced and even
radical ideas for his time. In the 1850's he opposed serfdom, struck
up personal friendships with anarchists, did what he could to
ease the lot of Siberian political prisoners and dreamed of a
Russian-American alliance that would dominate the North Pacific. Mikhail Bakunin, the founder of modern anarchism, wrote
in 1860: "Muraviev is the only man among all those who have
power and influence in Russia who can and must fully and without the least reservation be considered one of us."[4] Yet this same
Muraviev was a fanatical Russian expansionist, a man capable of
every kind of deception to accomplish his goals. In retrospect it
seems clear that, in his combination of radical political views and
Russian expansionism, Muraviev was an early example of a human type the world has become familiar with more than once
since the Bolshevik Revolution.

In his confidential memoranda to his superiors, Muraviev made
no secret of his ambitions and plans. He wrote the Tsar in 1853:
"There can be no doubt that . . . we must gain control of
Sakhalin and the estuary of the Amur River." While China
reeled under the blows of her foes, he mused in a memorandum:
"If the defeat of China should entail the fall of her dynasty, this
outcome would of course be most favorable to Russia. . . . Our
neighbors, Manchuria and Mongolia, would become (in fact, if
not in name) our possessions, and Russia would finally acquire
all that she could here desire."[5]

Writing to the Grand Duke Constantine, Muraviev expressed
both his fears and his hopes as he surveyed the world scene.
Some of his musings have a contemporary ring if due account is
taken of altered circumstances:

While the Western powers could not inflict any serious loss on Russia in Europe, they might easily deprive her of Kamchatka and of the mouth of the Amur in the Far East. The Empire of China, now insignificant on account of its military weakness, might become dangerous under the influence and guidance of England and France—Siberia might even cease to be Russian. The loss of this vast region . . . could not be compensated by any victories or conquests in the West. It was therefore necessary to guard Kamchatka, Sakhalin, and the mouth of the Amur, thus also acquiring enduring influence on China.[6]

Muraviev's tactics were simplicity itself and won a vast area with virtually no fighting. He built up Russian forces in the Far East, intruded upon the Amur Valley, set up fortified posts and settlements along the river's banks and presented the Chinese with a *fait accompli* which the Chinese had to accept. In accomplishing all this Muraviev had valuable aid from Captain, later Admiral, Gennadi Nevelskoy, commander of the Russian naval force in the Far East during the 1850's. It was Nevelskoy who struck the first direct blow at Chinese dominion of the area, sailing up the Amur in 1850 and establishing a post he named Nikolayevsk in honor of the Tsar. The intrusion on Chinese sovereignty, enthusiastically backed by Muraviev, provoked heated debate in St. Petersburg. The debate was resolved by the Tsar's famous words: "Where the Russian flag has once been hoisted, it must not be lowered." The die was cast.

In the early 1850's Muraviev built up his military forces in the Far East, while Nevelskoy continued his exploration of the Amur and discovered that Sakhalin was an island, not a peninsula as had been thought. In the spring of 1854 Muraviev directed a large fleet of barges, rafts, and one steamer down the Amur, a fleet carrying more than 1,000 soldiers and their artillery. The local Chinese officials were appalled but overawed by this power and did nothing to stop this flagrant violation of the Treaty of Nerchinsk. The next year Muraviev led an even larger and more powerful fleet down the Amur, this time bringing along more than 8,000 persons as well as cattle to help set up permanent settlements. In 1856 a third expedition bringing still more soldiers, settlers and supplies for the new settlements on the Amur went down the river. This had now really become a Russian river, a fact recognized by the Tsar's *ukaz* of October 31, 1856 which set up a new administrative region, the Maritime Province, including the Amur territory, Kamchatka and the Okhotsk coast. In 1867 Muraviev sent a fourth expedition down the river, bringing more Cossack infantry plus cavalry troops. Russia had lost the Crimean War far to the west during the time these expeditions had seized a new region, but these Far Eastern gains were at least a partial compensation.

Occupied with war against France and England and struggle against the Taiping rebels, the Peking government could do little except protest. Finally it sent Prince I Shan to negotiate with Muraviev at the Chinese town of Aigun. In 1689, at Nerchinsk, the Chinese had been able to impose their will upon the Russians because they had had the preponderance of military force. Now the shoe was on the other foot. Muraviev made plain his intention of having Russian ownership of the area north of the Amur, regardless of what the Treaty of Nerchinsk said. Behind his words was a well armed force of more than 20,000 men, while the Chinese troops in the area were relatively few in number and very poorly equipped. Moreover, there was a Russian fleet near Aigun and Muraviev used the threat that it might act as an effective bargaining counter. On May 28, 1858, the Treaty of Aigun was finally signed. In this treaty China ceded to Russia the left bank of the Amur River down to the Ussuri, while the area between the Ussuri and the Pacific Ocean was to belong in common to the two nations until the issues here were decided at a future date. Some 185,000 square miles had been won by Russia. It is characteristic of much of Russian policy in China in the nineteenth and early twentieth centuries that this act of imperialism was presented to the Chinese as an expression of Russian anxiety to "protect" China against a supposed threat from England. What the Chinese thought of the treaty was indicated by Peking's angry reaction. I Shan was dismissed and denounced "for stupidity and overstepping his authority."

In June 1858, the month following the Treaty of Aigun, another Russian-Chinese treaty was signed in Tientsin. The Russian negotiator here was Admiral Evfimi Putyatin, whose negotiating authority was confined to commercial matters. By this treaty Russia was granted commercial rights in China similar to those enjoyed by England and other Western powers. It could trade with China by sea as well as overland, and its ships could use Shanghai, Canton, Amoy, Ningpo and other open ports available to the Western powers. The treaty provided for a regular monthly courier service between Kyakhta and Peking, confirmed Russia's right to send envoys to Peking and permitted Russian consuls to reside in the open ports. These consuls, like their Western European counterparts, were given extraterritorial jurisdiction over Russian citizens violating Chinese laws.

But Putyatin's treaty, negotiated and signed before he knew of the gains at Aigun, had not solved the territorial problem. The Aigun Treaty was not ratified and instead the Chinese threatened to halt trade with Russia at Kyakhta and in Sinkiang. Chinese sources put out word that Aigun had been only an expression of the Emperor's "good will toward the poor Russian settlers, and his willingness to allow them to reside in some places of the Amur Basin and to cultivate the lands that were not occupied by anybody else." The negotiations on these matters carried out by a new Russian envoy, General Nikolai Ignatiev, became so heated that he left Peking in May 1860, effectively breaking off diplomatic negotiations.

Here history played into Russia's hands. The Chinese government was weak and in disorder under the cumulative blows of the British and the French on the one hand, and of the Taiping rebels on the other. At Tientsin in 1858 Putyatin's treaty had been one of four similar treaties the Chinese had signed with Russia, Britain, France, and the United States. But they had signed only after being subjected to extreme Western diplomatic and military pressure. Ignatiev had had no difficulty in 1859 in exchanging ratification documents for the Treaty of Tientsin with the Chinese, but the British and French ran into what they considered provocative delays in getting their treaties finally ratified. As a result, fighting broke out between the Chinese and the Anglo-French forces. This fighting culminated in the Western capture of Tientsin and Peking in the late summer and early fall of 1860. The looting and destruction of the beautiful Summer Palace of the Emperor in Peking by the victors shocked the Chinese but they were helpless.

At this point General Ignatiev, now back in Peking, re-entered the picture and accomplished one of the most skillful feats of diplomatic double-dealing in history. Some such possibility appears to have been envisaged in St. Petersburg when he was first given his assignment in 1859. Admiral Putyatin had suggested that Russia try to gain advantages from China's military weakness *vis-à-vis* the British and French by offering military aid to the Peking government. Hence Ignatiev brought experts in various military fields with him. His instructions called for him to try to mediate between the Western powers and the Chinese, and in particular to try to prevent the Manchu dynasty—with which all Russian-Chinese treaties had been signed—from collapsing. But if the Manchus did fall from power, he was to try to keep Manchuria, Mongolia and the Kashgar area in northwest China for Russia.

When the Anglo-French allies reached the Peking area, Ignatiev showed the British commander a detailed map of the city and recommended the capital's north gate as the weakest spot in its defenses. The British commander later testified that the map was of "great value." Almost simultaneously Ignatiev offered his services as mediator to the Peking government. As the price for his services he demanded not only ratification of the Treaty of Aigun but also extension of the Russian-Chinese boundary line along the Ussuri River to the limits of Korea and the establishment of Russian consulates in several cities. The Chinese accepted his proposition. In the days that followed, Ignatiev was the "never-failing counselor" to the British general as well as the mediator expecting rich rewards from the Chinese. After the latter had conceded to the British the desired principle of Western diplomatic residence in Peking, Ignatiev persuaded the British general that Peking was unsafe in winter and that he should leave as soon as possible. Once the allied troops had left, Ignatiev was free to deal with the Chinese, who paid his price by accepting the Treaty of Peking, signed on November 14, 1860.[7]

The Treaty of Peking brought the Russians major territorial and other gains. Its first article completed the work begun in Aigun two years earlier by making Russian the whole area between the Ussuri River and the Pacific Ocean, adding an additional 133,000 square miles to Russian territory. The boundaries of Russia were thus brought to the frontier of Korea, and the earlier Russian founding of the city of Vladivostok (Rule of the East) at a magnificent harbor on the Pacific in this region was retroactively legalized. An even larger territorial gain was made in Central Asia. There the Chinese surrendered their claim to almost 350,000 square miles of territory by agreeing that the boundary between Sinkiang and Russian Central Asia be set along the line of permanent pasture markers, or pickets, the Chinese had set up to limit pasture use by the Kazakh nomads. Later the Chinese tried in vain to have the border follow the temporary pasture pickets which really marked the limits of Chinese territorial claims, but by then it was too late. The Treaty of Tarbagatai in 1864 finally delimited the boundary in this area on the principles agreed to at Peking.

The non-territorial gains were also significant. Russian merchants were given the right to travel for trade purposes from Kyakhta to Peking, trading en route in the cities of Urga and Kalgan. Russia was permitted to maintain a consulate in Urga. In Sinkiang, where an earlier agreement had allowed Russian-Chinese trade at Kuldja and Tarbagatai, trade was permitted also at Kashgar and Russian consulates were permitted to function in all three of these cities. Citizens of each country, the treaty provided, were to be allowed in the other and "in places open for trade can carry on commercial activities completely freely, without any limitations from local authorities; they can also freely visit at any time markets, shops, or homes of local merchants, sell and buy different goods at wholesale or retail, for money or by means of barter, and borrow or lend on the basis of mutual trust." Russian extraterritorial rights over Russian citizens in China were confirmed.

The Russian territorial gains at China's expense which were won by the Treaties of Aigun and Peking were, of course, typical examples of imperialist encroachment on a weak Asian power. At the time, the duplicity employed by the Tsar's representatives was not considered particularly extraordinary, and it was taken for granted that the strong took advantage of the weak. But now, slightly more than a century later, both the world balances of forces and generally accepted standards of international morality have changed. In early 1963 the Chinese government publicly called into question the validity of the gains made by the Tsar in 1858 and 1860, gains remaining under Soviet rule. Soviet historians appear to have anticipated such a challenge. In the *Diplomatichesky Slovar* (Diplomatic Dictionary) issued in 1960, Soviet historians asserted that the Aigun Treaty "returned to Russia the territory given to China by the Treaty of Nerchinsk." And as though preparing for a Chinese attack on the Aigun settlement, they gave this account to rationalize and justify the territorial gains made:

In 1861 the Russian government informed the Chinese imperial government that, guarding the mouth of the Amur and Sakhalin from occupation by other powers and taking account of the fact that in this area no border had been established, it had taken measures to erect fortifications. The appearance of the British fleet off the Kamchatka coast during the Crimean War forced the Russian government to hasten the solution of the Amur problem. Muraviev, who was charged with the negotiations, convinced the Chinese representatives of the necessity of demarcation at the Amur, citing the danger both for Russia and for China of English penetration into the lower Amur and the difficulty of defending this region which lacked roads and had no communications along the Amur. Not seeing any advantage from having the left bank of the Amur and understanding that it could not defend the Amur region against English encroachment with its own forces, the Peking government reached agreement with Russia.[8]

The facts, as we have seen, were more complicated and less flattering to Russia's straightforwardness than this account.

We have seen that by a series of treaties—Nerchinsk, Kyakhta, Aigun and Peking—the Russian-Chinese border was defined from the western end of Mongolia to the Pacific Ocean. But a new major border between the two countries came into being in the nineteenth century, in Central Asia. That border, not finally fixed until near the end of the century, today divides Soviet Central Asia from Sinkiang. Located in the heart of Asia, the territory involved was the country of the Western Mongols in the eighteenth century and the scene of their frequent wars with the Chinese. In the second half of the nineteenth century this was a land of Moslem peoples—Kalmyks, Uzbeks, Kirghiz and others. The contest between Russia and China here was part of a greater struggle, for Britain then looked askance at the Russian advance in this region, fearing Russian aggression against India. The Russians in turn suspected British schemes to use the Moslem peoples of Sinkiang to displace the newly won Russian power over the similar Moslem peoples of Russian Central Asia. This larger struggle thus pitted Russians against British over a vast region from Persia to China, but we shall focus upon the Russian-Chinese aspects of the matter.

Russian interest in this area began as early as the late eighteenth century, when Russian traders penetrated into western China from Siberia and began trading at Kuldja and Tarbagatai. A Russian, Putimisev, reconnoitered the area in 1811 and reported that Russian textiles and leather were being exchanged at Kuldja for Chinese silver and for Chinese supplies needed by a Russian garrison on the Irtysh River in Siberia. Later Russian trade caravans came from Semipalatinsk and Petropavlovsk, leaving in July or August of one year, taking 50 to 60 days for their journey, and returning to Siberia in March of the following year. Chinese caravans in turn took the Russian goods to Peking through Urumchi and Lanchow. The trade in these cities was small compared to that at Kyakhta, but it grew sharply around 1850. Theoretically this was a barter trade, as at Kyakhta, but by 1851 the Russians were buying almost three times as much as they sold, paying for the deficit in silver or gold and receiving credit from Chinese merchants whose chief sales item was tea. By 1851 tea made up more than 90 per cent of Chinese sales to Russians in western China; the amount of tea sold here had grown very rapidly in the preceding decade. The Russians had no legal protection in this trade until 1851 and grumbled at the restrictions placed upon them by the Manchus. At Kuldja, for example, the Russian caravans had to stop outside the city at a special camp called Small Kuldja and often had to wait several months for word to arrive from Peking permitting them to trade. In 1851, however, a trade treaty was finally agreed on which legalized this trade and put the Russian merchants under the supervision of Russian consuls in both Kuldja and Tarbagatai. In 1860 as we noted above, a third major trading center in western China, the southern city of Kashgar, was opened to Russian trade by the Treaty of Peking.

Meanwhile, during the first half of the nineteenth century there was increasing Russian interest in and penetration of what is now Soviet Central Asia. In this vast desert area with its extremes of climate in summer and winter, the Russian advance was not easy despite the military weakness of such small medieval states as Khiva, Bokhara and Khokand. After some setbacks in earlier decades, the decisive Russian push came in the 1860's. The American Civil War played a part in this timing, since the difficulties of getting American cotton for Russian textile factories made influential industrial circles anxious to get control of the potential cotton-growing areas in Central Asia. By 1870, after the capture of Samarkand and Tashkent, much of Central Asia was under effective Russian control. The increasing Russian presence and strength in Central Asia provided the base from which pressure could be exerted for further expansion to the east at China's expense in Sinkiang.

We have discussed above the delimitation of the border between Sinkiang and Russian Central Asia by the Treaties of Peking (1860) and of Tarbagatai (1864) with the large Chinese territorial losses implied by the decision to follow the line of permanent pasture pickets. But in addition to these gains, the Russians also wanted control of the Ili Valley, a region which had been one of the great routes for trade and invasion in Asia for centuries. In 1857 General Gasfort, the Russian governor general of Western Siberia had declared: "The transformation of Kashgar into a state independent of China under a Russian protectorate would render a great service to its people, for whom the Sino-Manchurian tyranny has become insupportable. . . . We shall make ourselves masters of Central Asia, and we shall be able to hold all the Khans in respect, which will facilitate our march forward."[9]

A Moslem revolt in Sinkiang in 1864 finally gave the Russians their opportunity to penetrate the Ili Valley, though its first effect was to induce the Chinese negotiators to accept the Treaty of Tarbagatai. The Manchu rule over these Moslem peoples was very severe and there had been numerous unsuccessful revolts earlier in the century. This 1864 uprising soon came under the leadership of a talented adventurer of humble origin, a former dancing boy, Yakub Beg. By 1869 Yakub Beg's "Emirate of Djety-shaar" embraced almost all of Sinkiang; the Manchu forces controlled only a thin northern strip of the area. Emboldened by these successes, Yakub Beg dreamed of creating a vast new Moslem empire in the heart of Asia, an empire which would embrace not only Sinkiang but also much or all of Russian Central Asia. To the British, worried about a possible continued

Russian push south toward India, the appearance of Yakub Beg's new realm suggested interesting possibilities of a union between Britain and Islam to create a strong buffer area shielding India from the Russians. The latter had little love for Yakub Beg. He had fought against them in Central Asia before coming to Sinkiang. They recognized the explosive possibilities his continued success might have among the Moslems subject to the Tsar. Moreover, the Russians saw no point in offending the Manchu emperors, who had proved so pliable in earlier years, by trying any major intrigues with Yakub Beg. Peking intended to reconquer Sinkiang and needed only time to regain its strength after the debilitating wars with the Western powers and the exhausting struggle against the Taiping rebellion. But events showed that it had also occurred to the Russians that Yakub Beg might be exploited to get more Chinese territory.

The opportunity came in 1871 when Yakub Beg's forces appeared to threaten Kuldja. Instead, Russian troops took the city and a substantial area in the vicinity. The Russian governor general of Turkestan, Kauffman, informed St. Petersburg he had done so to keep British influence out of the region. The Russian foreign office sought to allay alarm in Peking by assuring the authorities there that its forces had merely moved in to restore order and would return the area when Chinese forces were strong enough to return and take over full control. Understandably, many historians suspect St. Petersburg said this blandly, considering it unlikely that Peking's forces in this distant region would ever become strong enough to require fulfillment of this promise. Certainly when the Chinese began negotiations for the region's return in 1872 the Russians had no difficulty in finding reasons for delaying their withdrawal indefinitely. In that same year, too, the Russians made a trade agreement with Yakub Beg opening up his territory for the first time to Tsarist merchants.

In the early 1870's Yakub Beg attempted a complex balancing act. He sought support from the British and accepted arms and a title from the Sultan of Turkey, a move suggesting he was making Sinkiang a vassal state of Russia's bitter enemy on the Bosporus. In 1874 and 1875 Russian troops were therefore concentrated for a possible attack against Kashgar in southern Sinkiang and in 1876 the Russians demanded and got from Yakub Beg strategic mountain passes to the west of Kashgar. At the same time, however, the Russians moved to help the Chinese forces mobilizing against Yakub Beg under the famous general Tso Tung-tang, supplying Tso with necessary grain. In 1876 and 1877 Tso's forces moved quickly and effectively. By the end of 1877 Yakub Beg was dead—a suicide or poisoned, the facts are unclear—and all of Sinkiang was under Chinese control except for the Russian-held enclave around Kuldja. Two Mohammedan leaders who had tried to preserve fragments of Yakub Beg's domain fled into Russia and their repatriation was denied the Chinese on the ground that they were political refugees.

The Chinese began pressing in 1878 for Russian withdrawal from Kuldja and finally after some delays negotiations were opened in St. Petersburg. The Chinese envoy, Chung How, had had some prior international experience but was completely incapable of driving a hard bargain with the Russians. This was proved in the summer of 1879 when he signed the very disadvantageous draft Treaty of Livadia. In this treaty the Russians agreed to vacate the Kuldja area in return for the following: the Tekes Valley—a large, rich territory in the southwestern portion of the occupied area—and passes through the mountains; permission for Russian merchants to be exempt from all duties in trading in Mongolia and Sinkiang; Chinese consent to the opening of Russian consulates in seven additional Sinkiang cities; and payment by China to Russia of 5,000,000 rubles to defray Russian occupation costs.

China was shocked when the terms agreed to at Livadia became known. Not only did Peking repudiate the agreement but it recalled its envoy, imprisoned him and sentenced him to decapitation. He was saved only by appeals for mercy from Queen Victoria and other European notables. An important and influential war party sprang up in Peking demanding that China stand firm at any cost. The redoubtable Tso Tung-tang himself memorialized the Emperor with these words:

It seems that Russia intends to make Ili (Kuldja) a Russian colony. . . . When a country is defeated in war it may be obliged to cede territory and to sue for peace. Why should China sacrifice an important area to satisfy Russia's greed? It would be like throwing a bone to a dog to prevent it from biting. But when the bone has been eaten up, the dog would still want to bite. The loss at present is apparent and the trouble in the future will be endless.[10]

The eccentric British general Charles G. Gordon entered the scene in the spring of 1880. He had a good reputation in China for his services to the Emperor in helping put down the Taiping Rebellion. His advice to the Chinese government was that it avoid war against Russia at all cost. To do this, he urged, it should agree to pay an indemnity. If war came, he predicted, the Russians would be able to occupy Peking in two months and China's only chance of success would come if it were willing to undergo long years of guerrilla warfare. The Russian actions in massing a large army near Kuldja and assembling a large fleet in the Pacific helped convince the Chinese that negotiation was wiser than war in this situation.

The result was that Tseng Chi-tse, the Chinese minister in Britain, was sent to St. Petersburg to renew negotiations. Accompanied by a Briton and a Frenchman, Tseng found upon his arrival that the Russians were arrogant and inclined to try to get the Treaty of Livadia accepted after all. But Tseng was persistent, conciliatory and firm on essentials. Moreover, the Russians had a healthy respect for Tso's troops and their capabilities if turned against relatively empty Siberia. The result of negotiations finally was the Treaty of St. Petersburg signed in 1881. This treaty was considered by the Chinese at the time as a victory of sorts, since Russia agreed to give up most of the Tekes Valley and the mountain passes, and to keep only a small area west of the Holkutz River. The number of new Russian consulates was reduced, as was the area in which Russian merchants were to enjoy free trade. Against this the Russians secured an increase in the Chinese indemnity payment from the 5,000,000 rubles of Livadia to 9,000,000 rubles.

Thus Chinese sovereignty in Sinkiang was restored and the border with Russia finally demarcated without the major losses that had taken place elsewhere. For several decades thereafter, Sinkiang was relatively quiet in Russia-Chinese relations. In part this was because Russia found more promising possibilities for expansion at China's expense elsewere. But in part it was because in the 1890's the Russians and the British improved their relations in the area, an improvement symbolized by Russian War Minister General Kuropatkin's report to the Tsar in 1900: "India in the twentieth century would be a burden for Russia. In Asia there is arising a struggle of the non-Christian regions against the Christian ones. In this struggle we are on the side of England."[11]

CHAPTER IV

Russian Imperialism in Victory and Defeat

"RUSSIA, with her territory adjoining ours, aiming to nibble away our territory like a silkworm, may be considered a threat at our bosom."[1] This was the evaluation of the Russian menace to China given the Emperor Hsien-feng in 1861 by his chief foreign affairs counselors. Some 35 years later, in the mid-1890's, it was clear to many observers that Russia was done with nibbling and was looking forward to taking great mouthfuls of territory from China. Li Hung-chang, the wily diplomat who conducted much of China's foreign policy in the late nineteenth century, wrote sadly in 1896 that Russia wanted "to control us in all our home affairs."[2] United States Ambassador to Russia Clifton Breckinridge had been even more blunt a year earlier when he wrote Washington that "Russia is ready for the partition of China."[3] His judgment was sound. He had anticipated a policy which was stated in these terms by one of the highest—and most cautious—Tsarist officials of the time, Finance Minister Serge Witte:

> The more inert countries in Asia will fall prey to the powerful invaders and will be divided up between them. . . . The problem of each country concerned is to obtain as large a share as possible of the inheritance of the outlived oriental states, especially of the Chinese Colossus. Russia, both geographically and historically, has the undisputed right to the lion's share of the expected prey. . . . The absorption by Russia of a considerable portion of the Chinese Empire is only a matter of time.[4]

New forces were stirring vigorously in both Russia and China in the years that ended the nineteenth century. In Russia the energies that had been liberated with the end of serfdom in the 1860's were reaching maturity and producing a flood tide of change. The country was industrializing rapidly, filling the cities with thousands of peasants turned proletarian and increasing the numbers and influence of the urban bourgeoisie. Influential figures around the Tsar were looking for new worlds to conquer, anxious to cover their names with glory and to find new markets for Russia's rising industrial production. Their thoughts turned naturally toward the Far East, where China's evident decay presented tempting opportunities. Count Witte's program hoped even for an eventual Russian protectorate over all China, to be achieved by a steady peaceful penetration which would culminate in the attainment of dominant influence over the Chinese court in Peking.

In China, ideas of reform and change were in the air. Farsighted men saw that, to survive, the country would have to imitate Japan by abandoning old ways and learning from the West the essentials for a strong modern state. But for the most part the conservatives lead by the Dowager Empress were in the saddle, fighting reform and change. These conservatives clearly saw the threat the forces of change posed to the continuance of the now very degenerate and Sinified Manchu dynasty. With little military power, the best that Chinese statesmen could do was to try to divide and conquer, to inflame jealousies and rivalries among the various Western imperialist nations so that China's interests might be served. But once the full extent of Chinese military weakness was revealed nakedly in the mid-1890's, this effort proved insufficient.

Korea in the 1880's provided an example of how the Chinese thought they might protect their patrimony. The hermit kingdom was nominally a vassal of China, but Japan had penetrated the area in the 1870's and had won the opening of diplomatic relations and the opening of some Korean ports for Japanese merchant ships. China was not displeased, therefore, when in the early 1880's several Western nations also secured some rights in and made treaties with Korea. But the chief struggle was between China and Japan, the latter favored by those Koreans who wanted reforms and modernization. In late 1884 the Japanese organized a *coup d'état* in Seoul to put their own men in power, but this was put down by Chinese troops. Both sides poured troops into Korea and a war seemed in the offing, but in April 1885 the dispute was settled peacefully. Both sides agreed to withdraw their troops and to permit the Korean king to hire officers from some third power. That third power, not unexpectedly in view of the geographic situation, turned out to be Russia. The result was a secret Russian-Korean agreement in which the Russians offered Korea protection and military instructors in return for the lease of a port in southeastern Korea, Port Lazarev. Learning of this, the British moved quickly to try to prevent a Russian protectorate over Korea. The British navy occupied Port Hamilton, an island off the coast of southern Korea. In the diplomatic fracas that followed, the Koreans decided not to ratify the treaty, the Russians promised not to threaten Korea's independence, and the British withdrew from Port Hamilton. The policy of setting "barbarian against barbarian" had worked.

As the 1890's began, the chief thrust of Russian Far Eastern policy was concentrated upon a new and most important project: the Trans-Siberian Railroad designed to connect western Russia with Vladivostok. Military, political and economic reasons all played a role in this momentous decision. From the strategic point of view, the railroad would for the first time make it relatively easy to ship additional Russian troops and supplies to the Far East and thus to help defend it. Moreover, the railroad was looked upon as a means of increasing the strength of the Russian position in the competition with its rivals for influence and territorial gains in China. From the economic point of view, the railroad offered great possibilities for remedying the great weakness of Russia's trade with China. The nature of that weakness is vividly shown by the statistics. During a typical year of the 1880's, the value of Russian imports from China was more than ten times as great as the value of exports. The average annual trade deficit in these years was over 23,000,000 rubles. Russia bought large quantities of Chinese tea for its entire population plus large amounts of essential supplies for the inhabitants of the Russian Far East. But Russian goods had a hard time finding Chinese markets. Competitive Western European goods could be sold much more cheaply in China because they were delivered by the cheaper water route. By cutting the time and cost of delivering Russian manufactured goods from European Russia to China, the Trans-Siberian Railroad offered attractive perspectives for Russian manufacturers and merchants.

Once the decision to build the Trans-Siberian had been made, the problem of its route to Vladivostok immediately arose. If it followed the Russian border across Siberia, it would have to sweep north along the great bend of the Amur River and be longer by hundreds of miles than a railroad line following the straightest, shortest route. But the straightest, shortest route to Vladivostok would have to go through Manchuria, opening prospects for greatly increased influence in that rich area, as well as for savings on railroad construction costs. How was Russia to get permission to build a railroad across Manchuria? This problem was very much in the minds of Russian policy makers in the first half of the 1890's.

The opportunity for solving the problem was provided by the short war of 1894–1895 between Japan and China. The Japanese won easily, demonstrating China's military weakness more clearly than ever before. At the Shimonoseki peace conference, the Japanese demanded they be given Formosa, the Pescadores Islands and the area around Port Arthur in Manchuria's Liaotung Peninsula. Tokyo asked also for payment of a large indemnity by China and Chinese recognition of Korea's independence. Aroused by the prospect of Japanese intrusion into Manchuria, Russia's foreign minister wrote the Tsar in early April 1895 suggesting that Russia organize an international intervention against this Japanese encroachment. The foreign minister's note declared: "Our aim is twofold: acquisition of an ice-free port on the Pacific, and the annexation of a part of Manchuria as a right of way for the Trans-Siberian Railroad." Nicholas II replied: "Russia absolutely needs a port free and open throughout the whole year. This port must be located on the mainland (southeastern Korea) and must certainly be connected with our possessions by a strip of land."[5] The need for ports open to navigation all year round was of course an old theme in Russian history, one used to justify territorial expansion in Europe and Asia.

To realize these plans, Russia was to pose as the defender of China. Together with Germany and France, therefore, on April 23, 1895 Russia presented what was in effect an ultimatum to the

Japanese, a demand that they renounce the Liaotung Peninsula or take the consequences. Deciding they could not afford to fight Russia, Germany and France, the Japanese agreed to give up the Liaotung Peninsula in return for an increased monetary payment from China. To help China pay the indemnity to Japan, a joint Franco-Russian loan was negotiated. The grandiose plans behind these moves were indicated by the charter of a new bank formed that same year, 1895. This Russo-Chinese Bank's charter looked forward to the time when it might coin money, collect taxes, secure railroad concessions and engage in other farflung operations throughout China. Much of the capital for the new bank came from the great French banks, but the Russo-Chinese Bank was, as a Russian diplomat noted, "in reality but a slightly disguised branch of the Russian Treasury."

Despite this good beginning for the Russian plans, matters did not go smoothly. For one thing, other powers were alarmed by the prospect of rapid Franco-Russian penetration of China. As a result, the Chinese were able to get a British-German loan to supplement the earlier Franco-Russian advance. Moreover, there was opposition in Russia to Witte's scheme for building a railroad across Manchuria. Most important, the Chinese in early 1896 were proving recalcitrant to Russia's suggestions as to how she should be rewarded for her help in 1895. By April 1896 the Russian ambassador in Peking reported home that his effort to get the Manchurian right of way had been fruitless, and it was necessary "to make the Chinese Government decisively understand that a refusal will directly result in the most disastrous consequences to China."[6]

The story was to have a happy ending for the Russians, however, when Li Hung-chang came to St. Petersburg to attend the coronation of Tsar Nicholas II. Under great pressure—including the offer of a bribe of $1,500,000—Li finally negotiated a secret treaty with Russia. This provided for a 15-year defensive alliance between the two countries to be operative in the event of Japanese aggression against Russian territory in East Asia, against China, or against Korea. The key point of this treaty was Article IV, which read:

In order to facilitate for the Russian land forces access to the points under menace and to assure the means of existence, the Chinese Government consents to the construction of a railway

across the Chinese provinces of Amur and Kirin in the direction of Vladivostok.

The junction of this railway with the railways of Russia shall
not serve as a pretext for any encroachment on Chinese territory, nor for an attempt against the sovereign rights of His
Majesty, the Emperor of China.[7]

In September 1896 the contract for what was to be called the
Chinese Eastern Railroad was finally signed between the Chinese
government and the Russo-Chinese Bank. The Chinese tried to
put many safeguards into this agreement. Even in the earlier St.
Petersburg negotiations, Li had refused to give the railroad concession to the Russian government. Nevertheless, the railroad
soon became a major instrument of Russian penetration into Manchuria since the railroad company itself quickly became only a
thinly disguised instrument of the Russian government. St. Petersburg had scored a major triumph. This was to become increasingly evident in later years, as all pretense that the railroad was a
joint Russian-Chinese venture was almost completely dropped.
The railroad company became in effect a Russian colonial administration in Manchuria, administering the large right-of-way
territory through which the rail line ran, operating its own
strong police force which constituted in effect a private army
on Chinese territory, collecting taxes and governing the cities and
towns which grew up along the railroad. What was intended
became evident even at the very beginning, when the sale of
shares in the Chinese Eastern Railroad Company was conducted
in such a way that would-be individual purchasers were shut out
and the Russian treasury got them all. Much of the money for
actually building the line, however, came from France in the
form of loans.

The Russian successes naturally increased the appetites of the
other great powers, and the Germans acted energetically in 1897.
Using the murder of two German missionaries as an excuse,
German forces occupied Kiaochow in mid-November 1897.
Shortly afterward, the Tsar decided to seize Dairen and Port
Arthur on the Liaotung Peninsula, the very same area the Rus-
sians had prevented the Japanese from getting in 1895. Witte
objected to this, fearing the impact of Chinese anger on the
Chinese Eastern Railroad, but the decision was taken, neverthe-
less, and executed by Russia's Far Eastern fleet. Under subse-

quent Russian pressure, the Chinese government was compelled to lease the territory to Russia for 25 years and to permit the building of a branch line of the Chinese Eastern Railroad from Harbin to Port Arthur and Dairen. France and Britain moved similarly to get their share of the loot. The process of partitioning China was in full swing. After the event, Witte wrote: "Our seizure of the Kwantung region was an act of unprecedented perfidy." Both hypocrisy and bribery were used to facilitate the major Russian *coup* at Port Arthur. Thus, several times in late 1897 and early 1898 the Russian government assured the Chinese that the occupation was temporary, that the Russian fleet's only purpose was to protect China against German aggression, and that the Russians would withdraw as soon as the Germans got out of Kiaochow. The result of all this maneuvering and deception was that Russia extracted from China greater gains in this area in 1898 than St. Petersburg had prevented Japan from acquiring in 1895.

The partition of China appeared to draw nearer as the year 1900 approached and each of the contenders moved to tighten its hold over the section of China it had picked for its own. Spheres of influence were marked out and the Chinese government was forced to declare she would not "alienate" one or another province to any other foreign power but the one at whose bidding the Chinese were acting at the moment. France got the island of Hainan. Britain extended its hold over the Yangtze Valley. Japan won assurances about Fukien. Then, to make assurance doubly sure—or to try to, anyway—the British and the Russians in April 1899 recognized each other's spheres of influence. Under the pretext of agreement on zones for building railroads, the Russians recognized British dominance in the Yangtze Valley, while the British recognized Russian primacy in the area "north of the Great Chinese Wall." In this situation the United States naturally feared for the future of its trade, investments and other economic activities in a China which might soon become simply a collection of foreign colonies. Moreover, the United States itself had no leased ports or spheres of influence to guard. Therefore, Secretary of State John Hay announced the Open Door doctrine, aimed at giving American merchants and investors rights of access to Chinese markets equal to the access enjoyed by merchants and investors of the powers controlling the different spheres of influence and leased ports. The American Secretary of State had Russia very much in mind when he moved in this way to try to protect China's territorial integrity and American rights in China. The Russians, it need hardly be added, were not pleased, but after some delay they agreed to the Hay idea in words at least, though some of the words were ambiguous.

Very important, too, were the Russian efforts in the late 1890's to make Korea a vassal state. The Japanese victory in 1895 had forced the Chinese to recognize Korean independence. Tokyo began to strengthen its influence in Korea under the cloak of supporting Korean reformers, provoking disturbances which induced the King of Korea in February 1896 to take refuge in the Russian embassy in Seoul. Despite Japanese opposition, this enabled the Russians to turn Korea into a virtual Russian protectorate for a time. Russian officers were sent to train the Korean army, lumber and mining concessions were granted Russians, and in May 1896 the Korean king was even induced to ask the new Tsar, Nicholas II, to place Korea formally under Russian protection. The Tsar agreed, but his foreign minister managed to persuade him not to make a decision that might mean war with Japan. The Korean king left the Russian embassy in February 1897 and continued to work with his former protectors. The Korean government formed in September 1897 had a pro-Russian chief and all seemed to be going as the Russian minister in Seoul, Alexis Speyer, wanted it. But early in 1898 the king turned against the Russians. When Speyer demanded the removal of some anti-Russian figures from the government, threatening otherwise to withdraw the Russian military instructors from Korea, the king rejected the demand and the officers had to leave. The newly opened Russian-Korean Bank was ordered closed. The Koreans were using the rivalry between Russia and Japan to try to obtain a maximum of independence for themselves.

These events coincided roughly with St. Petersburg's success in leasing the Liaotung Peninsula from China and thus getting for itself—as we have noted—a privilege Russia had denied Japan in 1895. St. Petersburg decided to soften the latter blow to Tokyo by concessions in Korea. The result was the Nishi-Rosen Protocol of April 1898 in which both parties recognized Korean independence and promised not to interfere in Korean internal affairs. The same treaty also gave Japan predominant economic rights in

Korea, equivalent to a monopoly position. But the very next year the Russian government took over vast timber concessions in Korea from private Russian interests; these they expanded in 1901. The Tsar in the early 1900's was still determined to make Korea a Russian province. He was working with advisers who had outlined a fantastic scheme to him: the conquest of Korea by troops brought into that country in the guise of lumberjacks to work the vast timber concessions the Russian government had obtained. Korea, therefore, was another battleground in the Russian effort to seize as much of China's historic empire as possible.

In Russia at the beginning of the twentieth century, foreign policy was ultimately made by the Tsar. The high officials surrounding him were essentially advisers who could suggest policies, conduct wars of memoranda against each other and otherwise intrigue to gain the Tsar's adoption of their ideas. But once the Tsar had made his decision, all officials had to obey the line he had set or else leave their posts. We have noted the role of Witte in influencing policy; the Tsar also gave much attention to the views of War Minister General Alexei Kuropatkin, a hero of the conquest of Central Asia. In the decade from 1895 to 1905 Russia had three foreign ministers: in order, Prince Lobanov-Rostovsky, Mikhail Muraviev and Count Vladimir Lamsdorff.

In the late 1890's, Witte tended to be the most cautious of the Tsar's advisers on the Far East, urging concentration on economic penetration and avoidance of armed conflict. General Kuropatkin tended to be the most aggressive adviser, confident of the strength of Russian arms and willing to use them against a China whose weakness had been shown up in the Sino-Japanese War. It is characteristic of Kuropatkin that when he got news of the Boxer Rebellion in 1900, he was overjoyed. "I am very glad!" he told Witte then. "This will give us an excuse for seizing Manchuria." He had dreams of repeating his Central Asian triumphs against China. Witte, troubled by long-range considerations, worried that "if we assault China with fire and sword, we are forever making China our sworn enemy."

But even Kuropatkin was put in the shade in the early 1900's by a new group of adventurous imperialists who caught the Tsar's ear and began influencing his policy. The group was led by Privy Councilor A. M. Bezobrazov, who dreamed of Russia ruling the entire yellow race. Among its most important members was General Eugen Alexeyev, reputedly an illegitimate son of Alexander II. The conflicts among these advisers and cliques produced confusion and bewilderment among both Russians and non-Russians. Ambassadors abroad and other high government officials frequently did not know what the Tsar's policy really was, and as a result often gave out misinformation based on ignorance (though at other times misinformation was disseminated deliberately). The anger this situation produced abroad was vividly mirrored by American Secretary of State Hay when he wrote President Theodore Roosevelt in 1903 about the difficulties of negotiating with Russia, and commented: "Dealing with a government with whom mendacity is a science is an extremely difficult and delicate matter. . . . We are not charged with the cure of the Russian soul and we may let them go to the devil at their own sweet will."[8] While the influence of different advisers rose and fell, and different cliques held the upper hand at different times, the decisive element was the determination of Nicholas II to spread the dominion of Russia in Asia as widely and as rapidly as prudently possible. It was to prove a very expensive determination, one which helped lay the groundwork for the end of the Romanov dynasty and the Tsar's own execution.

But neither the Tsar nor any of his advisers knew what lay ahead when the Boxer Rebellion reached its climax in 1900 and opened the door to what seemed to be great further advances. The Boxer movement was a primitive but powerful Chinese grassroots reaction against the nation's humiliation at the hands of foreigners and the growing impact of these strangers upon traditional Chinese life. The Boxer ideology combined genuine patriotism, nationalistic xenophobia and religious fantasy to produce a movement whose members felt it their holy mission to kill the foreigners and the Chinese converts to Christianity. Many Boxers believed naively that observance of Boxer rituals would guarantee each individual Boxer's personal immunity to bullets, knives, spears or other hostile weapons. It is still a curious point as to how the Boxers arranged their apparently often convincing public demonstrations of their supposed invulnerability to hostile weapons. When a Boxer was struck down by these weapons, it was explained that he had presumably failed to believe ardently enough or had made a mistake in carrying out the prescribed complicated ritual. Millions came to believe that the Boxers and their magic could rid China of the cursed foreigners. Among those who placed their faith in the Boxers for a time was the ruler of China, the Dowager Empress, a fact that was to have great international political significance when she put the Chinese armed forces on the side of the Boxers in 1900.

So far as the Russians were concerned, the Boxer Rebellion had two aspects. One, the less important, was participation in the international force which marched on Peking in mid-1900 and lifted the Chinese siege of the foreign diplomats and their legation quarter in that city. The second aspect was the Russian use of Boxer activity in Manchuria to put that whole rich province under Russian military occupation.

The allied force of almost 20,000 men who marched on Peking from Tientsin included about 4,000 Russian soldiers under General Linevich. The polyglot relief force was plagued by national jealousies, confusion, misunderstandings and other ills to be expected of such a hastily created enterprise. Moreover, when the Russians were the first to break into Peking, some of their glory-hungry allies smarted under this feat and accused them of duplicity in not keeping to the plan of campaign. There is dispute on this point, but one fact is clear: the Russians joined enthusiastically with all the allies in looting Peking. Count Witte wrote in his memoirs:

> It was rumored that Russian army officers took a part in the looting, and I must say, to our shame, that our agent in Peking unofficially confirmed these rumors to me. One lieutenant general, who had received the Cross of St. George for the capture of Peking [apparently General Linevich] returned to his post in the Amur region with ten trunks full of valuables from the looted Peking palaces. Unfortunately, the general's example was followed by other army men.[9]

Perhaps the most ironical incident of the looting was the Russian removal of the original text of the Russian-Chinese treaty of alliance from the bedroom of the Dowager Empress who had escaped from the city before its capture by the relief force. Later, Russian authorities returned the document to the Chinese as "evidence" that Russia remained faithful to the alliance.[10]

In November 1900 the Russian armed forces used their power to force the Chinese to give them a concession of land in Tientsin, an example immediately followed by Japan, Austria, France, Belgium and Germany. Russian ambitions in the heart of China were also vividly indicated when Russian armed forces seized the Peking-Tientsin and Tientsin-Shanhaikwan rail lines. This alarmed the other European powers, particularly Britain, and their pressure forced the Russians to surrender these key rail arteries.

Remembering the precedent of 1895, when Russia's demonstrative friendship for China paved the way for major Russian gains in Manchuria, Russia's allies were dismayed shortly after the siege of Peking diplomats had been relieved when the Russian minister announced the Russian troops would be recalled from Peking to Tientsin. Russia asserted that its only interest was to help restore order and a proper legal government in China. Thus the Russians sought to distinguish themselves from the other "imperialists" with whom they had worked so closely in the preceding weeks. We must turn to Manchuria, however, to understand why St. Petersburg was so anxious to impress the Chinese with its friendliness.

The Boxer movement, and its temporary backing by the Peking government in mid-1900, had profound repercussions in Manchuria, where many of the native population hated and feared the Russian penetration. The railroads under construction there were attacked and badly damaged. Chinese troops attacked Russian ships on the Amur River, bombarded Blagoveshchensk on the Russian side of the river, and even burned down Russian churches in Manchuria. Panic-stricken, Russians fled the province into Siberia or into the Port Arthur area where Russian troops were stationed. At Blagoveshchensk, the local Russian authorities retaliated in a particularly dreadful fashion, driving several thousand Chinese—men, women and children—into the Amur, where they drowned. St. Petersburg moved swiftly to take military advantage of the situation thus created. Russian troops moved into Manchuria and within a short period controlled the entire province, having routed the Chinese forces easily. The stage seemed set for the annexation of Manchuria, or something close to it.

Russian intentions in Manchuria became even clearer in November 1900 when the local Russian commander, General Alexeyev, forced the local Chinese authorities under Tseng-chi to accept a humiliating agreement. This provided that, though Chinese civil administration was to be restored in Manchuria, Chinese troops should be disbanded and disarmed and their military supplies turned over to Russian authorities. The agreement also authorized the stationing of Russian troops along the railroad right of way as guards. This naturally alarmed the Chinese authorities in Peking, and even drew opposition from Witte in St. Petersburg. The Chinese leaked the contents of the Alexeyev-Tseng agreement to the West and it was published in the *Times* of London on January 3, 1901, provoking consternation and protest in Western Europe, the United States and Japan. But the expansionists still held the upper hand in St. Petersburg, a fact shown by the contents of a draft Chinese-Russian treaty handed the Chinese ambassador by Russian Foreign Minister Lamsdorff in February 1901. This new draft went even further than the Alexeyev-Tseng agreement. It included such provisions as the requirement of Russian-Chinese consultation over the number of Chinese troops to be permitted in Manchuria after the Chinese Eastern Railroad was completed; prohibition of Chinese arms imports into Manchuria; the Russian right to secure the dismissal of any high-ranking Chinese official in Manchuria; and Chinese agreement to get Russian permission before giving any other nation railroad, mining or other concessions in the whole vast border area of China from Sinkiang through Mongolia and Manchuria. The Chinese leaked these new demands to the West and the international situation promptly showed the effects of the shock. Britain, Germany and Japan advised the Chinese not to sign the treaty. Threats of war against Russia began to be heard, especially from Japan.[11]

Li Hung-chang, who was directing China's foreign policy, was playing a complicated game. Having been promised a million-ruble bribe by the Russian government, he put on a show of advocating signature of the Russian draft agreement; the other powers all regarded him as a paid Russian agent. But at the same time he told the British representative that the Chinese government would be willing to communicate the Russian demands "and place itself in the hands of the powers for protection against Russia, whose demands it could not deny and whose constant threats terrified it." Japan in particular seemed to be anxious to go to war to prevent the Chinese capitulation to the Russian de-

mands, but the other major powers also urged the Chinese to refuse their signature and in various ways communicated their
displeasure to the Russians. The result was a Russian retreat. First
they presented a revised draft in which, for example, the Chinese
commitment to give no concessions to other powers was limited
to Manchuria rather than to the entire Sino-Russian border area
of Manchuria, Mongolia and Sinkiang. Finally in April 1901 the
Russians gave up completely for the moment. Count Lamsdorff
announced that the draft treaty was being withdrawn and denied that Russia had ever had any desire to violate China's sovereignty or territorial integrity. He denounced the interference
of other powers and said that Russian troops would remain in
Manchuria until China had a more stable government able and
willing to negotiate a treaty for withdrawal of Russian troops.
The Russians had been checkmated for the moment in their efforts to get further legal rights in China, but their troops still
ruled Manchuria.

The alarm raised among the other powers by this Russian
maneuvering did not end, and its most concrete result was the
Anglo-Japanese Alliance of January 1902, a treaty aimed at curb-
ing Russian imperialism both in China and in Korea. Its immediate implication was that Russia would have to go to war with
both Japan and England if it sought to continue its drive for
Manchuria along the lines of late 1900 and 1901.

Shortly before the Anglo-Japanese Alliance, in the fall of
1901, the Russians had been negotiating with Li Hung-chang
what finally seemed like an acceptable treaty. This provided for
the withdrawal of Russian troops from Manchuria by 1902 and
included permission for Chinese troops to be in Manchuria. But
at the last moment the Chinese were told they would have to sign
a secret agreement giving the Russo-Chinese Bank what amounted
to a monopoly on the economic development of Manchuria. The
Russians offered a 300,000 ruble bribe to Li if he would agree, but
he stormed that "he could never dare to accept the responsibility
for such an agreement which gives over to the Bank all Manchuria." Li died suddenly on November 4. The American envoy
in Peking reported to his government that only a few hours before Li's death, the Russian minister went to Li's house and tried
to have the official seals affixed on the treaty in the presence of
the dying statesman, but he had come too late since the seals had

already been given to another official. Early in 1902 the United States learned that the Chinese government was prepared to sign an agreement for evacuation of Russian troops which would give the Russo-Chinese Bank exclusive privileges for industrial development in Manchuria. The United States protested vigorously; Secretary of State Hay went so far as to say that if these privileges were granted, the United States "would be left in a position so painful as to be intolerable." This fervent United States opposition, together with the threat posed by the Anglo-Japanese Treaty, left the Russians no choice but to drop the demand for the bank to have these special privileges. The Russian-Chinese agreement finally signed on April 8, 1902 was far better for the Chinese than any earlier version. In this treaty Russia recognized Chinese sovereignty over Manchuria and promised to withdraw her troops from Manchuria in three stages over a period of 18 months. The reoccupation of Manchuria by Chinese troops was permitted, but only after the Russians had agreed as to the number of these troops and where they might be stationed.

From the Russo-Chinese Treaty of 1902 to the outbreak of the Russo-Japanese War in February 1904, the formation of Russian policy toward China was dominated much of the time by the fierce struggle at the apex of Russian power in St. Petersburg. Witte, supported increasingly by Foreign Minister Lamsdorff and even by General Kuropatkin, the defense minister, was for a relatively cautious policy of economic infiltration into China. Witte wanted to avoid war with Japan, and was even willing to sacrifice Korea to Japan. The palace clique of adventurers under Bezobrazov, which included the influential interior minister, Plehve, favored a much bolder policy.

Bezobrazov wrote the Tsar: "The Far East is still in a period when a stubborn struggle is necessary in order to assure the consolidation of our realm; domination by us is the ultimate aim of this struggle; without such domination we are not able either to rule the yellow race or control the inimical influence of our European rivals." The Bezobrazov group used its influence to stall the evacuation of Manchuria and to put new demands before China.

The first stage of the evacuation took place smoothly on October 8, 1902, but at Newchwang in Manchuria Russia continued to supervise the customs, the local administration and the judiciary, and to collect taxes. At other Manchurian ports, the Russians set up their own independent customs service. The second stage of the evacuation, scheduled for April 1903, did not take place. Instead, the Russian minister in Peking, Lesar, presented a list of seven new demands to the Chinese. The Russians demanded that no additional treaty ports or foreign consuls be allowed in Manchuria, that no foreigners other than Russians be employed in the North China public service and that no territory in Manchuria be transferred to any foreign power. The Chinese made these demands known to the West, and the United States, Britain and Japan denounced the Russian conditions, simultaneously warning China not to grant them. Count Lamsdorff categorically denied to the American ambassador that any such demands had been made. It was this denial which made Secretary of State Hay explode about Russia having a "government with whom mendacity is a science." The United States was vitally interested because it wanted the opening of Manchurian ports to American ships and trade. The Chinese said they would be glad to grant the United States' desires, but that the Russians would not let them and would use any such action as an excuse for not withdrawing their troops. Russian Ambassador Cassini in Washington, on the other hand, said his country had no objections. This was a game of diplomatic doubletalk.

The basic decision on Russian policy in Manchuria was made after a special conference on February 7, 1903 between the Tsar and his advisers. Witte and Lamsdorff demanded agreement with Japan and withdrawal of Russian claims to Korea and southern Manchuria, but the Tsar decided against them. On July 30, 1903, he named General Alexeyev to a new post, viceroy of the Far East. This removed Far Eastern policy and armies from the jurisdiction of the ministers of foreign affairs and war, and put them instead under one of the key members of the imperialistic Bezobrazov clique. In effect two rival Russian governments existed, each intriguing against the other for the Tsar's favor. It was an ideal situation for confusion.

At about the same time in the summer of 1903, the Japanese suggested joint consultation about the two countries' Far Eastern interests. Tokyo submitted a draft treaty providing nominally for respecting the independence and territorial integrity of China and Korea. But the crux of the proposal was a section calling for reciprocal recognition of Japan's "preponderant interests in Korea and Russia's special interest in railway enterprises in Manchuria, and of the right of Japan to take in Korea and of Russia to take in Manchuria such measures as may be necessary for the protection of their respective interests." This set off a bitter fight in St. Petersburg between those like General Kuropatkin who thought the proposed treaty was acceptable and the members of the Bezobrazov clique who were determined not to surrender Russian designs on Korea.

The United States was involved in all this, too, because it was pressing China to sign a trade agreement which would open Mukden and Antung to foreign trade and permit the appointment of American consuls in Manchuria. Russian opposition was so intense that United States Minister Conger wrote the State Department despairingly: "What's the use? Russia is too big, too crafty, too cruel for us to fight. She will conquer in the end. Why not give up now and be friendly?"[12]

The date for complete Russian evacuation from Manchuria, October 8, 1903, was ignored by St. Petersburg, but the signing of the Chinese-American commercial treaty regarding Manchuria on that day brought howls of protest from the Russian expansionists. From Port Arthur, General Alexeyev's group assailed the agreement as "unfriendly and undiplomatic." Bezobrazov himself declared Russia intended to remain in Manchuria and "had no idea of permitting other nations to have equal commercial privileges with Russia there." These influential figures brought the same spirit into the negotiations with Japan. The Japanese amended their original proposal and suggested a neutral zone along the Manchurian-Korean border. The Bezobrazov group fought determinedly against even the modified Japanese position, refusing to give up the Yalu lumbering concession in Korea for which such high hopes were held. As a result the Tokyo proposals were rejected, but the Tsar wanted to continue negotiations and hoped to avoid war. The Russians' arrogance, their refusal to make significant concessions and their obstinate maintenance of illegal forces in Manchuria finally convinced the Japanese they could hope for no deal with St. Petersburg. On February 8, 1904, the Japanese fleet off Port Arthur began the Russo-Japanese War with a surprise attack on the Russian ships anchored off the port. If Americans had remembered this event, they might have avoided a similar Japanese surprise attack at Pearl Harbor on December 7, 1941.

Rarely has a nation miscalculated as completely as the Russian government did in the Russo-Japanese War. One of those who had favored the war, reactionary Minister of Interior Plehve, had declared: "We need a small victorious war to stem the tide of revolution." But the war actually helped bring on a near-revolution in 1905 and speeded up the decay of the Tsarist system. Its generals and admirals were shown to be incompetent; scandals in connection with troops and supplies exposed the corruption in the bureaucracy; and military defeat followed military defeat on both land and sea. We need not go into details of the war here. Suffice it to say that much of the land fighting between Russian and Japanese troops took place in Manchuria where the Russians suffered defeat time and again. Port Arthur surrendered on January 1, 1905. The great battle of Mukden in February and March, involving a total of 750,000 combatants, ended in Japanese victory. The final blow to Russian military hopes came in May 1905 when the Russian Baltic fleet arrived in the Pacific and was annihilated by Admiral Togo's forces at Tsushima. At home the war was widely unpopular among the Russian masses. Defeatist sentiments were very common among leftist and liberal forces. When Father Gapon led a workers' march on the Winter Palace, the demonstrators were met by a barrage of bullets. This outrage set off a wave of political strikes and agrarian disturbances which ultimately forced the Tsar to grant the first Russian Constitution and the establishment of the Duma.

Witte and Rosen represented Russia at the negotiations which began with Japan in Portsmouth, New Hampshire on August 9, 1905. The final peace treaty signed there showed what a major victory the Japanese had won. Russia recognized the paramount Japanese political, military and economic interests in Korea; Russia also agreed to withdraw its troops from Manchuria, and, subject to China's consent, transferred the Liaotung Peninsula lease—including Port Arthur and Dairen—to Japan, which also got free of charge the Russian-built railroads in the south of Manchuria. Russia ceded the southern part of Sakhalin Island to Japan and gave Japanese citizens fishing rights in the seas adjacent to Russia in the Pacific. The whole Russian Far Eastern drive, begun so brilliantly in 1895, seemed to have collapsed.

CHAPTER V

Tsarist Russia's Last Gains

FOR BOTH Russia and China, the years 1905–1917 were tumultuous. In Russia the period began with an unsuccessful revolution and ended with two successful ones, the first of which toppled the Tsar while the second installed Bolshevik power. In China these were the years in which the centuries-old Manchu dynasty met its doom and was replaced by a weak and strife-ridden republic. But from the point of view of Russian-Chinese relations, the chief theme of this period was the same as earlier. Russian territorial encroachment on China continued as before, actually making some of its major gains in the years just preceding the end of the Romanov dynasty. Anyone who thought in 1905 that Russia's defeat by Japan and the extensive concessions made to Tokyo in the Treaty of Portsmouth spelled the end of St. Petersburg's pressure on China soon learned differently. What changed after 1905 was the direction of Russian pressure for new gains at China's expense; at the same time St. Petersburg used these years to improve and strengthen its position in northern Manchuria, the area in which the Russian presence was permitted to remain by the provisions of the Portsmouth Treaty.

The key to the 1905–1917 period was Russian-Japanese cooperation. Though strained at times, this cooperation dominated both countries' relations with China. The two countries moved together, aiming to divide northern China between themselves while fighting off both Chinese resistance and possible competitive encroachment by other powers, notably the United States. In Tokyo and St. Petersburg there were influential men who saw that in defenseless China's huge territory and resources there was more than enough for both nations, if they would work together rather than fight each other. The Japanese wanted Russian sup-

80

port as they turned Korea into a colony and fastened their hold more securely on southern Manchuria. The Russians wanted similar Japanese backing as they turned northern Manchuria into virtually a Russian colony and started extending the colonization process into other areas of northern China adjacent to Russian borders. Each country distrusted the other, of course, and kept a sharp eye out to make sure the other did not make any unexpected gains. Rivalry and jealousy between them went hand in hand with cooperation.

Four secret Japanese-Russian treaties—in 1907, 1910, 1912 and 1916—spelled out the details of the two nations' alliance against China and against others who would rival them in feeding off North China. The 1907 agreement saw Japan recognize Russia's primacy in northern Manchuria and Russia's "special interests" in Outer Mongolia, while Russia promised to respect Japan's primacy in Korea and southern Manchuria. In the 1910 agreement each side gave the other a free hand in its assigned portion of Manchuria, and both sides agreed to take "common action" should either's "special interests" in Manchuria be threatened. The 1912 agreement provided for the definition of the two powers' spheres of influence in Inner Mongolia. The 1916 agreement reached during World War I provided for an alliance against any third power "which may be hostile to Russia or Japan" and which might threaten to win political dominance over China. The treaty was certainly aimed at Germany, and probably also at the United States.

One of the key factors driving the Russians and Japanese together during this period was their fear of the United States, which they saw striving for major economic and political penetration of Manchuria. A moving spirit in these American efforts was young Willard Straight. As American consul in Mukden from 1906 to 1908 he tried to arrange massive American investment in Manchuria, arguing this would both help protect China's territorial integrity and serve the interests of the United States. Another key figure was American railroad magnate Edward H. Harriman. The latter, whose son W. Averell Harriman was to play a key role in Soviet-American relations a half century later, envisioned a great globe-circling transportation system which would be facilitated by American ownership of either the Trans-Siberian Railroad, the Japanese-owned South Manchuria Railroad, or both. J. P. Morgan and Company and Kuhn Loeb and Company were also involved in these efforts, which had sympathetic support from the Taft administration. President Taft himself had declared that American foreign policy in the Far East "may well be made to include active intervention to secure for our merchandise and our capitalists opportunity for profitable investment which shall inure to the benefit of both countries concerned."[1] These efforts failed, primarily because the Russo-Japanese partnership effectively kept Manchuria a preserve for those two nations and their financial and commercial interests.

In China the key event of this period was the fall in 1912, after more than 250 years of power, of the Manchu dynasty. The men who led this revolution were moved very largely by nationalistic motives. They were appalled by the degeneracy and incompetence of Manchu rule, and they resented bitterly the repeated humiliations China had received at foreign hands. Sun Yat-sen and other revolutionary leaders dreamed of a new China, militarily, politically and economically strong, which could take what they considered its rightful place in the world community.

But the immediate impact of the revolution was fighting, disunity and fragmentation of political power over the country. To the greedy foreign powers watching the developing events, the Chinese Revolution seemed to offer new opportunities for further gains at China's expense. The Russian foreign ministry made this judgment as events unfolded: "From the point of view of our interests, the dissolution of the present Chinese Empire would be desirable in more than one respect. Even in the event that various parts of China will not become entirely independent, there will develop between them a rivalry which will weaken them."

Russia took advantage of China's weakness before and after the fall of the Manchus to buttress its position in northern Manchuria. The result was described in these words by a Russian general in 1914:

> The Chinese Eastern Railway Administration represents, in the full sense of the word, a *colonial government* with all functions inherent to it. The manager of the railway administers at the same time the territory of the zone together with its population through all branches and in all respects; he is even

endowed with the power of diplomatic relations, for which there is a special department in the structure of the administration.[2]

There was complete Russian political and economic control of the railway zone through Manchuria and the extensive lands adjoining the railway and annexed to the zone. Russian laws and Russian courts functioned in the zone; police and military power were in the hands of Russians, and a great new Russian city grew up at Harbin, the key station on the line. Using the railroad as a base, the Russians pressed economic penetration of Manchuria as rapidly as possible. Russian ships won the right to use the extensive Manchurian river system, and the Sungari River traffic became an important part of the Chinese Eastern Railroad's activities. The railroad opened up numerous coal mines and lumbering camps in Manchuria, too, and operated a large network of schools, libraries and clubs throughout its zone as well. This was a Russian empire within China, complete with a large-scale missionary enterprise aimed at disseminating Christianity among the Chinese.

The opening up of northern Manchuria by the Russian railroad had major consequences, however, which St. Petersburg may not have anticipated and which increased concern among many Russians as time went on. About 2,000,000 people lived in northern Manchuria in the 1890's; by 1914 the figure was about 8,000,000. All but about 100,000 or 200,000 of these were Chinese attracted by the new economic opportunities created in the wake of the railroad, which could bring the area's products quickly and cheaply to markets. Chinese farmers began to work the soil, and the soybean soon became a major export crop. And as Chinese settlers moved north of the railroad and began farming the areas near the Russian border, the possibilities this opened for the future began to trouble some officials. One former manager of the railroad complained that his country had spent 800,000,000 rubles to settle 200,000 Russians and 15,000,000 Chinese in Manchuria. In southern Manchuria, where the Japanese-sponsored economic development was even more intensive, the Chinese population grew still more rapidly. Manchuria as a whole had had about 8,000,000 people in 1890; by 1920 it had 23,000,000.

We need not enter here into the detailed maneuvering by which the original Russian private railroad concession for Manchuria granted by Li Hung-chang in 1896 became the Russian economic empire and Tsarist colonial area of 1914. Suffice it to say that the tactics were no prettier than similar imperialistic ventures elsewhere. The Russians stretched their legal rights to the maximum and then exceeded them. They could do so successfully during these years because neither before nor after the Chinese Revolution could China resist successfully. The balance of power favoring the Russians was too uneven.

The most directly favorable impact of the Chinese Revolution, from Russia's point of view, was felt in Outer Mongolia. As we have seen, the boundary between Russia and Mongolia had been fixed in the Treaty of Kyakhta in the early eighteenth century. The next two centuries there were relatively quiet since the Chinese regarded this vast, arid region as a buffer zone between China and Russia. The relatively primitive Mongol people lived as nomadic herdsmen in a feudal society which was ruled by princes claiming descent from Genghis Khan as well as by Buddhist religious leaders. The prevailing Lamaism had turned a large fraction of the Mongolian adult males into monks living a life the very antithesis of that led by their ancestors, who had once conquered almost all of Europe and Asia. Small colonies of Chinese merchants living in the few cities of the region handled much of Mongolia's trade and exercised powerful economic influence through credits extended to the poverty-stricken herdsmen. About 5,000 Russians lived in the area before the Chinese Revolution, engaging in trade against the Chinese competition, operating some leather factories and trying to exploit gold deposits.

Russian expansionist intentions toward Mongolia were expressed most frankly about 1910 by the *Journal of Commerce and Industry*, the organ of the Russian industrialists:

Mongolia and Northern Manchuria naturally gravitate, geographically and economically, toward Russia. . . . We must do business there and control their markets. Moreover, our frontier with China is unnatural, sinuous, difficult to defend, and completely contrary to physico-geographical conditions. A natural boundary of Russia should consist of the deserts of Mongolia (Gobi). Those lifeless seas of sand can be compared to the oceans which separate peoples and states. Also two different and absolutely incompatible races, like the yellow and the European, ought to be separated by real obstacles to a mass invasion. If we do not think about that at present, and if we allow the Chinese to control Mongolia and Manchuria, then the roads which are to be constructed by them through the desert, close to us along the Russian frontier, would be utilized to strengthen their economic and political position to such an extent that we Russians will be pushed backward to the Urals.[3]

Russian interest and increased activity in Mongolia after 1904 soon discovered fertile ground in the growing discontent of the Mongols. This was the product of increased Manchu activity in the area, which the native people saw as a threat. The key move was the decision to open Mongolia to Chinese settlement, followed by the beginning of systematic efforts to encourage large-scale Chinese colonization of Mongolia. Plans were also announced for stationing permanent Chinese garrisons in the area, for initiating Chinese mining enterprises, for a railroad and for a new Chinese industrial bank in Mongolia. Moreover, in 1910, a new Chinese *amban* or governor in Urga, capital of Outer Mongolia, began setting up a large network of government bureaus and schools. The Mongols did not like the prospect of increased Chinese immigration and tighter Chinese controls. The Mongol princes feared the lessening of their power as the new Chinese bureaucracy expanded. And all the Mongols disliked the new heavy taxes levied to support the burgeoning Chinese establishment. The Mongol leaders began to think of independence, of carving out a new vast Mongolian nation embracing all the related Mongol peoples. All this fitted in well with the Russian plans, and with the Russian fears that the new Manchu activity in Mongolia was primarily directed against the rising Russian influence there. Russian agents in Mongolia took care, therefore, to inflame this dissatisfaction and to encourage the Mongols to look to Russia for help in gaining independence from China. But there were also important voices to be heard in St. Petersburg about 1910 warning against too much involvement in Mongolian affairs and against excessive risks there.

It was with mixed emotions, therefore, that St. Petersburg received a delegation sent by the *khutukhtu* (living Buddha) and princes of Mongolia in August 1911. The delegation wanted Russian support for Mongolian independence and against Chinese efforts to change the status quo in Mongolia. A special conference

of high Russian officials decided that it would be inexpedient to
support Mongolian independence, since this would involve complications which could divert Russian energies from Europe. But
it was decided to support the Mongols in trying to maintain their
own way of life and to protect the delegation and those who had
sent them. A concrete measure taken was the sending of 200
Russian soldiers with machine guns to the Russian consulate in
Urga. But the attitude of more ambitious Russian circles was
typified by a Captain Makushek who was appointed to head the
secret Russian convoy taking the Mongolian delegates home.
He suggested using the Russian trading firms in Mongolia to
set up a secret network of arms depots there. He proposed following this with the organization of partisan detachments which
would stage an armed demonstration making possible the seizure
of power in the area.

It was the activists who won out in the months that followed.
Encouraged by the Chinese Revolution, the Mongols decided to
revolt. They asked for and got from the Russians some 15,000
rifles, 7,000,000 cartridges, and 15,000 sabers in November 1911.
The Russian war ministry, which had its Irkutsk military district
deliver the arms, described the delivery as that of "private business
firearms." At the beginning of December the Mongols carried out
a *coup d'état* in Urga, disarming the small detachment of Chinese
soldiers there and forcing the Chinese governor to take refuge
in the Russian consulate, from which he was subsequently permitted to leave in Russian military custody for Peking via Siberia.
On December 16, the formation of a new independent "Empire
of Mongolia" was proclaimed with the Urga *khutukhtu* as its
head, administering a government of five ministries—war, foreign
affairs, interior, finance and justice. All Chinese merchants were
expelled from Mongolia at the same time.

Though Russian diplomatic pressure protected them against
the weak new Chinese government that succeeded the Manchus
in 1912, the Mongols were soon embroiled in bitter arguments
with the Russians. The Mongols wanted a really independent all-
Mongol state, combining Inner and Outer Mongolia, as well as
the area of Barga in Manchuria whose inhabitants had expelled
the Chinese in January 1912 and submitted to the Urga *khutukhtu's* rule. But the Russians opposed union of Inner and Outer
Mongolia since this development would conflict with their secret

treaty commitments to Japan. Moreover, the Russians also opposed the efforts of the Mongols to establish diplomatic and other contacts with states besides Russia and China, fearing the entry of competitors for commercial and political influence in Outer Mongolia. It took hard bargaining to get the Russo-Mongolian Treaty of November 3, 1912 concluded, and the Mongols were no longer very happy about the friend and protector they had turned to. The treaty did promise that Russia would help Mongolia "preserve her present autonomy and also her right to keep her national army, forbidding entry to Chinese armies and colonization of her lands by the Chinese." Mongolia in turn gave Russian subjects extensive privileges to live and engage in economic activities anywhere in Mongolia. A Russian postal service in Mongolia was also agreed to in the treaty. No rights denied Russians could be given to citizens of any third power. Given the great disparity of economic and political development between Russians and Mongols, it is clear the treaty amounted to creation of a Russian political and economic protectorate in Mongolia.

The news of the Russian-Mongolian Treaty created a storm in China. The new Chinese government denied that any valid treaty could be entered into between Russia and a part of China. The Chinese foreign office refused to accept a copy of the treaty from the Russians. Mass protest demonstrations took place throughout China and both high officials and ordinary citizens demanded the dispatch of armed forces to win back Outer Mongolia, even at the risk of provoking war with Russia. A Chinese military buildup began on the borders of Outer Mongolia, but Russia warned Peking that entry of troops into Outer Mongolia would mean war. Feeling rose so high that the Chinese foreign minister had to leave his post and flee Peking to ensure his safety. But the hard reality was that China was in no position to challenge the Russians militarily. It had no alternative but to try to salvage as much as possible by diplomatic means.

Very hard bargaining followed between Russia and China. A draft treaty agreed to in May 1913 was rejected by the Chinese in July. But finally a Russian-Chinese Declaration was made in November; the document was far from palatable to the Chinese but it was accepted as the best possible by Yuan Shih-kai, who had established what amounted to personal dictatorial rule over China.

The declaration represented an exchange of Russia's recognition of China's suzerainty—but not sovereignty—over Outer Mongolia in return for China's recognition of Outer Mongolia's autonomy, its right to carry on its own internal administration and to settle for itself all questions of commercial and industrial relations with other nations. The last provision in effect legalized the sweeping economic concessions the Russians had won a year earlier in their agreement with the Mongols. China promised to keep troops out of Outer Mongolia and to refrain from colonization, while the Russians promised to keep no troops other than consular guards there. China agreed to accept Russian good offices to help settle the question of its future relations with Mongolia. Territorial and political matters concerning Mongolia were to be settled at a tripartite Russian-Mongolian-Chinese conference. In effect, therefore, a joint Russian-Chinese protectorate over Mongolia was set up, one in which the Russians were the senior partners.

The Mongols were furious in their turn since this agreement provided neither for their full independence nor for the union of Inner and Outer Mongolia. To help soothe the Mongols, the Russians gave them three separate loans totalling over 5,000,000 rubles during 1913–1914. These were intended to pay for reorganizing the administration of Outer Mongolia and for establishing and arming a Mongolian army. To help assure repayment of the loans, the Russians insisted on and secured the Mongols' acceptance of a Russian financial adviser. This adviser, S. A. Kozin, became virtual economic ruler of Outer Mongolia, exercising his functions with the help of an extensive staff of Russian experts. His work was subsequently aided by the formation of a Russian-controlled Mongolian National Bank which had a monopoly on the issuance of currency in Outer Mongolia.

This chapter of Outer Mongolia's history was finally wound up by the tripartite Sino-Russian-Mongolian Agreement signed in June 1915 at Kyakhta after nine months of negotiation. In effect, this incorporated the two earlier agreements, recognizing Outer Mongolia's autonomy under China's suzerainty. Mongolia was given the right to make treaties and agreements of an economic nature but could not make agreements with foreign powers on political or territorial matters. On the latter questions Russia and China had to agree through negotiations with Outer Mongolian participation. As a concession to China, the Mongols agreed that the ruler of Outer Mongolia should receive his title from the president of China. The legal framework was complete for an Outer Mongolia dominated by Russia but nominally part of China.

In one corner of Mongolia, Russia played an even bolder hand at the time of the Chinese Revolution than it played in the rest of Outer Mongolia. This was the northwestern portion of Mongolia termed the Uryankhai district originally and later called Tannu-Tuva. The 60,000 nomadic Mongols there lived in a region roughly the size of Great Britain. They were even more backward than their fellow Mongols and even more vulnerable to the Russian penetration which began when Russian merchants entered the area in the 1860's. It reached a mass basis at the end of the nineteenth century when thousands of Russian peasants began migrating to the area, seizing or leasing land for their farms. Russian settlers and merchants in the area exerted pressure on St. Petersburg to annex the area, but the Tsar's regime was cautious. Its researchers had found China's legal claim to the area incontestable, and there was fear of adverse British reaction to any overt moves. Hence, for a time the Russian government contented itself with backing the establishment of Russian cultural institutions in the area and with sending in a small number of troops.

The Chinese Revolution encouraged a new look at the problem, and the Russian embassy in Peking began urging vigorous action to annex the region. The Tsar agreed, and planning got under way despite the realization that such action would face opposition from both the Mongols and the Chinese. The latter, of course, regarded all of Mongolia as their territory and were still bitter over the Russian maneuvers in Outer Mongolia. The Mongols also regarded Tannu-Tuva as part of their realm. But Tannu-Tuva was too far from Peking for the Chinese to do anything about Russian plans there, and the Mongols were too weak and too dependent upon the Russians.

In 1913 two regional Mongol chiefs were persuaded to appeal to the Tsar to take Tannu-Tuva under his protection. After some debate in St. Petersburg, it was decided to establish a protectorate over the area rather than annex it outright. The plan, a Russian official wrote later, "consisted of the quiet occupation of the region by Russians and the acquisition of *de facto* possession." On July 4, 1914 the Mongol *amban* of the area pledged that Tannu-Tuva would have no independent contact with any other country, thanked the Tsar for accepting the role of protector, promised to submit to the Tsar all local disputes and begged the Russian ruler "to leave to our Uryankhai population their customs, the Buddhist religion which they practice, their way of life, self-government, ranks, and nomad camps, permitting no special alterations which would tend toward a loss of power." Shortly afterward World War I broke out, ending fear of foreign concern over Russian actions in the area. The result was the installation of virtually complete Russian control, including the adoption of Russian civil and criminal codes as the law of the area. Russian immigration into the region was stepped up, and the local Mongol pressure for incorporation into Outer Mongolia was fought ruthlessly. Outer Mongolia's plea for permission to have its agents enter Tannu-Tuva was refused completely in 1916. On the eve of the Russian Revolution, Tannu-Tuva was for all practical purposes part of Russia.

On the border of Russia and Outer Mongolia in northwest Manchuria, the Barga area was the scene of other Russian intrigues aimed at taking advantage of China's troubles at the time of the revolution. The Barguts, a Mongol people, also felt threatened and feared for the future of their nomadic cattle-tending society as the bars to Chinese immigration were lifted. As in Outer Mongolia, it was the war of the nomad against the farmer all over again. Events reached a crisis in Barga in 1911 when the Peking government ordered all schools conducted in Chinese. This resulted in an uprising which swiftly expelled the Chinese troops and pledged allegiance to the Urga *khutukhtu*. The Russians supported the Barguts and effectively warned the Chinese republican government against sending troops into the area. But the Russians opposed the union of Barga with Outer Mongolia. Their plan was to keep the area a part of northern Manchuria, which they hoped to annex. Meanwhile the Russians exerted pressure on China to grant Barga autonomy and to give the Russians priority in any railroad building there. In 1915 China gave in to most of these demands and Barga became a "special district" of China; Chinese immigration was limited and Chinese troops could be sent into the area only after advance notice to Russia. Russian influence was dominant in the area when the situation was radically changed by the dramatic events of 1917.

In Sinkiang, too, the Chinese Revolution produced new Russian activity, including the sending of Russian troops into some parts of the area. China demanded the withdrawal of the Russian troops but again could do nothing effective about it. In reply the Russians demanded the withdrawal of Chinese authority from much of the area and the granting to Russians of the right to settle in the area, demands China rejected. But the real result of the Chinese Revolution was the effective severing of bonds between Sinkiang and Peking, with the result that the area's governor, Yeng Tseng-hsin, ruled with little check. Nothing dramatic happened in the area before the Russian Revolution set new forces into motion.

On the eve of the Tsarist regime's downfall in early 1917, northern Manchuria and Outer Mongolia were essentially Russian protectorates. Russian influence also played an appreciable role in Sinkiang, though a less important one than in the first two areas. Writing about that time, the great Chinese revolutionary leader Sun Yat-sen estimated that this vast Russian sphere of interest in China made up 42 per cent of the country's land area. Britain on the other hand had substantial influence over 28 per cent of China, and Japan and France each had spheres of influence over about 5 per cent of China's territory. But the Russian sphere was primarily an area of mountains, deserts and poor grasslands, a region supporting only 3 or 4 per cent of China's people. If the Romanov dynasty had survived, the likelihood that it would sooner or later have absorbed northern Manchuria, Outer Mongolia and Sinkiang into the Russian empire seems high. But the Romanovs did not survive as Russia's rulers beyond March 1917. And little more than six months later the Bolsheviks took power. The complications that this fundamental development introduced into China's relations with Russia will concern us for the rest of this history.

CHAPTER VI

Soviet Power vs. Chinese Nationalism
in the 1920's

"WHEN the next Chinese general comes to Moscow and shouts, 'Hail to the World Revolution,' better send at once for the G.P.U. [the Soviet secret police]. All that any of them wants is rifles."[1] These bitter and disillusioned words were spoken in the late 1920's by Michael Borodin shortly after his career as chief Kremlin agent in China had ended in an historic debacle. He was paying unwilling tribute to a Chinese general, Chiang Kai-shek, who had outwitted Stalin and administered a crushing defeat to Soviet designs in China. That defeat, inflicted in 1927, was the key event in Russian-Chinese relations between the Bolshevik Revolution and the outbreak of World War II.

In the Petrograd of November 1917, during the "ten days that shook the world," Lenin and his comrades can have given little if any serious thought to China. In the months that followed their seizure of power, these men were concerned with Europe primarily. There were the highly developed capitalist countries with their hordes of proletarians. In these countries, Marxist theory had predicted, Socialism would triumph first. Lenin and Trotsky waited, eager and impatient for revolutions in Germany, France and Britain to bring the beleaguered Bolsheviks of Russia much-needed help. They had no reason in those early months to harbor any great expectations about China. Its vast peasant masses—sunk in what Marx and Engels had called "the idiocy of rural life"— had been almost completely ignored in the earlier Europe-centered analyses of Marxist theoreticians. In China itself there were few, even among the scholars, who knew anything of the Socialist theories for which Lenin stood. But the passage of a few years was to change the perspectives in both countries. Soviet attention turned more and more to the East, particularly to China, as it became clear that the hoped-for European revolutionary triumph was a fantasy. And in China the Bolshevik Revolution soon came to seem like a beacon of hope and inspiration to a portion of the Chinese intelligentsia that had never before taken Marx or Marxism seriously. Thereafter the creation of a Chinese Communist party, completely ruled by Moscow in its early years, required but a small step.

It did not take long for the basic dilemma of Moscow's China policy to emerge. On the one hand the new Bolshevik rulers were the heirs of the Tsars, commanding a national state whose imperialistic aggression against China had won vast gains in Manchuria and other Chinese border lands as well as important privileges—concession areas in some key Chinese cities, Boxer indemnity payments and the like—in China proper. On the other hand, these same men saw themselves as leaders of a world revolutionary movement appealing to the oppressed and downtrodden everywhere. What should their attitude be toward those areas and peoples which had suffered from Russian imperialism and oppression?

The problems flowing from this dilemma were masked at first by the fact that Soviet weakness in Asia gave the Kremlin no practical possibility of seeking to defend Tsarist-won positions in China. Thus there were no initial barriers to a flow of public statements and declarations projecting an image of revolutionary fervor, idealism and zeal for justice and equality. In the early phases of the Russian civil war after 1917, after all, most of Siberia was held by Kolchak and other anti-Soviet Russian military leaders, as well as by Japanese, Chinese and American troops. In northern Manchuria, Chinese troops took over the Chinese Eastern Railroad zone with the help of the anti-Bolshevik Russian management. In Sinkiang and Outer Mongolia, too, Chinese power was able to reassert itself in the vacuum left by the weakness of a Russia torn by bloody domestic strife. To Lenin and his colleagues, fighting for the revolution's survival in the heart of their country, the disappearance of Tsarist spheres of influence in China was initially a matter of little importance. They sought instead to turn the loss into a propaganda weapon.

Typical of this early Soviet attitude was the declaration issued by Deputy People's Commissar for Foreign Affairs Leo Karakhan on July 25, 1919 to the Chinese nation. This statement declared that the Soviet government early in its existence had called for negotiations with China "to annul the treaty of 1896, the Peking protocol of 1901, and all agreements concluded with Japan between 1907 and 1916; that is, to return to the Chinese people everything that was taken from them by the Tsarist Government independently, or together with the Japanese and the Allies." The heart of the Karakhan Declaration was contained in these paragraphs:

> The Soviet Government has renounced the conquests made by the Tsarist Government which deprived China of Manchuria and other areas. Let the peoples living in those areas themselves decide within the frontiers of which State they wish to dwell, and what form of government they wish to establish in their own countries.

> The Soviet Government returns to the Chinese people without compensation of any kind the Chinese Eastern Railway, and all mining concessions, forestry, and gold mines which were seized from them by the government of Tsars, that of Kerensky, and the outlaws Horvath, Semenov, Kolchak, the Russian generals, merchants and capitalists.

> The Soviet Government renounces the receipt from China of the 1900 Boxer rebellion indemnity. . . .

> The Soviet Government abolishes all special privileges and gives up all factories owned by Russian merchants on Chinese soil. Not one Russian official, priest, or missionary shall be able to interfere in Chinese affairs, and if he commits a crime, he should be subject to the justice of the local courts. . . .

> If the Chinese people wish, like the Russian people, to become free and to avoid the fate which the Allies prepared for them at Versailles, a fate designed to turn China into a second Korea or a second India, they must understand that their only allies and brothers in the struggle for freedom are the Russian workers and peasants and their Red Army.[2]

This sweeping renunciation of Russia's imperialist gains in China was intended to, and did, arouse wide enthusiasm in China. But it is indicative of the confusion and difficulties reigning in the period that the recognized Chinese government in Peking did not receive the text of the Karakhan Declaration until March 1920, more than eight months after its release. The text received in Peking from a Soviet official in Siberia contained the second paragraph quoted above, a paragraph whose favorable impact on Chinese public opinion was particularly strong. But the official Soviet version of the declaration—published in August 1919—lacks this paragraph and Soviet sources have often denied that this renunciation of the Chinese Eastern Railroad was ever actually made. What seems to have happened is this: the paragraph was at least in an early version of the declaration, one drawn up when the battles in Siberia were not going well for the Bolsheviks. But later, when time came to publish the declaration, Soviet successes against Kolchak had so changed the situation that Moscow officials were far less ready to surrender historic Russian rights in the railroad than they had been earlier. Hence the paragraph was omitted in the published version.

Two years after the Karakhan Declaration, however, the Soviet government began following a policy in Outer Mongolia which looked to many Chinese like simply a repetition of the Tsarist policy of a decade earlier. The crudity with which Lenin's regime turned Outer Mongolia into the first Soviet puppet state was all the more glaring because of the promises which had been made to the Mongols in August 1919. Then, the Soviet government had spoken in these terms to the people of Outer Mongolia:

> The Russian people have renounced all treaties with the Japanese and Chinese governments which deal with Mongolia. Mongolia is henceforth a free country. Russian advisers, Tsarist consuls, bankers and the rich who have mastered the Mongolian people by means of force and gold and robbed them of their last possessions must be driven out of Mongolia.

> All institutions of authority and law in Mongolia must henceforth belong to the Mongolian people. Not a single foreigner has the right to interfere with Mongolian affairs.[3]

The reality of the situation in Outer Mongolia in late 1919, however, was that Chinese rule had been reimposed upon the area, and the dominating Russian position won five years earlier had been essentially wiped out. Chinese troops under General Hsu Shu-tseng had seized control of Urga and forced the *khutukhtu's* government to petition Peking to be readmitted to the Chinese republic. Not only was Mongolia's autonomy ended but the Mongols were disarmed, their use of Russian currency was prohibited, and they were compelled to turn again to the use of

Chinese financial and trading services. Heavy taxes were levied on the Mongols for the support of the Chinese forces in the area, and they were dunned for the payment of old debts—plus accumulated interest—owed Chinese merchants at the time of the 1911 Mongolian revolt. The Chinese policy, in short, was one ideally suited to alienate the Mongols.

All this created a situation in which it became possible for a strange adventurer, Baron Ungern Sternberg, to rule briefly over Mongolia. A former Tsarist officer, the baron entered Mongolia with a force of several thousand troops in October 1920 after the larger Russian anti-Communist army in which he had served had been defeated. His first attempt to capture Urga from the Chinese was repulsed, but late in 1920 and early in 1921 several thousand Mongols joined his army, seeing in it the means of liberating their country from Chinese rule.

The baron's forces captured Urga in February 1921, effectively and abruptly ending Chinese rule over Outer Mongolia. Sternberg's rule was brief but bloody and tinged with fantasy. His troops engaged in wholesale massacres of his opponents, and the baron himself dreamed of a career as a new Attila conquering Asia for the Asiatics, and then Europe for the fallen Hohenzollern and Romanov monarchies. Reality dealt harshly with this madman who had boasted that "with my Mongols I shall go to Lisbon." When he tried to invade Siberia, he was quickly defeated by Soviet forces, taken prisoner and executed, all before the year's end.

These events set the stage for the resumption of Russian control over Mongolia. A façade of legality was cast over the intervention by the creation of a tiny Mongolian People's Revolutionary party which met in the border town of Kyakhta in March 1921 and proclaimed a "Provisional Revolutionary Government of Mongolia." This "government" appealed for Soviet help to annihilate the baron's forces, help which was quickly and enthusiastically supplied. The Soviet forces and their Mongolian puppets marched into Urga in July 1921 and Outer Mongolia became the first Soviet satellite. A Soviet-Mongolian Treaty signed in November 1921 gave the Russians such privileges as the right to establish postal and telephone communications in Outer Mongolia and promised them the cession of land needed for the construction of railroads in Mongolia. In an effort to avoid

Chinese anger, the treaty was kept secret for a time and a Soviet envoy in Peking, Alexander Paikes, directly denied that any such treaty had been concluded. When the fact of the treaty became clear, Chinese anger was very great. Soviet Russia appeared to be following Tsarist Russia's policy of trying to detach Outer Mongolia from China. The bitter Chinese reaction was summed up this way in an official note of May 1922:

> The Soviet Government has repeatedly declared to the Chinese Government: . . . that the Soviet Government renounces all encroachments of Chinese territory and all concessions within China, and that the Soviet Government will unconditionally and forever return what has been forcibly seized from China by the former Imperial Russian Government. . . .

> Now the Soviet Government has suddenly gone back on its own word and, secretly and without any right, concluded a treaty with Mongolia. Such action on the part of the Soviet Government is similar to the policy the former Imperial Russian Government assumed toward China.[4]

The major significance of the Mongolian incident was that it marked the emergence of an active Soviet policy in relations with China. Gone were the times when Moscow had to accept diminution or elimination of the old advantages won by the Tsars because it was too busy defending Bolshevik power within Russia itself. Now the anti-Bolshevik forces had been largely defeated and economic strength was increasing again within Russia. Energy was now available for salvaging at least part of the old Russian power in China, and ambitions were being nursed in Moscow for achievements there far surpassing anything the Tsars had accomplished. The Romanovs had had only the conventional instruments of military power and diplomatic pressure to accomplish their aims. The Soviet state—as later events in the 1920's showed—had and could use these instruments, too. But in addition it had at its command a force of which the Romanovs never even dreamed: the attractive power of Communist ideology. The Chinese adherents of this ideology could be manipulated by the men in the Kremlin who simultaneously ruled both Russia and the Communist movement. The new concepts maturing in Moscow were summed up by Lenin's observation that "Russia, India, China, etc. contain a mighty majority of the population. And precisely this majority of the population is, with unexpected rapidity in recent years, being drawn into the fight for its own freedom." His conclusion was that this phenomenon meant "the final victory of socialism is fully and unconditionally secured."[5]

Chaotic conditions in China during the early 1920's offered the Soviet Union, both as a state and as the fount of the world Communist movement, rich opportunities. China in these years was an arena for the contending ambitions of several warlords and their private armies which controlled different portions of a divided nation. The government at Peking, recognized by foreign powers, exercised no real sovereignty beyond the area controlled by the warlord ruling there at any moment. A rival aspirant to national power existed in South China, at Canton, in the shape of a government often related to or headed by Sun Yat-sen and his Kuomintang. But Sun Yat-sen, too, was dependent on warlord favor. Among the intellectuals, nationalism was at a fever pitch. Angered by their country's repeated humiliation at the hands of foreign powers and convinced that China's traditional institutions were useless for meeting the needs of the twentieth century, the Chinese intelligentsia looked abroad eagerly for ideas and organizational forms that might permit the building of a new, strong and prosperous China. Among the urban masses, a new mood of militancy was evidenced by the spread of trade unions and the outbreak of major strikes. Lenin noted early in this period that "in China there is raging hatred against the Japanese, also against the Americans."[6]

For those who shaped Soviet strategy and tactics toward China in the early 1920's, the ultimate objective was a Communist China. But that seemed distant indeed in an overwhelmingly rural country, a nation where powerful foreign interests—notably those of Britain and Japan—existed. The course decided upon, therefore, was a three-pronged one aimed at securing immediate objectives while still laying the groundwork that might make possible the ultimate goal. Between 1921 and 1924 substantial progress was made by Moscow in all three major directions of its China policy.

Effort number one was aimed at normalizing Soviet relations with the internationally recognized Chinese government in Peking, establishing good relations with key warlords elsewhere, and generally cultivating the conservative forces in China. In pursuing this policy, Moscow had in mind winning back as much as possible of the old Russian position on the Chinese Eastern Railroad in the Manchuria controlled by warlord Chang Tso-lin, and also securing opportunities for the spread of Soviet influence in the areas controlled by these conservative elements. Among the northern warlords that Moscow wooed, the so-called Christian general, Feng Yu-hsiang, was particularly willing to be cooperative on a number of occasions. As a reward he received substantial stocks of Russian weapons and munitions for his troops and was given refuge in Moscow for a time during 1926.

A series of Soviet attempts to normalize relations with Peking failed during 1920–1923. The first effort had been made by M. I. Yurin, a delegate representing the Far Eastern Republic, a nominally independent and supposedly non-Communist state the Bolsheviks operated for a time in eastern Siberia. Yurin was able to get Peking to revoke its recognition of the old Tsarist diplomats, but he finally left empty-handed, frustrated by Chinese anger at the Soviet entry into Outer Mongolia. In December 1921 a mission formally representing Moscow arrived in Peking under the leadership of Alexander Paikes. Paikes also had to go home empty-handed in mid-1922; Chinese anger had exploded when his denial that a Soviet-Mongolian treaty had been signed was found to be false. Paikes was followed in August 1922 by the highest level Soviet diplomat to visit Peking, Adolf Joffe, a man nominally empowered to settle all issues in dispute. The Joffe mission began well, and Chinese public opinion was favorably impressed by a series of public statements, interviews and speeches Joffe gave emphasizing Russia's desire to help China against foreign imperialists and to respect fully China's sovereign rights. But the Chinese insisted that Russian troops evacuate Mongolia and that Moscow carry out what Peking regarded as the Karakhan Declaration's promise to turn over the Chinese Eastern Railroad to China. Joffe, too, therefore had to leave without any agreement. Only after Leo Karakhan himself—the author of the Karakhan Declaration of 1919 and of a similar statement issued in 1920—arrived in Peking in mid-1923 was it finally possible to resolve the impasse and reach an agreement, and then only after a half year of hard bargaining, some of it extremely ugly.

The Sino-Soviet Treaty Karakhan concluded in 1924 represented a major victory for Moscow. It was made possible by the steadily increasing Soviet strength and by the weakening position of the Peking regime, which found itself under heavy attacks from domestic enemies, some of them supported by the Russians. Events were to prove that the verbal concessions given the Chinese in this treaty were often meaningless in practice. The practical effect of the treaty was to give the Russians a substantial fraction of the rights in China which the Tsars had won, which had been temporarily lost in the chaotic early years following the Bolshevik Revolution. Many Chinese realized this and the Peking regime refused to ratify the first version of the treaty reached in negotiations between Karakhan and C. T. Wang. Karakhan's first reaction to the refusal was in the classic imperialist tradition. He gave the Chinese government a three-day ultimatum, warning that if the treaty were not ratified Russia would break off the negotiations and China alone would bear "the responsibility for all the ensuing consequences." The threat did not succeed fully, but negotiations were resumed and the final treaty differed only slightly from the original.

The key provisions of the new treaty were these: China and Russia resumed diplomatic relations. The Soviet government agreed to nullify all Tsarist agreements and treaties affecting the sovereign rights of China. The Soviet Union recognized Outer Mongolia as part of China's sovereign realm, and agreed to withdraw its troops as soon as various questions involved were agreed upon at a subsequent conference. The Soviet and Chinese governments would jointly administer the Chinese Eastern Railroad as a commercial enterprise, while the road's future would be more fully settled at the scheduled subsequent conference. The Soviet government agreed to renounce the Russian share of the Boxer indemnity and the former Russian extraterritorial rights in China, but it received certain consular, church and other Russian property in China.

Later, in September 1924, Karakhan signed a supplementary agreement in Mukden with the real master of Manchuria, Chang Tso-lin. This incorporated much of the earlier agreement, as well as some provisions covering points affecting the railroad, such as the setting up of a joint commission to dispose of the road's profits. Joint Sino-Soviet management of the railroad began on October 3, 1924. Karakhan now boasted openly of his triumph: "At present the Soviet Union is gaining a firm foothold in the

Far East by occupying one of the most important positions of which its enemies were trying to deprive it. In addition to the political, economic and other advantages, the Soviet Union has recuperated [sic], on October 3, a property which according to the most conservative estimate is worth over a half billion rubles."[7]

The other two major Soviet policy lines in China during the early and middle 1920's were so closely interlinked that we may consider them together here. One line sought to and did create a Chinese Communist party subject to the discipline and direction of the Communist International headquarters in Moscow. The other line was the encouragement given to Sun Yat-sen's Kuomintang, a nationalistic, non-Marxist middle-class organization. The Soviet effort, which failed in 1927, was to provide organizational and material help to the Kuomintang so that it could ultimately gain control of all China in a situation where it would be greatly indebted, and presumably friendly, to the Soviet Union. Simultaneously the Chinese Communists were instructed to join the Kuomintang and gain as much influence and as high place in the Kuomintang as they could, looking forward ultimately to the time when the Communists would displace the Kuomintang as the masters of China. In this Soviet plan Sun Yat-sen—and after his death Chiang Kai-shek—was to be the Kerensky of China.

What was attempted in China was a particular application of the general tactics Lenin had spelled out in 1920, at the Second Congress of the Communist International, for use in the then vast colonial realm ruled by the West. In this area, Lenin knew, there was virtually no proletariat and the mass of the people were peasants. He saw the middle classes in these countries struggling for national independence, an objective in whose realization he believed Communists could profitably participate. But he worried about the danger that the Communists might be submerged in the ensuing united front and might therefore be prevented from pursuing their own more revolutionary ends, which must ultimately turn them against their bourgeois allies. Here is the way Lenin's Theses on the National and Colonial Question, adopted by the Comintern in mid-1920, put the matter:

In regard to the more backward countries and nations, with prevailing feudal or patriarchal and patriarchal-peasant relations, it is especially necessary to bear in mind the following:

(a) All Communist parties must give active support to the revolutionary liberation movements in these countries. . . .

(d) In backward countries it is especially important to support the peasant movements against the landowners, large-scale land ownership and all feudal survivals. . . .

(e) It is likewise necessary to fight the attempts to cloak with Communist garb the revolutionary movements for liberation in the backward countries which are not truly communist. It is the duty of the Communist International to support the revolutionary movements in the colonies and in the backward countries, for the exclusive purpose of grouping together the various elements of the future proletarian parties . . . in all the backward countries, and educating them to the consciousness of their specific tasks—i.e., the tasks of fighting the bourgeois-democratic tendencies within their respective nationalities. *The Communist International must be ready to establish temporary relationships and even alliances with the bourgeois democracy of the colonies and backward countries. It must not, however, amalgamate with it. It must retain the independent character of the proletarian movement, even though this movement be in the embryonic stage* [italics added]. . . .[8]

Even when Lenin presented these theses he met opposition from Communists who feared that their movement would lose by these tactics, and who wanted to focus on exclusive development of the Communist party in each such country. M. N. Roy, an Indian Communist who also played a prominent role later in China, led the opposition, but Lenin answered: "The Hindu Communists are duty-bound to support the bourgeois liberation movement, without, however, merging with it."[9] The issues thus raised in 1920 were to become of major importance a half decade later as the Soviet-supported forces in China surged forward and controlled more and more of that vast country. And the application of this tactic under Chinese conditions was to play a significant role in the Soviet power struggle between Stalin and Leon Trotsky.

A tiny group of intellectuals founded the Chinese Communist party at the beginning of the 1920's. Under the leadership of two

Peking University professors, Chen Tu-hsiu and Li Ta-chao, the founders saw in Marxism-Leninism and the Soviet example the ideology and the pattern for a rebirth of China. These professors and their students were originally primarily nationalists, disillusioned and bitter with the West for what they regarded as the betrayal of China at the Versailles Conference. They saw the Soviet Union as the friend and helper of the exploited and oppressed colonial and semi-colonial nations such as China. Moreover, Lenin had won in Russia. Might not his tactics, his ideology and his program win in China? These were dizzying and inspiring perspectives for the professors and students who were the nucleus of the Chinese Communist party. Three decades later one of the student members of the group, Mao Tse-tung, became ruler of all mainland China as the head of the vast and powerful organization which had grown from this tiny start.

A major role in forming and shaping the new Chinese Communist party was played from the very beginning by a series of Communist International agents. The first to get results was a Russian, Gregory Voitinsky, who helped finance and form first the Chinese Socialist Youth Corps in August 1920 and then, a month later, the Chinese Communist party itself. The second was a Dutchman, Maring, who attended the party's first congress in July 1921 and made a deal with the current Peking warlord of the time, Wu Pei-fu, which gave the Communists free organizational rein in the area in exchange for Communist support of Wu against his warlord rivals. These pioneers, Voitinsky and Maring, and the men who came from Moscow after them in the 1920's trained the Chinese Communists in Marxism-Leninism, transmitted Moscow's orders on strategy and tactics, and generally acted as ideological and political governors of the party. However, the contempt that many in Moscow felt for the fledgling Chinese Communists was vividly expressed in 1922 by Karl Radek at the Fourth Comintern Congress:

> The comrades working at Canton and Shanghai have failed to associate themselves with the working masses. . . . Many of our comrades out there locked themselves up in their studies and studied Marx and Lenin as they had once studied Confucius. . . . You must understand, comrades, that neither the question of socialism nor of the Soviet republic are now the order of the day. . . . The immediate task is: (1) To organize

the young working class; (2) To regulate its relations with the revolutionary bourgeoisie elements in order to organize the struggle against the European and Asiatic imperialism.[10]

The "revolutionary bourgeoisie elements" Radek and his fellow Muscovites had in mind were the members of the Kuomintang under Sun Yat-sen, who had briefly a decade earlier been the first president of the Republic of China. As early as 1912 Lenin had praised Sun Yat-sen's ideas, seeing him as a leader of the progressive bourgeoisie anxious to break the grip of both foreign imperialism and native feudalism on China. Sun's ideas of nationalism, democracy and economic welfare owed much to his study of Western history and institutions, and he was certainly not a Marxist. But Sun and his followers had prestige and fame in China in the early 1920's, and therefore political potentialities far exceeding anything the infant Chinese Communist party could claim at the time. Moscow calculated that if the Kuomintang's military, organizational and political weaknesses could be rectified, Sun Yat-sen and his followers could be made the rulers of China. And if the Chinese Communists played their cards right in working with Sun, so Moscow reasoned, Sun would prove only a transitional figure and the way would have been prepared for the Red flag to fly over all China. To accomplish this goal, the first steps were clearly to persuade Sun to work with the Communists and with Russia, and to induce the Chinese Communists to work with Sun. In the first case, Sun's antipathy to Marxism and his distaste for the Russian moves in Outer Mongolia had to be overcome, a task which was eased by the lack of interest the Western powers showed in helping the Kuomintang. In the second case the Kremlin had to overcome the Chinese Communists' reluctance to work with a bourgeois leader and the preference of many of them to concentrate on building up the Communist party. The Chinese Communists' objections to collaboration with the Kuomintang ended only after their unhappy experience in the Peking area where warlord Wu Pei-fu's soldiers destroyed the alliance with the Communists by massacring a group of railroad workers the Communists had organized. This helped convince them that the working class movement in China was too weak to try to remake their country alone.

The chance of persuading Sun to work with Russia improved in November 1921 when the Comintern agent Maring briefed the Kuomintang leader on the latest developments in Moscow's realm. Here is how Sun described the impact of this meeting on him:

I had been very skeptical that Marxism—pure Communism— could be carried out after the Soviet revolution . . . Russian industry and commerce are not very developed, and Communism, unable to succeed in isolation, still has a long way to go to be realized. Now I have just learned from Maring that Soviet Russia, after having a go at Communism, ran into deep difficulties and therefore switched to the New Economic Policy. The spirit of this New Economic Policy coincides with the Principle of People's Livelihood which I advocate. I am very glad that Soviet Russia has embarked on a policy which corresponds to my principle and am strengthened in the belief that my principle can be entirely realized and must ultimately succeed.[11]

Negotiations with Sun continued during 1922. He was suspicious of the Communists and wanted to be sure he would not be harboring a Trojan Horse if he collaborated with them. He told Maring at a later meeting: "If the Communist party enters the Kuomintang, it must submit to discipline and not criticize the Kuomintang openly. If the Communists do not submit to the Kuomintang, I shall expel them; and if Soviet Russia should give them secret protection, I shall oppose Soviet Russia."[12]

The negotiations were finally concluded in January 1923 when Adolf Joffe and Sun Yat-sen reached agreement that members of the Chinese Communist party would be admitted to the Kuomintang. Their statement said:

Dr. Sun Yat-sen holds that the Communist order, or even the Soviet system cannot actually be introduced into China, because there do not exist here the conditions for the successful establishment of either Communism or Sovietism. This view is entirely shared by M. Joffe, who is further of the opinion that China's paramount and pressing problem is to achieve national unification and attain full national independence, and regarding this task he had assured Dr. Sun Yat-sen that China has the warmest sympathy of the Russian people and can count on the support of Russia.[13]

Joffe also pledged Russia to renounce all Tsarist treaties, while Sun agreed to back a "temporary" reorganization of the Chinese

Eastern Railroad under joint Sino-Soviet management. Joffe assured Sun that Russia had no imperialistic aims in Outer Mongolia and would not "cause it to secede from China." Sun accepted this and responded that immediate evacuation of Russian troops from that area was not "either imperative or in the real interest of China."

Events moved swiftly to get results from the tripartite Soviet Russia–Kuomintang–Chinese Communist party alliance. That summer of 1923 Sun Yat-sen ordered his young aide, General Chiang Kai-shek, to go to Moscow, learn what he could there and negotiate for Soviet military assistance. When Chiang returned, he became head of the Whampoa Military Academy whose function was to train officers for the Kuomintang army. To help the academy, Moscow provided 3,000,000 rubles as well as some 40 Soviet officers as instructors and advisers for a curriculum which combined political indoctrination with technical military training. At least equally important was the arrival of Michael Borodin in China in September 1923. Nominally a correspondent for the Soviet news agency Rosta, he was actually intended to be chief adviser to Sun Yat-sen. His task was nothing less than the complete remolding of the Kuomintang and its forces along strictly centralized and tightly disciplined Soviet lines, thus revolutionizing this hitherto loosely organized and extremely weak organization. Borodin, who had once been a school principal in Chicago and whose chief qualification for being sent to China was his knowledge of English, drew up the constitution of the Kuomintang, wrote its manifesto and suggested its organizational structure. He taught the Kuomintang how to spread effective propaganda by promising the masses redress of their grievances and improvement of their conditions. With Borodin came other Russian military and civilian experts, as well as a flow of arms and money to the Kuomintang. The transfusion of Soviet knowledge, experience, techniques and resources was to prove even more effective than Moscow had expected. Not only did it permit the Kuomintang to gain its further triumphs but it laid the organizational groundwork which later permitted the Kuomintang leadership under Chiang Kai-shek—after Sun Yat-sen's death —to defeat the Soviet design for China and for a time almost completely to destroy the Chinese Communist party. None of this was foreseen by the Moscow leaders, who even admitted the

Kuomintang to the Communist International as a "sympathizer member."

In the mid-1920's the agreements and preparations of 1923–1924 bore rich fruit for a time. The Kuomintang grew stronger politically and militarily and after 1925 it rapidly extended its sway over China's territory, defeating the armies of some warlords and winning over others as its prospects for triumph became clearer. The Communists in the Kuomintang also gained greatly in these years. They dominated many of the lower Kuomintang party units and won great influence over the workers, peasants and students in the expanding areas of Kuomintang control. To Stalin in Moscow all seemed to be going well and according to plan, a conviction strengthened in him by Leon Trotsky's opposition to his China policy. To Trotsky, the correct policy in China was one which would have emphasized an independent Communist party, one following a line of strictly revolutionary practice based upon the organization of Chinese Soviets of workers and peasants. There were many Chinese Communists who shared Trotsky's misgivings and wanted to break with the Kuomintang. They knew that they were spreading Kuomintang propaganda and ideas, not Communist propaganda and ideas, while acting as Kuomintang agents. These Chinese Communists knew also that, for all their strength among the masses, they were very weak in the Kuomintang army, many of whose officers came from landowners' families and therefore looked with horror upon the prospect of peasant revolts and land seizures. But Stalin, confident of his own genius and determined to give no ground to Trotsky in the internal Kremlin power struggle, persevered in his pro-Kuomintang policy, time and again rebuffing Chinese Communist pleas for a change.

Within the Kuomintang there were also differences of opinion and misgivings on continued cooperation with the Communists. To an influential group of right wingers it seemed as though the Communists were taking over the Kuomintang. This group—known as the Western Hills group*—demanded expulsion of the Communists from the Kuomintang and dismissal of Borodin and all the other Russian advisers. The result was a Kuomintang split and the Western Hills group formed its own separate national

---

* They were named for the Western Hills near Peking, where the members met in December 1925 and formulated their policy.

organization. Much cleverer was Chiang Kai-shek. In words he praised the utility of the alliance with the Soviet Union and the advantages of having the Communists within the Kuomintang. But his real attitude became clear—for those with eyes to see—on March 20, 1926, when he arrested the Communist political commissars attached to his troops and put his Soviet advisers under house arrest. This put Canton under his firm control. This accomplished, he proceeded to make apologies and patch things up, but the power remained his. Two months later he rammed through a resolution barring Communists from all top Kuomintang posts and forbidding them to criticize Kuomintang doctrine. The mutterings of Communist discontent grew louder, but Stalin was deaf to them, and Borodin refused to give the Communists the Soviet arms they wanted to create their own military forces. Stalin was confident he would know when the proper time came for the break between Chiang and the Chinese Communists. Events were to prove Chiang Kai-shek the shrewder tactician.

The climax of this struggle came in April 1927 when Chiang's army stood at the gates of a Shanghai ruled by Communist-controlled workers. Moscow ordered that he be admitted to Shanghai unopposed, warning against any clashes and suggesting the workers hide their weapons. At dawn on April 12, Chiang's troops struck. They easily overcame the workers' resistance and then began a reign of terror against all Communists, real or imagined. This "purification movement" went on for many months, and its massacre of Communists and their sympathizers, particularly in Shanghai, Nanking and Canton, did much to break the substantial strength Chinese Communism had amassed in the great cities. The Communists preserved a position for a time in the so-called Wuhan (named for the Chinese cities of Wuchang, Hankow, and Hanyang) government, where they were allied with the left wing of the Kuomintang, but this blew up in June 1927 when Moscow ordered the Communists to back peasant land seizures, to "destroy the present unreliable generals," and oust the members of the Kuomintang Central Committee. Informed of these orders by the indiscretion of the Indian Communist Roy, the Wuhan leaders joined forces with Chiang Kai-shek and the break between the Kuomintang and Moscow became complete. Stalin's policy thus ended in a debacle. Borodin left

China for Moscow in July 1927 and subsequent Communist efforts—such as the great rising in Canton the following December—were drowned in blood. By the end of 1928, Chiang controlled most of China and the Chinese Communists—the few who were left—were a powerless, hunted fragment of a once powerful political force.

In Manchuria during the middle and late 1920's another Soviet-Chinese drama was being enacted, this one over the Chinese Eastern Railroad. Moscow's 1924 treaty with the Peking government and its Mukden Agreement with the Manchurian administration of Marshal Chang Tso-lin had provided for joint Sino-Soviet management of the railroad as a commercial venture. Once this was begun, irritations and disputes multiplied so that the railroad was a continuing source of Sino-Soviet hostility. To the Chinese it soon seemed that the new Soviet officials were behaving exactly like the old Tsarist Russian officials before 1917 and with the same basic purpose: to establish Russian hegemony over the railroad zone and northern Manchuria. The Chinese complained, with more than a little justice, that the nominally equal control exercised by Soviet and Chinese officials over the railroad was a mockery, a façade hiding the reality of virtually unchecked Soviet control over the line's day-by-day operations. The Chinese felt, too, that the railroad was being looted by its Soviet management in a variety of ways for the benefit of the Soviet Union, of Russian workers on the line and of the Communist cause. Most important, the Chinese felt the Soviet control of the railroad was being employed as a weapon to advance Soviet interests in China and to try to affect the course of the military and political struggles going on in North China in these years. In late 1925 and early 1926, for example, the Soviet general manager Ivanov tried to stop the transportation, without immediate cash payment, of Chinese military forces on the railroad. To Chang Tso-lin this seemed a transparent effort to impede his military movements against the rebel General Kuo Sung-lin who was widely suspected of being a Russian puppet. In retaliation, Marshal Chang had Ivanov and three other high Russian officials arrested, and for a time the Chinese ran the railroad until the dispute was patched up by a compromise formula. Soviet relations with Chang

Tso-lin worsened further in April 1927. At that time the Manchurian warlord, then in control of Peking, raided the Soviet embassy, arrested Communist leaders there and seized many documents.* In retaliation, the Soviet government ordered its envoy in Peking and his staff home, though Soviet consuls and representatives remained in many other Chinese cities.

The twin disputes over management of the C.E.R. and the spread of Communist propaganda reached a crisis in mid-1929. Chinese police raided the Soviet consulate in Harbin, arrested numerous Soviet citizens there and seized documents which the police reported showed a Russian plot to secure the violent overthrow of the Nationalist government. In retaliation the Soviet government suspended the diplomatic immunity of Chinese diplomats on its territory. Finally, on July 10 and 11, the Chinese took over control of the railroad and its entire communications system. They arrested and deported the highest Russian managers of the C.E.R. and closed down various Soviet agencies in Manchuria as well as different organizations of the C.E.R.'s employees. Moscow's answer was to break off all diplomatic relations with China (except in Sinkiang, which was effectively independent of Chiang Kai-shek's regime) and to suspend all railroad communication between Russia and China.

This was the start of an undeclared, but at times very real and bloody, war between Russia and China over the next several months. A series of violent border clashes took place between the forces of both nations and Soviet planes bombed strategic points in Manchuria, while pro-Soviet Outer Mongolian forces attacked in the region of Hailar. Military events in this war reached a climax in the autumn of 1929. In October combined Soviet sea, air and land forces destroyed the Chinese Sungari River fleet and captured Tungkiang. The following month Soviet land forces captured the cities of Manchouli and Chalainor after heavy fighting. China's military strength was clearly inadequate to cope with the Soviet forces, a fact the Manchurian authorities

---

* The Peking police later published what it said were translations of the seized documents. This produced a tremendous stir because the published materials appeared to expose direct Soviet involvement in efforts to set up a Communist government in China, and use of Soviet diplomats in China to foster this end. Naturally the Soviet government denounced the published documents as forgeries, but they did have a great impact on Chinese public opinion, and it is likely many of them were authentic.

recognized in December when they agreed to the Khabarovsk Protocol. This document amounted to a complete surrender by the Chinese, since it provided for restoration of the original status of the C.E.R. before the Chinese takeover of the previous July. According to official Chinese reports, the struggle had cost China some 10,000 lives and about half a billion dollars in property loss.

The Soviet military success in Manchuria was accompanied, however, by political embarrassment. Even within the Communist movement, there were many who asked whether Russia's military moves to protect its hold on the C.E.R. were not simply in the old imperialist tradition and a far cry, in particular, from the spirit of the Karakhan Declarations. The Chinese Communist party's leadership dutifully supported Moscow in the dispute, advancing the slogan "Protect the Soviet Union." But more of a justification was needed. Hence the argument was advanced that the Soviet position in the railroad was needed to protect the line from being taken over by the imperialists and also to make it easier eventually to transfer the line to the Chinese proletariat when the Chinese revolution would be victorious. These arguments were to be hastily forgotten a few years later, however, when the Soviet Union decided that in its own interest it should transfer the railroad to an imperialist power, Japan.

Thus, at the end of the 1920's Moscow could look back on a mixed but not unproductive period of its Chinese policy. China's starry-eyed *naïveté* about the Soviet Union and its beneficent intentions toward China had been shattered. So, too, had been Moscow's hopes of gaining a Communist China as a satellite. But Outer Mongolia had again been detached from China and made a satellite, while in Manchuria much of the old Tsarist position had been regained, first by diplomacy in 1924 and then by force of arms in 1929. It was not a record to be sneered at.

CHAPTER VII

Russia, China and Japan in the 1930's

FEAR of foreign attack dominated much of Soviet policy at home and abroad during the 1930's. The rising tides of Hitlerite military strength in Germany and Japanese conquest in Asia threatened to put Stalin's realm in a vise from which the Soviet Union might not be able to escape. At home, Stalin's response was a pitiless campaign to build Soviet military-economic power regardless of cost. In the Far East, his tactics went through intricate convolutions from appeasement of Japan at one extreme to undeclared war against Nipponese troops at the other. In the complex situation thus created, much of Stalin's China policy in this decade was a consequence of the needs created by his relations with Japan. The effort to use China in Russia's plans to resist Japan combined with the relative weakness of the Chinese Communists to make traditional Russian and Soviet hopes for the conquest of China of secondary importance during these years. The diversity of Stalin's tactics is indicated, however, by the fact that during this decade he surrendered the Russian position in Manchuria he had regained at such cost and effort in the 1920's, fought an undeclared war to keep Outer Mongolia under his wing and created a new Soviet satellite in China, the province of Sinkiang.

To create the vast Asian empire to which its militarists aspired, Japan had to conquer China, drive Russia away from the Pacific by seizing at least the Soviet Far East and evict Russia from its conquests in China. The easy Soviet victory over the Chinese in Manchuria in late 1929 showed the ambitious men in Tokyo where the weakest point in their intended victims' defenses was located. In September 1931 the Japanese army struck at the Manchurian walled city of Mukden, opening an offensive which brought all Manchuria—including the Russian sphere surrounding the Chinese Eastern Railroad—under Japanese control. In March 1932 the Japanese created their puppet state of Manchukuo. This easy triumph produced a deep impression in Moscow, where the inferiority of Soviet military strength *vis-à-vis* the Japanese in the Far East was well understood.

Stalin's response was two-fold. Insofar as his propaganda apparatus—working through the Chinese Communists and other instruments—could do so, it sought to stimulate Chinese resistance to Japan. But for the Soviet Union itself, a policy of appeasement was decided upon. Soviet weakness at home was at the root of this policy. In the first half of the 1930's, it should be remembered, Russia was going through twin ordeals. Stalin was simultaneously carrying out the beginning stages of forced industrialization and trying to impose the hated collective farm system upon his recalcitrant peasants. A war with Japan at this juncture might have resulted in more than disastrous military consequences in the Far East. It might have shaken Communist power in Russia as deeply as, or even more deeply than, the Russo-Japanese War shook the Tsarist regime in 1905.

The policy of appeasement showed itself in many ways. Russia declared its strict neutrality in the conflict between China and Japan. It accepted the replacement of Nationalist China's officials on the Chinese Eastern Railroad by Manchukuoan puppets. And finally, under Japanese harassment of the railroad's operations, Moscow decided to sell its interest in the Chinese Eastern to Manchukuo and its Japanese masters. The offer to sell was made in mid-1933, and Russia asked 250,000,000 gold rubles, equivalent to 650,000,000 yen. Then began an involved series of negotiations, punctuated by bitter words and harsh pressures from both sides. But the Japanese held the upper hand since they controlled the territory through which the railroad ran and could hamper its operation in many ways, as they did. In March 1935 the deal was finally concluded. The railroad was sold to Manchukuo for 140,000,000 yen plus a Manchukuoan promise to assume the payment of the retirement allowances due the line's employees. This was a price less than one-third the amount Moscow had originally asked.

Bowing to superior Japanese force, Russia had given up a foothold in Manchuria whose attainment and retention had been a major goal of both Tsarist and Soviet policy for almost half a century. Soviet Foreign Minister Maxim Litvinov justified the Soviet decision to sell by saying: "In the building of the road in Manchuria, in foreign territory, the Tsarist government unquestionably was pursuing imperialist aims. After the October revolution the road lost the significance it had for the people of the Russian empire as an instrument of penetration."[1] This was a very different tune indeed from the one Moscow and the Communist International had sung less than four years earlier when the Soviet Union was willing to, and did, fight an undeclared war with China to retain the Chinese Eastern Railroad. *Izvestiya* in 1935 answered in a vein similar to Litvinov's when the Chinese government protested the sale as a violation of the 1924 Sino-Soviet Treaty which had permitted re-establishment of the Soviet position on the Chinese Eastern. But, despite the Chinese protest, Soviet relations with Chiang Kai-shek's regime were already improving slowly; diplomatic relations between the two countries had been resumed in December 1932.

Any hopes Moscow may have had that its retreat from Manchuria would satisfy Japanese appetites soon faded. Difficulties arose quickly along the border between Manchuria and Siberia. Since much of it was not clearly demarcated, border disputes and clashes broke out, some of them reaching the magnitude of actual battles. Alarmed by growing Soviet military strength in the Far East, Japan demanded that Russia destroy the fortifications along the border with Manchukuo and neutralize it. Moscow refused the demand. It pointed out that the Trans-Siberian Railroad—the Soviet supply line to the Far East—ran very close to the border in many places, and could therefore easily be destroyed by a Japanese military blow if left undefended. In turn, Japan turned down Soviet suggestions for a nonaggression pact between the two countries. The rising tension was further intensified in November 1936 when Germany and Japan announced the Anti-Comintern Pact. Nominally this was directed at the subversive activities of the Communist International, and the published portions of the pact did not even mention the Soviet Union. But there could be little doubt in Moscow that this was actually a Berlin-Tokyo alliance aimed at encircling and defeating the Soviet Union.

Soviet-Japanese tension also climbed in the mid-1930's because of differences over Outer Mongolia, a Soviet satellite Tokyo schemed to detach from Moscow. Japanese occupation of Manchuria had brought Nippon's power to the eastern border of Outer Mongolia, another poorly demarcated boundary easily productive of territorial disputes and clashes. During 1933–1935 Japanese forces also advanced deep into Inner Mongolia, putting them into a position to exert pressure on Outer Mongolia from the south as well as the east. In 1934 Manchukuo proposed a mutual recognition agreement to the Outer Mongolian government in Ulan Bator (the city formerly known as Urga). This agreement proposed to establish Manchukuoan representation in Outer Mongolia and thus end the latter's isolation from the rest of the world. Moscow could hardly welcome this proposal. Its acceptance would have opened the Ulan Bator government to possible Japanese penetration and influence. Hence the Soviet Union saw to it that the idea was rejected. Instead, the Soviet Union promised informally to increase its direct military aid to Outer Mongolia in late 1934, just before the major battle over Lake Bor Nor in January 1935 between Mongolian and Manchukuoan forces. Diplomatic negotiations following this battle lasted many months during 1935, but failed to reach any agreement. The result was a new and increasingly frequent series of border clashes. With a Japanese attack upon Outer Mongolia apparently possible at any moment, Stalin announced publicly in February 1936 that the Soviet Union would come to the aid of Outer Mongolia if the Japanese should attack. Two months later it was revealed that Moscow and Ulan Bator had concluded a mutual assistance pact amounting to a military alliance. These moves all constituted an effective Soviet announcement that the period of Japanese appeasement was over. The story of the Chinese Eastern Railroad would not be repeated in Outer Mongolia. But the mutual assistance pact also made explicit what had been implicit but clear for many years: Outer Mongolia was a Soviet satellite and the 1924 Soviet promise to Peking to regard Outer Mongolia as part of China was long since dead. Chiang Kai-shek's government protested the 1936 treaty, pointing out that a Chinese province had no right to conclude an independent treaty with a foreign power. The protest was clearly only for the record, since Chiang had no power available to influence events in Outer Mongolia.

In Outer Mongolia, of course, the years between the early 1920's and the mid-1930's had been used to make the country completely dependent upon the Soviet Union. The power of the princes and lamas was smashed and the great bulk of their property taken away from them. During the early 1930's an effort was made to duplicate in Outer Mongolia the mass collectivization of agriculture that was taking place in the Soviet Union. But strong popular resistance and the difficulties encountered in trying to collectivize a mass of illiterate nomadic herdsmen forced a major retreat in 1932 and an end for a time to the collectivization efforts. The Soviet Union and its representatives in Outer Mongolia clearly dominated the area's economy and its foreign trade, however.

There was Soviet-Japanese competition also during the first half of the 1930's in a third major Chinese border area, Sinkiang. In this vast, thinly settled region of deserts, oases and mountains, most of the population consists of non-Chinese Moslem peoples— Kazakhs, Uigurs, Kirghiz, Uzbeks and others—closely related to the peoples of Soviet Central Asia. Japanese domination of Sinkiang thus would have posed an immediate and clear political threat to the Soviet position in the important areas immediately west of the Chinese border. The political, economic and military advantages of adding Sinkiang to the Soviet Union, or making it a satellite on the model of Outer Mongolia, must also have occurred to the Soviet leaders. Certainly their policy in the 1930's gave them a dominant position in Sinkiang that went far beyond the needs of defense against the Japanese threat.

Shrewd maneuvering by the Chinese governor of Sinkiang in the decade following the Bolshevik Revolution had prevented anything beyond restoration of the old Russian major trading presence in the area. Given the disorders which afflicted China proper during the 1920's, Sinkiang during that period enjoyed almost independent relations with the Soviet Union. Thus in 1927, when Chinese-Soviet relations were broken off, Sinkiang's consul general in the Soviet city of Semipalatinsk issued a public declaration that his office "has nothing in common with Central China. . . . This consulate is dependent upon Western China, which does not wish, in any case, to sever its friendship with the U.S.S.R."[2]

Two events at the beginning of the 1930's set the stage for the tremendous increase of Soviet influence which took place in Sinkiang during that decade. One was the completion of the Turkestan-Siberian Railroad (Turksib) connecting the Trans-Siberian Railroad with the major cities of Soviet Central Asia, including several very close to the Sinkiang border and lying on the main trade routes into the area. This immediately fortified the already great commercial advantages the Soviet Union enjoyed *vis-à-vis* Sinkiang. The second development was the outbreak of a major Moslem revolt against the Chinese governor of Sinkiang, Chin Shu-jen. This revolt, led by the brilliant General Ma Chung-ying, derived its strength from the real grievances of Sinkiang's Moslem majority against the exploitative and corrupt Chinese rule, but there is evidence that General Ma's forces had at least unofficial Japanese support and he had Japanese agents in his entourage. In this situation Governor Chin turned to Moscow for support, not even bothering to inform the Chiang Kai-shek regime of what he was doing. Apparently in return for Soviet promises of military assistance, he gave Soviet economic penetration of Sinkiang vast new scope in a secret trade agreement signed in October 1931. Customs duties on Soviet goods were reduced. Telegraph and radio communications facilities were set up under nominally joint Sinkiang-Soviet—but actually Soviet—auspices. Soviet commercial representatives were given freedom of movement in the province, and eight Soviet trade agencies were permitted to open their doors in Sinkiang's most important communities.

Governor Chin proved to be inadequate to deal with the thorny problems before him, and he fled the province in April 1933 when a mutiny broke out among White Russian troops in his forces. His successor, General Sheng Shih-tsai, was a remarkable figure who managed to rule for roughly a decade, skillfully riding the very turbulent and complex political currents that swept Sinkiang. General Sheng was in effect a Marxist warlord who revolutionized life in the province and preserved Chinese suzerainty with vast Soviet help. In response to Sheng's appeal for assistance against General Ma's Moslem forces, Moscow sent troops and planes into Sinkiang, and these guaranteed Sheng's victory in 1934. Alexander Barmine, a Soviet official who later defected to the West, described what happened as he saw it from his position as head of the Soviet organization in charge of secret military deliveries abroad:

> The Politburo ordered two brigades of G.P.U. troops with air units of the Red Army to clear the roads and liquidate the rebellion. Meanwhile, on the order of the Politburo, we shipped a number of planes and bombs to the borders of Sinkiang. There they were stuck for some time, as the road to Urumchi . . . was blocked by the rebels. Finally the command of the Red Army Air Force operating there took charge of this shipment. They delivered our cargoes, consigned to the governor, by dropping bombs on the rebel forces gathered round the capital, and by landing the planes right on the airfield of the besieged fortress. I was instructed to send the bill for the bombs, as well as the other goods, to the governor.[3]

Moscow's continued suspicion of General Sheng was evidenced after the victory when the defeated General Ma was given political asylum in the Soviet Union. His presence there gave Stalin an alternative Sinkiang leader, should Sheng break with the Soviet Union. This threat, plus Sheng's Marxist beliefs and his dependence upon the Soviet Union for economic and military aid, resulted in a Sinkiang foreign policy based upon "anti-imperialism" and "pro-Sovietism." Russian advisers swarmed into Sinkiang. Anti-Soviet elements were purged and a Sinkiang equivalent of the Soviet secret police was set up. Sinkiang, in short, became virtually a Soviet colony during the middle and late 1930's. General Sheng himself was ordered by Stalin to join, and did join, the Communist party of the Soviet Union. At the same time, however, Sinkiang made important strides in economic development and in provision of educational and medical facilities to the population. But in name Sinkiang remained a part of China, and events after 1937 showed that this had more than merely juridical importance.

We have seen that between 1930 and 1936 the Soviet Union, forced out of its major position in Manchuria and compelled to announce that it would go to war to defend its hold in Outer Mongolia against Japan, had established a major new position of political, economic and military dominance in Sinkiang. We must now turn to a fourth thread of the complex story of Soviet-Chinese relations in this period: the Chinese Communists whom we left defeated in the major cities by Chiang Kai-shek and his Kuomintang. Moscow could not admit that Stalin's tactics in China had brought disaster; it refused to admit defeat. Stalin blamed setbacks on the mistakes of Chinese Communist leaders and on the succession of Comintern representatives who had advised them. He spurred what remained of the Chinese Communist party on to raise armed revolution in the cities. To make sure that the Chinese Communist party remained loyal to him and followed his instructions, Stalin had that party's Sixth Congress held in Moscow in July 1928. But this did not help. Though Stalin purged Chinese party leaders and changed Comintern agents, the Chinese Communist party proved impotent against the forces of Chiang Kai-shek in the great cities—the centers of the Chinese proletariat—in the late 1920's and early 1930's. A measure of Moscow's desperation, as defeat followed defeat, was the installation in January 1931 of the so-called "Returned Students Clique" into the leadership of the Chinese party. These "callow Bolsheviks," as their opponents called them, were a group of young men who had studied at Moscow's Sun Yat-sen Academy and who had little practical knowledge of China. Their chief merit was their high status with the Comintern agent for China, the Russian Pavel Mif, who was the real ruler of what remained of the Chinese Communist party apparatus. Their elevation to the leadership is important for our purposes only because, as Charles B. McLane has pointed out, the meeting at which they were installed "is the last identifiable instance of outright Soviet intervention in the internal affairs of the Chinese Communist party."[4] (We shall see later that in the early 1960's evidence of Soviet intervention in Chinese Communist party internal affairs in 1959 became available.) But all this represented a dead end for Chinese Communism. Its real future, history was to show, was being prepared in China's vast rural areas.

The path that was to lead to a Communist China was first broken by Mao Tse-tung in 1927 when he turned to the rural areas of South China and began organizing peasant soviets. In the next few years he worked out in practice the basic elements that were to lead to victory: the seizure of fixed territorial bases;

the winning of peasant support by distributing the land of the richest peasants and drastically easing the burdens imposed by rural money lenders; the setting up of a Red Army which engaged in hit-and-run guerrilla warfare against numerically superior government forces; and tight Communist party control over and indoctrination of the population of the areas he controlled. Moscow was pleased and excited at the first news of the Chinese soviets. Initially it thought of these rural beginnings as merely a helpful sideshow to the main effort, which it thought must be made in the great cities. But as the soviet areas expanded in late 1929 and 1930, Moscow began to realize the full potentialities of this movement. It ordered the formation of a Chinese Soviet Republic on the Russian model. This new government was proclaimed at the First Congress of Chinese Soviets in Juikin, Kiangsi Province, in November 1931. Mao Tse-tung, named chairman of this new "republic," was now in fact the main leader of Chinese Communism, though he did not receive full, unchallenged recognition of his leadership until 1935.

During the next few years a bitter struggle was waged between Mao Tse-tung's forces and those of the Chiang Kai-shek regime. To Chiang, the task of eradicating these new centers of Communist power had top priority even over the struggle against Japan, and he sent army after army against the Communist military strength. The Communists for their part regarded the Kuomintang and the Japanese equally as their enemies, and called for war against both. In early 1933, after four major efforts by Chiang Kai-shek's troops had failed to liquidate the soviet areas, the Chinese Communists controlled some thirty districts in the Kiangsi, Fukien and Chekiang provinces of South China, in the areas north and northeast of Canton. The Chinese Red Army had about 300,000 men, many of them equipped with rifles and other weapons captured from the Kuomintang troops. But by October 1934 a new major campaign by Chiang Kai-shek—one in which full account had been taken of all the guerrilla stratagems Mao Tse-tung's forces had used earlier—forced the Chinese Communists to give up their South China base and to begin the epic in their history known as the Long March. Even anti-Communists grant that this trek of more than 5,000 miles was a saga of courage, discipline and faithfulness with few analogues in history. Harried by Chiang's troops much of the way, forced to climb major mountain ranges and to ford great rivers, often short of food and, in winter, suffering from extreme cold, the Chinese Communists had enormous losses during this hegira. Fewer than a third of the 100,000 men who had begun the trek completed it. Those who survived the ravages of battle, disease, hunger, cold and exposure finally ended their journey in October 1935 at the other end of China, in northern Shensi Province. They were now entrenched in one of the poorest, most primitive areas of China, in a hilly region whose million and a half peasants —almost all illiterate—barely raised enough food for themselves, let alone for the army of 20,000–30,000 Mao Tse-tung had led there.

It is uncertain how much knowledge of, and control over, Mao Tse-tung's activities Moscow enjoyed during these years, particularly during the difficult time of the Long March. At the very beginning of this period Moscow was certainly poorly in-formed. The official organ of the Comintern, the *International Press Correspondence* or *Inprecorr*, printed a long obituary of Mao Tse-tung in March 1930, reporting he had died of con-sumption. Three months later, at a Soviet Communist party congress, Stalin revealed he was not clear about the situation. He referred to reports of a Soviet government in China, and added: "I think that if this is true, there is nothing surprising about it."[5] Soviet information about the rural centers of Chinese Communist power and liaison with them improved later. But given the complex and difficult situations the Chinese Commu-nists often found themselves in, and the communications prob-lems which existed, there seems little likelihood that Moscow can have had the same close and unchallenged control in the 1930's that it had enjoyed in the 1920's.

In the first half of the 1930's, the Chinese Communists looked upon both the Japanese and Chiang Kai-shek's Kuomintang as their mortal enemies. They took it for granted that a struggle to the death must take place between the two main Chinese forces of that time and attacked Chiang Kai-shek frequently as a lackey of Japanese imperialism. But by 1935 Stalin saw clearly the dan-ger posed to the Soviet Union by the rise of Hitler's power in Germany and the menace of advancing Japanese strength east and south of the Soviet position in Asia. His response, made clear in August 1935 when the Seventh Congress of the Communist

International met in Moscow, was the decision to make the fight against fascism and imperialism the paramount goal of Communist parties everywhere, to make the "united front" tactic central everywhere and to have Communists unite with all possible forces that could help stem the rising power of Germany, Italy and Japan. In China this global decision meant that the Chinese Communists must seek a united front with Chiang Kai-shek, their hated enemy who had caused the death of thousands of Communists. Such a sharp turn in policy could not help but cause sharp disillusionment and bitterness among many of Mao's followers, as well as attempted opposition. An important factor, however, helped make this major policy reversal palatable for many party members. This was the fact that the new center of Chinese Communist strength in Shensi Province was directly in the path of Japanese expansion. In deciding to join forces with Chiang Kai-shek against Japan, Mao was not only following Moscow's instructions but also seeking to defend his own territorial base against an enemy even more formidable militarily than Chiang. But how was unity to be attained with a Chiang Kai-shek who still considered the Chinese Communists his enemies, sought to destroy their forces and feared and fought Russian designs in China?

Two developments, one in December 1936 and the second in July 1937, solved the problem. As a result of these events there was established both a Kuomintang–Chinese Communist united front against Japan, and a Chiang Kai-shek–Stalin military assistance agreement. In the space of little more than a decade, Kuomintang-Soviet relations had turned through a complete circle of 360 degrees.

The first event was the Sian crisis at the end of 1936. Visiting that city to put more heart into troops slated to begin a new drive against the Communists, Chiang Kai-shek was arrested by his own local commanders and presented with a list of eight demands. These amounted to a demand for an end to the civil war and a union of the Kuomintang and Chinese Communist forces for war against Japan. Moscow immediately made clear through its press that it considered the arrest a major blow against the struggle to unify China against Japan. The Chinese Communists joined the negotiations in Sian and helped substantially in the arrangements which finally permitted Chiang to return unharmed to his capital in Nanking. Chou En-lai, the chief Communist representative at Sian, thus provided substantial evidence of the sincerity of the Communists' desire to cooperate with Chiang. But the Kuomintang was by no means convinced that unity would be in its best interests or anything but a Trojan Horse technique.

The second event was the outbreak of full-fledged war between China and Japan in July 1937. Beginning at the Marco Polo Bridge on the outskirts of Peking, fighting soon spread to Tientsin, Shanghai and other centers. Japanese planes bombed the capital at Nanking. Chiang Kai-shek's efforts to delay or avoid all-out war with Japan now came to an end. A war began that was to last eight years and was ultimately to bring both the United States and Russia into conflict with Japan.

The war acted as a catalyst, bringing to fruition negotiations that had been going on for many months both between Chiang Kai-shek and Stalin and between the Kuomintang and the Chinese Communists. On August 21, 1937 the Chinese and Soviet governments signed a nonaggression pact whose practical effect was to pledge the Soviet government not to help Japan or to do anything which might help Japan, though Japan was not mentioned by name. The Soviet press at the same time was making clear Moscow's sympathy with and admiration of the Chinese resistance to the Japanese. A month later, on September 22, 1937, the Chinese Communist party issued a manifesto pledging itself to strive for the realization of Sun Yat-sen's Three People's Principles. This document announced the end of the party's effort to overthrow the Kuomintang regime by force, as well as promising an end to confiscation of land from landlords. The same manifesto abolished the Chinese Soviet Republic and announced that the Red Army had become a National Revolutionary Army under the control of the Military Affairs Commission of the National government. Chiang Kai-shek the next day hailed the Chinese Communist manifesto as "an outstanding instance of the triumph of national sentiment over every other consideration." A united front against Japan had come into being.

Moscow was the immediate beneficiary of the outbreak of the Chinese-Japanese War. The conflict occupied Japanese forces which might otherwise have been turned against the Soviet Union, and the fiercer the fighting the less likely was a Japanese attack against Soviet territory. The war also ended the possibility of Chiang Kai-shek making a deal with the Japanese, joining the anti-Comintern alliance and adding his forces to the German-Japanese bloc against the Soviet Union. Thus Moscow had every incentive to help the Chinese against the Japanese. The force of this incentive was increased by actual fighting between Soviet and Japanese forces. During July and August of 1938 bitter fighting between the two took place on the border at Chang-kufeng Hill near Posyet Bay not far from Vladivostok. Several hundred were dead or wounded before the fighting, and the border dispute, ended. Even more serious was the fighting on the Manchurian-Mongolian border. The battle there in the Nomon-han area pitted a mixed Mongolian-Soviet army against Japanese forces and resulted in thousands of casualties between May and September 1939. Russia effectively won both these tests of military strength on borders it had determined to defend. It seems reasonable to suppose that there would have been more such conflicts, and some might have ended differently, if so much of the Japanese strength had not been tied up in China proper.

The help the Soviet government gave China during the late 1930's was of several kinds. Soviet exports to Japan dropped precipitously. The Soviet delegate to the League of Nations spoke up frequently in that body for international condemnation of the Japanese aggression against China and for League of Nations moral and material assistance to China. But most important was the flow of Soviet arms, planes, munitions and military personnel to China from late 1937 on, a flow which halted only when Germany attacked the Soviet Union in June 1941.

At this point we must shift our attention to Sinkiang, the back door to China, which became the main channel for the flow of Soviet military and economic aid to Chiang Kai-shek during the late 1930's. We noted the Soviet military aid to Sheng Shih-tsai earlier in that decade which had enabled him to control Sin-kiang while opening the door wide to Soviet penetration. In the spring of 1937 Sheng faced another threat to his position from Moslem forces under General Ma Hu-shan, brother-in-law of the leader of the earlier rebellion. Once again Sheng appealed to Moscow and more than 5,000 troops, including an air unit and an armored regiment, responded to his call. Once again Soviet troops intervened on a major scale in a purely internal Chinese matter. Their intervention was successful, and this time many of the Soviet troops remained. Thus arose a strange situation in which a Chinese area existed virtually independent of the central Chinese government and garrisoned by Soviet troops; yet in these years this area played a key role in making possible continued Chinese resistance to the Japanese. Moreover, Sinkiang in this period provided a route for communication between the Chinese Communist leadership at Yenan and Moscow, a route Moscow used to forward money and presumably advice to Yenan. Also Moscow sent Chinese Communists, including a brother of Mao Tse-tung, to Sinkiang, men who soon occupied key positions in Sheng's regime. Soviet influence in Sinkiang rose sharply in the years that followed, particularly as the competitive British economic influence was driven out by a combination of government order and Soviet cut-price competition. Yet Stalin was careful not to turn Sinkiang over to the Chinese Communists, a policy made dramatically clear when he refused to let Sheng join the Chinese Communist party and ordered him to join the Russian party instead. It is hard to avoid the conclusion that Stalin saw Sinkiang's future in terms of a much closer tie to the Soviet Union than to China, even to a China that might eventually be ruled by Communists.

At first Soviet supplies were delivered by sea, traveling the long route from Odessa to Canton, but this channel was closed off when the Japanese occupied Canton in late 1938. This closing of the sea access to Nationalist China had been anticipated and all through 1938 hundreds of thousands of coolies labored to build a road from Tarbagatai on the Sinkiang border with Russia across some 3,000 miles to Chungking. Trucks, camels and assorted pack animals were used to move supplies over this long and difficult route. Roughly $300,000,000 in Soviet credits were given Chiang Kai-shek's regime to finance these deliveries during 1938–1940. Of key importance in the varied aid China received were hundreds of Soviet planes, Soviet fliers to fly them and Soviet instructors to train Chinese pilots. An incidental benefit to the Soviet Union was the fact that hundreds of its pilots thus received combat training under actual combat conditions. A high level Soviet military mission under General Cherepanov assisted the Nationalist government and Russian advisers were attached to many of the Chinese armies. At Urumchi, capital of Sinkiang, the Russians set up a plant to assemble the planes they were sending in, disguising the plant by calling it an "agricultural implements factory." Aviation schools with Soviet officers serving as instructors were set up in Urumchi and Chengtu, and a Soviet airbase was set up near Lanchow. To facilitate movement of persons and key freight between China and Russia, a joint Sino-Soviet airline was set up in 1939; Soviet pilots flew the route from Moscow and Alma-Ata to Urumchi and Hami, and Chinese pilots took over at Hami for the rest of the journey to Chungking.

Soviet security was Stalin's chief motive in sending this aid to China, and the search for this security drove him in August 1939 to conclude an agreement of friendship and nonaggression with Hitler Germany. The immediate impact upon China of this historic reversal of Soviet policy in the West was slight. Soviet deliveries of supplies continued, as did the public display of Soviet sympathy for the Chinese cause. Some in China reasoned that the pact actually was favorable to their nation. They argued that by guaranteeing Russia against attack from Germany—or so it was then believed—the treaty gave Moscow greater freedom to support the Chinese cause against the Japanese. But by 1940 Soviet relations with Japan appeared to be improving. Behind the scenes, Moscow was negotiating with Berlin over a possible agreement among Germany, Italy, Japan and the Soviet Union for division of much of the world among these powers. But Moscow wanted too much of the globe as its share, and by December 1940 Hitler had secretly decided to attack the Soviet Union. Negotiations collapsed, therefore, but Stalin continued to pursue an alternative, a direct agreement with Japan. From his point of view, the ideal situation would have been one in which Japan concentrated its aggressive plans in a southerly direction, into areas which would bring it into conflict with Britain and the United States. The Japanese, too, had reconsidered their earlier plans to attack the Soviet Union. They understood the lessons of their defeat on the Mongolian border in 1939. Moreover, the collapse of Western Europe before Hitler's armies in the spring of

1940 appeared to open a rich field for expansion in the French and Dutch colonial areas of Southeast Asia. It was against this background that Stalin reached his neutrality agreement with Japanese Foreign Minister Yosuke Matsuoka on April 13, 1941.

This agreement, which came as a terrible shock to the Chinese Nationalist government, pledged Russia and Japan to be neutral in the event of a conflict between either of them and a third power. Attached to this agreement was a frontier declaration in which the Japanese pledged to respect the territorial integrity of Outer Mongolia while the Soviet Union pledged itself similarly with respect to Manchukuo. The latter document came close to Soviet diplomatic recognition of Manchukuo and to Japanese recognition of Outer Mongolia as separate from China. The Chinese Nationalists protested, but in vain, for Stalin was convinced he had scored a major diplomatic triumph. He was so pleased that he escorted Matsuoka to the railroad station and publicly embraced him there several times, declaring, "We shall remain friends." He made a similar demonstrative show of friendship to the German ambassador. In the light of what happened later, it seems likely Stalin really believed that with his two treaties, with Germany in 1939 and with Japan in 1941, he had effectively protected his borders on the east and on the west.

By the time of the Soviet-Japanese Treaty, the atmosphere in China had already changed much for the worse from the height of the period of good feeling in 1937 and 1938. By 1941 there was already bitter, open enmity between the Nationalists and the Chinese Communists. The Nationalists charged that the Chinese Communist armies fought much more against Chiang Kai-shek's troops than against the Japanese and that they were using the new opportunities opened to them by the united front to increase their strength and to bring new areas and new millions of people under their control. The Chinese Communists hurled similar charges at the Nationalists, and this mutual bitterness reached a climax after Nationalist troops wiped out the Chinese Communists' New Fourth Army in January 1941. Thereafter, even the pretense of joint military action by Nationalist and Chinese Communist troops, was dropped.

Our information is most meager about relations between Moscow and the Chinese Communists in this period of the late 1930's. There were undoubtedly links and clandestine communications, but their importance is difficult to assess. It seems likely that Mao enjoyed considerable freedom of action during these years and was able to maneuver as he thought fit within the general limits set by overall Soviet and Comintern policy. The public record indicates that at key points in these years there were substantial differences between Moscow and Yenan. At the time of the New Fourth Army incident, for example, Moscow's public reaction was cautious and conciliatory toward Chiang Kai-shek, while Yenan exploded in anger. These differences reflected the fact that Moscow concentrated publicly upon keeping Chiang Kai-shek and his forces in action against the Japanese, while Mao was interested publicly both in the anti-Japanese struggle and in the future of his own Communist forces in what he deemed to be the inevitable struggle for China.

There is no need to exaggerate these differences or their significance. But it is interesting in retrospect that as early as 1939–1941 there was evidence suggesting that the Chinese Communists were more militant publicly than their Soviet brothers, and that they took positions which were neither simple repetition nor mere logical consequences of the publicly stated Moscow positions. It may have been that the Chinese Communists were responding in some way to secret orders from Moscow. If so, however, evidence proving this has been successfully hidden. The alternative explanation—that these were early signs of Chinese Communist independence—cannot be summarily dismissed.

CHAPTER VIII

World War II and Its Aftermath

WITHIN a short time after the Nazi invasion of the Soviet Union in June 1941, Stalin's regime was fighting for its life. As Soviet armies reeled back in confusion toward Moscow, there was no choice but to mobilize all Soviet energies for the vital objective of stopping Hitler. Soviet aims and ambitions in the Far East, including China, shrank to insignificance beside the need for survival in the West. Stalin's nightmare in those early weeks and months must have been the possibility of a Japanese strike at his rear while Hitler was advancing so swiftly. But Tokyo decided to ignore Berlin's pleas and to honor its still fresh neutrality agreement with Moscow. Instead, it gathered its energies for the conquest of the Anglo-American position in Asia and struck at Pearl Harbor on December 7, 1941, when the Nazis stood at the gates of Moscow. The choice was to prove disastrous for the Japanese, but it was great good fortune for the Soviet Union. From the end of 1941 until after the victory over Hitler, Moscow was the only major neutral in the Pacific theater of war, a neutral whose security from Japanese aggression was guaranteed by Japan's involvement in the struggle against the Western powers and China.

In the first two years after Hitler's attack, therefore, the Soviet Union sharply reduced its forces in Asian Russia as part of the general concentration of energy against the invaders in the West. The flow of supplies to the Chinese Nationalists halted shortly after the German invasion, an understandable move in view of Moscow's desperate situation in the early phases of the struggle. As regards China, the Soviet press appeared to continue the old line, emphasizing and approving of Chiang Kai-shek's resistance to the Japanese and taking a rather more optimistic view of the united front in China than the facts warranted. When Moscow disbanded the Communist International in May 1943, the Chinese Communists approved of the move and claimed their party had long been able to set its "political line independently and to carry it out in accordance with the concrete situation" in China. Mao Tse-tung wrote that the dissolution strengthened the Communist parties, "making them more national and more suited to the necessities of the war against Fascism."[1] Not until well after the victory at Stalingrad early in 1943 were there signs in Moscow of a new active interest and a new policy toward China.

Sinkiang was the one area of major Soviet-Chinese confrontation during the first two years after the Nazi invasion, and here Moscow had to pay heavily for the weakness of its Far Eastern position. Soviet influence in Sinkiang was pre-eminent in mid-1941. The area's trade was dominated by Soviet organizations, and Soviet geological surveys had given Moscow far more knowledge of Sinkiang's mineral riches than Chiang Kai-shek's government possessed. The Soviet Union was receiving significant amounts of oil and tungsten from installations operated under its control in Sinkiang, and preparations were under way to implement the "Tin Mines Agreement" Sheng Shih-tsai had signed with the Soviet government in November 1940. This agreement would have permitted creation of a major extraterritorial Soviet economic empire in Sinkiang. There were Soviet troops and Chinese Communist political and propaganda advisers in the area working with Sheng's government, and Marxist-Leninist and pro-Soviet statements abounded in Sheng's own pronouncements.

Almost a decade of Soviet domination of Sinkiang ended swiftly in mid-1942. At that time Sheng made a deal with Chiang Kai-shek's regime, purged the leading Communists from his entourage and turned against the Soviet Union. For the first time in many years, Sinkiang came under the rule of the central Chinese government. Whatever Sheng's motives in making this breathtaking reversal, it was the new power situation—Russia's complete military involvement in Europe and Chungking's increased strength as American aid shipments mounted after Pearl Harbor—that made possible the undermining of the Russian position. Moscow sought to fight back with diplomatic moves, going so far as to send a deputy commissar of foreign affairs to remote Urumchi to try to dissuade Sheng from his course. But the effort was in vain since all concerned knew Moscow was in no position to use the Red Army against Sheng Shih-tsai and his new Nationalist support. Moscow tried hard to get the Nationalists to agree to a joint exploitation of Sinkiang's oil resources, but Chungking refused. Finally, after protracted negotiations and bitter disputes, Soviet troops and technicians were evacuated early in 1944. We may suspect that Stalin's anger at losing this rich prize contributed to the ill will he showed later for the Kuomintang regime. Certainly he did not give up hope of regaining Sinkiang, for Soviet-supported Moslem rebels soon reappeared in the area and created new turmoil and difficulties for Chiang Kai-shek's appointees, who succeeded Sheng.

After the middle of 1943, the military situation in the West had improved enough so that Soviet thinking could return to the problems of Far Eastern and Chinese policy. Moreover, Soviet leaders had less need in this improved situation to hide their dislike for the Kuomintang. One straw in the wind appeared in August 1943 when an authoritative Soviet magazine, *War and the Working Class*, printed an article asserting "capitulators and defeatists" occupied key positions in Chiang's regime. It charged his forces were planning to ignite civil war to liquidate the Chinese Communist armies. At the Teheran Conference in late 1943 Stalin privately told President Roosevelt he thought the Chinese armies were of little military value largely because of the poor quality of the Chinese leaders. Even earlier, apparently, the Russians had made plain their unwillingness to meet at summit conferences with Chiang Kai-shek. Beginning with the spring of 1944 and continuing into 1945, more—and sharper—criticism of the Kuomintang appeared in the Soviet press. Once again, after a lapse of many years, the attention of Soviet readers was being directed systematically to the internal division in China and the supposed superiority of the "patriotic" and "progressive" Chinese Communists over the "reactionary" and "pro-Japanese" elements in the Kuomintang.

For the makers of United States policy during 1943, 1944 and early 1945, a prime goal was to draw the Soviet Union into the war against Japan. Shocked by the high and tragic price fierce Japanese resistance had extracted from American troops at

Guadalcanal, Iwo Jima and other celebrated battle sites, these policy makers anticipated that final storming of the Japanese home islands would require enormous human losses. As the war neared its close, moreover, American leaders grossly overestimated Japan's ability and will to resist, while failing to realize the full potentialities of the atomic bombs they were soon to employ. For these reasons, Roosevelt was willing to go to great lengths to bribe Stalin to enter the war against Japan. The United States government seemed unaware that the Soviet Union had such vital interests in the Far East and such great ambitions there —as revealed by the historic record—that it would have been inconceivable for Stalin to let the Anglo-American alliance alone defeat Japan and gain all the benefits following therefrom. In the accord that was reached on this matter, the bulk of the price Stalin demanded had to be paid by an ally, China, which was not even consulted or present when the fateful agreement was made at the Yalta Conference in February 1945. What Stalin demanded, and got, amounted to reversing most of the Russian and Soviet defeats in China during the preceding four decades so that Moscow's postwar position in China would be even stronger than St. Petersburg's had been at the beginning of the twentieth century, before the Russo-Japanese War. This remarkable secret agreement deserves to be printed here in full:

> The leaders of the three great powers—the Soviet Union, the United States of America and Great Britain—have agreed that in two or three months after Germany has surrendered and the war in Europe has terminated, the Soviet Union shall enter into the war against Japan on the side of the Allies on condition that:
>
> (1) The status quo in Outer Mongolia (the Mongolian Peoples Republic) shall be preserved;
>
> (2) The former rights of Russia violated by the treacherous attack of Japan in 1904 shall be restored, viz., (a) the southern part of Sakhalin as well as the islands adjacent to it shall be returned to the Soviet Union; (b) the commercial port of Dairen shall be internationalized, the preeminent interests of the Soviet Union in this port being safeguarded, and the lease of Port Arthur as a naval base of the U.S.S.R. restored; (c) the Chinese Eastern Railway and the South Manchuria Railway, which provides an outlet to Dairen, shall be jointly

operated by the establishment of a joint Soviet-Chinese company, it being understood that the preeminent interests of the Soviet Union shall be safeguarded and that China shall retain full sovereignty in Manchuria;

(3) The Kurile Islands shall be handed over to the Soviet Union.

It is understood that the agreement concerning Outer Mongolia and the ports and railroads referred to above will require concurrence of Generalissimo Chiang Kai-shek. The President will take measures in order to obtain this concurrence on advice from Marshal Stalin.

The heads of the three great powers have agreed that these claims of the Soviet Union shall be unquestionably fulfilled after Japan has been defeated.

For its part, the Soviet Union expresses its readiness to conclude with the National Government of China a pact of friendship and alliance between the U.S.S.R. and China in order to render assistance to China with its armed forces for the purpose of liberating China from the Japanese yoke.[2]

The concessions won by Stalin at Yalta would have warmed the hearts of Tsarist diplomats of the late nineteenth or early twentieth century. These concessions fitted neatly into the historic pattern of Russian efforts to secure political and economic advantages at the expense of China. They bore no trace either of any Marxist internationalism or of any human compassion for a sorely tried and long humiliated neighbor. Only China's weakness in 1945, combined with American pressure and Chiang Kai-shek's need for Russian favors in the situation that promised to emerge after Japan's surrender, made it possible for the Soviet Union to win the major victory that the ensuing agreements with Chiang Kai-shek's government represented.

Knowing how unpopular the implementation of the Yalta Agreement would be among the Chinese people, the Kuomintang representatives who negotiated with Vyacheslav Molotov and Stalin in Moscow in July and August of 1945 tried to engage in some hard bargaining. They rebuffed some Russian efforts to get advantages beyond what Yalta had provided, but even this success was only partial. Later events were to show the magnitude of the Soviet victory and how little Moscow's paper promises—

embodied in a treaty, four agreements, and two exchanges of notes between the two nations—were to mean in practice.

The Sino-Soviet Treaty of Friendship and Alliance pledged joint war against Japan until victory, and mutual support thereafter in the event of renewed Japanese attack. The railroad agreement set up the Chinese Changchun Railroad, combining the old Chinese Eastern and South Manchurian Railroads, to be jointly owned and operated for thirty years as a commercial enterprise in a manner similar to the arrangements made in 1924. Two other agreements were intended to govern the Soviet commercial presence in Dairen and the Soviet military presence in Port Arthur. A fourth agreement provided for Soviet rule over all zones of military operations on Chinese territory, and for the Chinese authorities to assume civil control over each zone as soon as it ceased to be an area of military operations. In the notes, the Soviet Union recognized the Kuomintang government as the "Central Government of China," promised to respect China's sovereignty over Manchuria, and asserted it had "no intention of interfering in the internal affairs of China." In another exchange of notes, Chiang Kai-shek's negotiators finally acquiesced in effect to the permanent separation of Outer Mongolia from China, agreeing to accept the results of a plebiscite if the Mongolians voted to become independent. There could be no doubt about the outcome of the plebiscite.

China, in short, had agreed to pay a heavy price, but if the Russians kept their part of the bargain the National government of China would regain control of all the areas from which the Japanese were to be evicted by Soviet troops. Ironically, all these agreements were signed on the day Japan announced its surrender, August 14, 1945.

Before we go on to examine how these agreements were implemented in fact, let us retrace our steps a bit and consider what had been happening to the Chinese Communists during 1941–1945. Their forces had experienced both victories and defeats against the Japanese and Kuomintang armies during these years, but on balance they had greatly extended their influence and power over many rural regions in North China. The Communist-ruled areas of China, the party claimed at its Seventh Congress in April 1945, had grown from 30,000 square miles in 1937 to 300,000 square miles. The population living in these expanding Communist-ruled areas was said to have increased from 2,000,000 in 1937 to 63,000,000 in 1941 and 95,000,000 in 1945. The Communists claimed a regular army of 910,000 men whose power was supplemented by several million militiamen. There probably was some exaggeration in all this, but it is clear that Communist power in China was far greater at the end of the war with Japan than it had been at the beginning, eight years earlier.

The Chinese Communists' "secret" lay in more than military organization and action. In the areas they took over after 1937, they were careful to follow a relatively moderate policy which brought benefits to the poorest peasants without entirely alienating the mass of middle and upper peasants. Thus, they reduced rents but did not abolish them; land was confiscated and rented to poor peasants but usually only if the owner was an absentee or collaborationist landlord; interest on peasant loans was lowered but, like rents, not abolished. The economy established in the Communist-ruled areas saw the existence side by side of private enterprises, cooperatives and state enterprises. Intensive use was made of propaganda, and mass organizations were set up to help mobilize popular support for Communist rule. Given the difficult wartime conditions and the attendant economic disorganization which prevailed in China in these years, the Chinese Communists scored impressive achievements in maintaining or increasing production in their areas and meeting local needs more or less equitably. All this impressed many foreigners very favorably. Many Western observers then argued that conditions in the Communist areas were superior to the inflation, demoralization and corruption that were rampant in many areas under Nationalist rule. That the Communist-ruled territories were also regions of totalitarian dictatorship seems to have escaped many foreign observers at the time, though not all were fooled by the formal democracy the Chinese Communists claimed to practice.

The rapid growth of the Chinese Communist party's membership after 1937 created problems because of the inexperience of the new members, their ignorance of Marxist-Leninist ideology and their non-proletarian origin. To meet these problems, a widespread ideological training and reform movement was carried out during 1942 and 1943. One idea emphasized then is worth remembering in view of later developments—the need "to make Marxism Chinese." Mao put the matter this way as early as November 1938:

> Chinese Communists are Marxian internationalists, but Marxism must be expressed in a national form for practical realization. There is no such thing as abstract Marxism, only concrete Marxism. What we call concrete Marxism is Marxism expressed in a national form. . . . It has become a problem which the entire country must thoroughly understand and resolve, to make Marxism Chinese, to see to it that in every manifestation it bears a Chinese character, that is to say, that it is applied according to China's special characteristics.[3]

This was a curious note to be sounded by a leading Communist during the Stalinist era. Its implications were to become of major importance two decades after those words were uttered, but in the early 1940's Mao was by no means a rebel. If proof of his submissiveness were needed it was provided by his recommendation that Chinese Communists use Stalin's *Short History* of the Soviet Communist party as their guide to Marxism-Leninism. He praised this Soviet document as "the best synthesis and summary of the century-old world Communist movement and the most perfect model in the world of a blending of theory and practice."[4]

But the outside world knew little or nothing of this at the time, and careful efforts were being made to suggest that the Chinese Communists were not Communists at all. Stalin told American Ambassador Harriman in June 1944 that "the Chinese Communists are not real Communists. They are 'margarine' Communists." Vyacheslav Molotov spoke in a similar vein two months later to two American envoys, one of whom reported:

> Molotov then spoke of the very impoverished conditions of the people in parts of China, some of whom called themselves Communists but were related to Communism in no way at all. It was merely a way of expressing dissatisfaction with their economic condition and they would forget this political inclination when their economic condition improved.[5]

Different but equally soothing words were being said in 1944, too, by Mao Tse-tung. Here is what he told a Western correspondent, Gunther Stein:

China cannot restrict herself to friendly relations with only one power or group of powers. . . . It would be just as wrong for China to rely only on the Union of Soviet Socialist Republics and snub the United States of America and Britain as it has been for Chungking, in recent years, to rely only on the United States of America while showing antipathy, suspicion and actual unfriendliness toward the Union of Soviet Socialist Republics and sometimes also toward Britain. . . .

I do not believe for one moment that conflict between the capitalistic world and the Union of Soviet Socialist Republics is inevitable. On the contrary, we Chinese Communists . . . are convinced that the capitalistic world and the Union of Soviet Socialist Republics can and will learn to cooperate closely in peace as in war, in spite of occasional difficulties. . . .

China can and must be one of the bridges between the two camps, instead of hoping to win foreign support as one of the zones of friction.[6]

Was all this mere camouflage and deception on both sides? In part, probably, it was. Both Stalin and Mao had every reason to want the Chinese Communists accepted as harmless agrarian reformers rather than real Communists. They were pressing for a coalition government for China, one which would end the Kuomintang dictatorship and give the Chinese Communists substantial voice in the fate of all China. Similar coalition governments were entered by Communists in many countries of Europe in the years immediately after these statements. All these plans could be frustrated if the West took fright at what might happen if the Chinese Communists gained in power. Yet two decades later it is tantalizing to recall that Mao Tse-tung once spoke out in public of China as "one of the bridges between the two camps" and denied the inevitability of war between the Soviet Union and the capitalist world.

At this point it is appropriate to introduce virtually the only piece of behind-the-scenes evidence we have on the relations between Moscow and the Chinese Communists in mid-1945. This is a famous statement made by Stalin in early 1948 to a high Yugoslav delegation visiting Moscow. Here is Milovan Djilas' version of the Stalin statement:

True, we, too, can make a mistake! Here, when the war with Japan ended, we invited the Chinese comrades to reach an agreement as to how a *modus vivendi* with Chiang Kai-shek might be found. They agreed with us in word, but in deed they did it their own way when they got home: they mustered their forces and struck. It has been shown that they were right, and not we.[7]

This suggests that at the end of the Japanese war, Moscow did not expect—and perhaps did not want—any quick conquest of China by the Chinese Communists. Certainly there were Russian national goals in Manchuria which could be more gracefully served if extracted from the Nationalist government than if demanded from Communists. The Chinese Communists may have been partially responding to Stalin's advice when they engaged in major negotiations with the Nationalists in the late summer of 1945 (Mao Tse-tung participated directly in these) and in early 1946. At times the Chinese Communists made concessions in these negotiations but these efforts to restore unity came to naught, leaving the question of who would rule China to be decided by force of arms.

Our attention must now turn to Manchuria, into which large Soviet forces poured in August 1945 after Moscow's declaration of war on Japan—a declaration which, significantly, did not wait on China's agreement to the Yalta demands. Full Soviet military victory and occupation of Manchuria were quickly achieved. Now that Stalin held Manchuria, he proceeded to do as he saw fit, with only minimal concern for the agreements he had reached with Chiang Kai-shek's envoys in mid-August.

First priority was given to removing from Manchuria—which the Japanese had built into a major base of heavy industry—as much machinery, raw materials and other wealth as possible. The identical policy was being followed at the same time in Soviet-occupied Germany and Eastern Europe. The Soviet economy had been terribly depleted by four years of war, by enemy occupation and looting of the rich western regions of the Soviet Union and by application of a scorched-earth policy first by the retreating Russians and then by the retreating Germans. Stalin was determined to, and did, get billions of dollars worth of the goods needed to rehabilitate and reconstruct the Soviet Union from the areas his troops occupied. The mission headed by Edwin W.

Pauley which visited Manchuria in mid-1946 estimated that the direct damage done there by the Soviet removals was equal to $858,000,000, while direct and indirect damage altogether amounted to over $2,000,000,000. The Russians took stockpiles of food and other materials, some complete installations, the best and newest machine tools and most of the power-generating and related equipment in Manchuria. The Soviet Union justified these seizures on the ground that they were war booty and therefore properly Soviet property. *Izvestiya* in early 1947 denounced the Pauley Report as slanderous and claimed that the industrial portion of the war booty seized by the Red Army in Manchuria was worth only $97,000,000.[8]

Soviet aspirations in Manchuria went far beyond these seizures, however. Moscow envisaged securing a permanent major economic foothold in the area through winning Chiang Kai-shek's agreement to future "joint" Soviet-Chinese operation of what had been the vast Japanese economic empire in Manchuria, including iron and coal mines, gold mines, arsenals, electric power plants, chemical and machinery factories and the like. The Nationalist government, backed by the United States, resisted these far-reaching demands, since it realized that such major Soviet economic penetration—together with the Soviet position on the Chinese Changchun Railroad—would go far toward turning Manchuria into an economic dependency of the Soviet Union, with profound political implications.

But the central question in Manchuria in the months immediately after the Japanese surrender was the question of who would rule after the Soviet troops evacuated the area. The Sino-Soviet agreements of August 1945 had provided for complete Soviet evacuation of Manchuria three months after Japan's formal surrender, which took place on September 2, 1945. Moreover, the agreements had seemed to make clear that the Russians would turn over the administration of the areas they evacuated to Nationalist officials. The reality turned out to be quite different. Using a variety of pretexts and devices, the Soviet officials in Manchuria hindered and prevented Nationalist officials and troops from taking over. At the same time, they cooperated with the Chinese Communist forces that poured into Manchuria and, clearly with Soviet connivance, took over vast stores of Japanese arms and supplies that remained after the surrender and disarming of Nippon's armies. Finally Nationalist troops had to fight their way into Manchuria against stiff Communist resistance at the Shanhaikwan Pass. Soviet troops remained in Manchuria until May 1946. When they finally left, the evacuation had been completed in such a manner that the Chinese Communists controlled roughly two-thirds of Manchuria, including such major cities as Harbin, Kirin and Tsitsihar. A provisional Communist regime was established in northern Manchuria. It engaged in brisk trade and other economic relations with the Soviet Union, and its representatives worked with Soviet officials to operate the section of the Chinese Changchun Railroad within the Communist-controlled territory. In the southern portion of Manchuria, where the Nationalists controlled such cities as Mukden, Changchun and Fushun, friction between Soviet railroad officials and Chiang Kai-shek's regime forced the Russians to leave Mukden and return home in 1946. At Dairen and Port Arthur, the Soviet government simply refused to permit the landing of Nationalist troops and officials, using various pretexts, including the argument that the war with Japan was not officially over because no peace treaty had been signed.

Thus, by the summer of 1946, a year after Japan's surrender, the Soviet government could look with satisfaction upon the gains from its short involvement in the Far Eastern phase of World War II. At minimal cost it had won the recognized Chinese government's acceptance of an independent—though obviously Soviet-dominated—Outer Mongolia. The area of Manchuria bordering on the Soviet Union was governed by a Chinese Communist regime completely dependent economically upon the Soviet Union, from which it received such essentials as machinery, metals, petroleum, medicines, sugar, paper, textiles and other products in return for soybeans and other agricultural goods. At Dairen and Port Arthur, Soviet troops were solidly entrenched in a position that had historically been recognized as of major strategic importance. And in North Korea a Communist regime controlled the entire area north of the thirty-eighth parallel. The position, in short, was one ideally suited to give the Soviet Union maximum security against any possible threat from the new American positions in South Korea and Japan, as well as pro-

viding potential jumping-off points for possible future expansion
of Soviet and Communist power.

Only in Sinkiang, among the border areas adjoining Chinese
territory, did the Soviet Union have an unsatisfactory position
from its own point of view in 1946. But even there important
gains had been made in a partial recovery from the debacle
caused by Sheng Shih-tsai's defection in the early 1940's. The
restoration of Nationalist control had brought with it economic
difficulties, inflation and renewed Chinese exploitation of the
non-Chinese peoples. The resulting dissatisfaction soon erupted
into a civil war. An Eastern Turkestan Republic was proclaimed
whose forces won a major victory over the Chinese Nationalists
near Wusu in early September 1945. There is evidence suggesting
the Soviet Union provided material aid for the rebels, and in late
1945 and early 1946 the Soviet consul acted as a "mediator" between the Chinese and non-Chinese forces. An agreement finally
signed in June 1946 gave the rebels near-independence in three
key areas of Sinkiang, permitting them even to maintain their
own armed forces and police units. Confused fighting broke out
again in 1947 as splits developed among the Moslem groups and
new differences emerged between the Moslems and the Chinese.
There was military action also on the border between Outer
Mongolia and Sinkiang. Russian pressure for economic concessions continued in Sinkiang, and in 1949 the Soviet Union tried
to get Nationalist consent to Soviet control of Sinkiang's mineral
resources for fifty years. The Nationalist governor refused, but
even as Communist Chinese troops approached Sinkiang, Moscow
appears to have tried one last gambit. According to what a repu-
table American scholar terms a "reliable source," the Soviet consul in Urumchi approached a Nationalist general and suggested he
declare Sinkiang independent on the model of Outer Mongolia.
The Soviet envoy reportedly said: "If you will do this, we will
order the Chinese Communists not to continue their advance into
Sinkiang." The offer was refused, and shortly afterward the
Chinese Communists took over Sinkiang.[9] Given the earlier history of Soviet machinations in Sinkiang, this effort to snatch the
province away from Chinese—even Chinese Communist—control
does not seem unlikely.

There is no need here to go deeply into the involved military
and diplomatic developments in 1947, 1948 and 1949 which pre-

ceded the Chinese Communist conquest of China's mainland and
the proclamation on October 1, 1949 of the Chinese Peoples Republic, or Communist China. Mao Tse-tung's forces gathered
strength in Manchuria and then swept southward in 1948 and
1949 until they were masters of the mainland. To what extent
the Soviet Union aided Mao's forces with munitions, weapons,
supplies and advisers is a debatable matter, except, of course,
insofar as it relates to the initial aid given in 1945–1946 toward
establishment of the Chinese Communist position in Manchuria
itself. The charges filed by the Nationalist government's representative in the United Nations against the Soviet Union and the
furious debate this provoked are now mere footnotes to history,
and do not merit extended treatment.

Early in 1949 the Soviet Union engaged in formal intergovern-
mental trade negotiations with the Chinese Communist authorities
in Manchuria. The Manchurian Communist leader, Kao Kang,
visited Moscow and signed a trade agreement in this period. Elsewhere in China, however, Soviet diplomatic representatives to
the Nationalist regime behaved very correctly as Communist
forces captured one major city after another in 1949. Soviet
consulates were closed in such captured cities, and on occasion
their officials retreated with the Nationalists. The only foreign
ambassador to follow the Nationalist government when it abandoned Nanking and went to Canton was Soviet Ambassador
Roshchin. This comedy was ended the day after the formal
national Chinese Communist government was formed. Moscow
announced its recognition of the new regime and severed all
diplomatic relations with the Nationalists.

A new era of Chinese history, and of the history of Soviet-
Chinese relations, had begun.

CHAPTER IX

The Two Communist Flowers

"SOVIET COMMUNISM has bloomed a Soviet flower and Chinese Communism a Chinese one. Both are equally Communism, but their flowers are of different hues."[1] Chen Yi, Communist China's foreign minister, used these words in November 1960 to sum up the similarities and differences between his country and the Soviet Union. In this brief passage, voiced eleven years after the formation of the Chinese Peoples Republic, one of that nation's highest officials was asserting the equality of Chinese and Soviet Communism, underlining the fact that they were not identical and tracing their basic difference back to their national origins. The case for the importance of national as well as ideological factors in the relations among Communists could hardly have been stated more succinctly.

But when the formal relationship between the Soviet Union and the newly constituted Chinese Peoples Republic began in 1949, neither side was anxious to call attention to any possible future differences between them. Rather, a concerted public effort was made to suggest the identity of all their interests. In June 1949, just before his national government was formed, Mao Tse-tung enunciated his famous "lean to one side" policy. China must "either lean to the side of imperialism or to the side of socialism. . . . Neutrality is a hoax. No third path exists," he declared. In this situation China had to ally itself with the Soviet Union in "an international united front." From the Soviet side came similar expressions of amity.

But behind the public façade of unity, both Stalin and Mao must have been troubled about the prospects facing them. An unprecedented chapter in the history of relations between their two countries was beginning in 1949. Neither man can have harbored any illusions about the past history of Russian—including Stalinist —imperialism in China. Stalin can hardly have taken it for granted that a Communist regime in China must necessarily mean security and peace on his southern and Central Asian frontiers. Chronically suspicious, as Khrushchev later noted, Stalin was beginning diplomatic relations with Communist China at the height of his quarrel with Yugoslavia, a quarrel which had demonstrated that a Communist government in another nation need not necessarily be a subservient regime. The possibility that China might become another Yugoslavia must have crossed his mind. Moreover, he knew then—as he had told the Yugoslavs in early 1948—that the Chinese had proved their independence and won their revolution by disobeying his advice at the end of World War II. It would be surprising if Stalin, reviewing the new problems about to arise before him in late 1949, did not regret that Chiang Kai-shek had been beaten so decisively. From Russia's point of view a weak, divided China enmeshed in the agonies of civil war might well have seemed preferable to a united China which would certainly embark as soon as possible upon a program of economic and military development.

Similar forebodings must have occurred to Mao. He knew well the history of Russian-Chinese relations, the humiliations his nation had suffered time and again at Russian hands. He could personally remember the arrogance of Borodin and the other Moscow envoys who had directed the Stalinist strategy that resulted in the catastrophe of 1927. He must have known that his claims to have made Marxism Chinese and to have charted a new creative development of Marxism-Leninism could only inspire jealousy and distrust in the Moscow dictator who demanded, and was accustomed to receiving, the most abject servility and sycophantic praise from those around him. And Mao could hardly have been ignorant in late 1949 of the Stalinist intrigues in Sinkiang where, as noted earlier, Russian efforts to obtain a special position and even detach the province from China kept up virtually to the time of the Chinese Communist takeover.

Yet both men were certainly well aware of the forces that drew them together. One factor was their common allegiance to Marxism-Leninism and to the dream of the future Communist world. Public discord between them, both men must have realized, would do violent injury to the *mystique* of Communism, an important element in the system of power on which both depended. Moreover, there was their common hatred and fear of the United States. Stalin saw the United States as his prime antagonist on the world scene. Mao viewed it as the evil power that had sought to keep Chiang Kai-shek in power, which might yet join with Chiang in an attempt to reconquer the mainland. In this context both Mao and Stalin must have seen very clearly the major political and military advantages of unity against the American Colossus.

Stalin could, nonetheless, be confident that for the immediate future at least he could bend the Chinese to his will. China's weakness, as she emerged for the first time from decades of internal convulsion, civil war and war against a foreign foe, gave Mao reason to tread softly in his relations with Stalin. Inflation and goods shortages were rampant in China. Its heavy industry, never very big by world standards, was in ruins and producing minuscule amounts. Mao's mass armies had proved adequate to defeat Chiang Kai-shek's demoralized forces, but neither in arms nor in training of men and officers were they a modern force for an era when nuclear weapons were already in being. To become a major power, Communist China would need enormous amounts of economic, technical and military aid. In the political situation of late 1949, Mao had only Stalin to look to for the needed help.

This analysis of the mixed feelings on both sides seems abundantly confirmed by what we now know of the historic negotiations between Mao and Stalin. These stretched on in Moscow for almost two months between mid-December 1949 and mid-February 1950. This was no simple matter of Stalin imposing his will upon a servile puppet. Given China's great weakness and enormous needs then, Mao must have put up surprisingly stubborn resistance to Stalin's demands and defended China's national interests as best he could. The result was a compromise which can hardly have satisfied either side fully. Seven years later, in December 1956, the Chinese Communists accused Stalin of "a tendency toward great-nation chauvinism" and said he "himself lacked a spirit of equality" toward other countries of the Socialist camp. We may suspect their experiences in these Moscow negotiations helped them to reach that conclusion, though they naturally said nothing at the time.

The basic document signed in Moscow on February 14, 1950

was a 30-year treaty of friendship, alliance and mutual assistance clearly directed at the common enemy, the United States. It called for common action to prevent "aggression" by "Japan or any other state that may collaborate with Japan directly or indirectly" and for each power to "render military and other assistance by all means at its disposal" to the other, should the latter become involved in war with "Japan or any state allied with her." The same treaty also provided for consultation "in regard to all important international problems affecting the common interests of China and the Soviet Union."

A second agreement tackled the ticklish problems of the Russian presence on the Chinese Changchun Railroad and in Port Arthur and Dairen. Here Mao scored major victories. Stalin agreed to surrender all rights of joint ownership and operation in the railroad, without compensation, by the end of 1952. In the interim period, the Chinese smashed the old system by which the Russians had dominated the railroad. Mao did this by the simple expedient of winning agreement to an annual alternation of Soviet and Chinese citizens in all the key posts. It was agreed, too, that Soviet troops would be withdrawn from Port Arthur by the end of 1952, but interim civil authority would be Chinese while military affairs would be presided over by a joint Chinese-Soviet military commission with equal representation from both sides. China pledged itself to compensate the Soviet Union "for expenses which it has incurred in restoring and constructing installations since 1945." The fate of Dairen was left undetermined, but it was noted that the Chinese administered the area and it was agreed to turn over to the Peking regime all property "temporarily administered by or leased to the Soviet Union . . . in the course of 1950." Here were major victories for Chinese nationalism and its goal of removing the Russian presence and Russian power from Chinese soil.

A credit agreement provided for the Soviet Union to lend China $300,000,000, in five equal annual amounts during 1950–1954. The loan was to carry a one per cent annual interest charge and was to be repaid in ten equal annual installments beginning in 1954. This was a niggardly amount in relation to China's needs. Two years earlier Stalin had granted Poland—with a territory and population far, far smaller than China's—a loan of $450,000,-000. The contrast must support the suspicion that Stalin's anger at Chinese stubbornness made him give them the minimum amount possible.

In the official *communiqué* announcing the signing of these agreements, several additional important points were made. It was announced that both governments "confirm the fully guaranteed independent situation of the Mongolian Peoples Republic as a result of the 1945 referendum" and that Communist China would establish diplomatic relations with the Ulan Bator government. Mao Tse-tung had had to accept the Soviet severance of Outer Mongolia from China, but he had established a diplomatic channel for contact with that area, breaking the long-time Russian diplomatic monopoly in Ulan Bator and gaining an opportunity to rebuild Chinese influence there. The *communiqué* also announced a Soviet promise to return to China without payment all Japanese property seized in Manchuria, as well as to turn over to China the buildings of the former Russian military enclave in Peking.[2]

Were these the only agreements reached in the Moscow negotiations? Probably not, for certainly there must have been at least preliminary accord on setting up joint Sino-Soviet companies in China. In March 1950 the formation of two of these companies was announced and news of a third followed the next month. A fourth was formed in July 1951. The first two joint companies represented Chinese concessions to the Soviet demand for economic influence in Sinkiang. They were empowered to search for and produce oil and non-ferrous metals respectively in that area. But unlike the pattern of Soviet exploitation set under Sheng Shih-tsai in Sinkiang, in these joint enterprises power was shared through a system of alternating key posts between Chinese and Soviet officials. Similar alternation was provided for in the third agreement, which set up a civil aviation company to fly the three main air routes between the two countries along the lines Chita-Peking, Irkutsk-Peking, and Alma-Ata-Peking. The fourth company was set up to engage in ship construction and ship repair in Dairen. This provided a basis for a continued Russian foothold in that city, whose fate had been left undecided in the Moscow negotiations. As later events showed, the Chinese regarded all four of these companies as examples of Soviet economic imperialism and got rid of them as soon as they could.

It seems almost certain that the plans for North Korea to invade

South Korea were discussed in the Moscow meetings, too. Evidence later became available of the transfer of Korean soldiers from the Chinese to the North Korean army in the first half of 1950, perhaps around 50,000 in all. Mao and Stalin could hardly have disagreed about the desirability of ousting a pro-American South Korean government, though presumably they could not have foreseen the difficulties that were to arise in the attempt. Ironically it was Sino-Soviet cooperation that was indirectly to make possible the United Nations defense of Korea that began after the North Korean invasion of mid-1950. If a Soviet representative had been present at the Security Council meeting on this issue, he could have vetoed the decision to send United Nations forces into Korea. But the Soviet representative was absent, boycotting the body because it included a representative of Nationalist China—now confined in authority primarily to Taiwan—rather than of the new Peking government.

In the three years that remained of Stalin's life after the basic Sino-Soviet agreements of February 1950 had been signed, it was the Korean War that dominated the relationship, especially after the entrance of Chinese "volunteers" into the conflict. We may doubt that the Chinese were entirely happy that after the North Korean debacle had brought United Nations—including United States—troops to the Yalu River, it was China alone that had to bear the brunt of trying to save Korea from the "imperialists." But once they had decided to intervene, they were in no position to grumble at the absence of Soviet comrades fighting beside them. Rather, their participation in the conflict greatly increased China's dependence upon the Soviet Union for weapons, munitions and supplies, particularly airplane fuel. Not only were the Chinese troops being used as cannon fodder in a war effort that also served Soviet interests, but the Soviet Union apparently gave its help on a credit basis, not as a gift. In 1957 Lung Yun, a vice chairman of China's National Defense Council, complained in public: "It is unreasonable for China to bear all the expenses of the resist-America aid-Korea war." He went on to remind his audience that "during the second world war, the United States granted loans and leases to her allies. Later some of these allies refused to pay back the loans while the United States excused some from repayment. It will take us more than ten years to repay the loans from the Soviet Union if we ever repay them. Besides we have to pay interest to the Soviet Union. China fought for socialism, but look at the result!"[3] Lung was denounced for his "anti-Soviet" attitude, but his assertion of facts went unchallenged.

The Chinese also benefited from the alliance during the fighting because the threat of possible Soviet intervention undoubtedly helped bring about the United Nations and United States decision not to carry the fight beyond Korea's borders into China proper. But the real gains the war brought to the Peking regime were the spur to national pride from the successes achieved against the American and other U.N. troops, the impetus the war gave to national unity and patriotism inside China during a difficult period of the new government's development and the opportunity the entrance of the "volunteers" gave for making possible permanent Chinese influence in North Korea. The Soviet Union had earlier tried to keep North Korea as its own monopoly area despite Korea's long history as a Chinese dependency.

At the end of 1952 the Soviet Union did turn over its interest and role in the Chinese Changchun Railroad to Peking as had been promised, but it did not evacuate Port Arthur as planned. The exact role the Korean War played in the latter development we do not know, nor do we know what—if any—bitterness the matter may have aroused, but in September 1952 a Chinese note to Moscow asked the Russians to maintain their troops in Port Arthur until the conclusion of a peace treaty with Japan. The Soviet Union, not surprisingly, agreed. Two years later it was revealed that at the same time the postponement of the Soviet exit from Port Arthur had been agreed upon, the Soviet Union, Outer Mongolia and China had agreed to build a new railroad connecting Chinese territory with Ulan Bator and through that city with the Soviet Union. The suspicion must arise that Mao won this secret agreement—a concession opening Outer Mongolia to further possible economic and other influence from China—as a *quid pro quo* for permitting the maintenance of the Soviet military position in Port Arthur.

In the years 1950–1953 Soviet-Chinese cooperation economically, culturally and politically continued on many fronts. A major campaign was begun in China to spread friendship toward the Soviet Union and to popularize the Russian language and Russian culture. The Sino-Soviet Friendship Association reported it had almost 40,000,000 members by the end of 1952. Many Soviet books were translated into Chinese and published there. Increasing numbers of Soviet specialists in many fields—civilian and military—came to China to help train Chinese technicians, as well as to help in Chinese economic reconstruction. Chinese students were sent to the Soviet Union in large numbers to study in Soviet schools and factories. In short, a massive dose of pro-Soviet indoctrination plus Soviet technical knowledge was being injected into China.

Soviet-Chinese trade rose rapidly in these years as Chinese production recovered and China's program for economic reconstruction and development grew. This was essentially an exchange of Chinese foods and raw materials for Soviet machinery and other manufactured products plus petroleum in which China has been historically deficient. The data on this trade during 1950–1953 follow:

Year	Soviet Exports to China	Soviet Imports from China (*millions of dollars*)[a]	Chinese Trade Deficit
1950	388.2	191.3	196.9
1951	476.3	331.9	144.4
1952	550.2	413.7	136.5
1953	705.5	474.7	230.8

[a] Converted into dollars at the official rate of four rubles to the dollar.

The relative share of Soviet trade in all Chinese trade, a Soviet source reports, rose from 23.4 per cent in 1950 to 51.5 per cent in 1952.[4] These data show that in the first four years of trade between the two countries the Chinese trade deficit exceeded $700,000,000, or more than twice as much as the five-year $300,-000,000 credit agreed upon in 1950. These figures probably do not include the value of Soviet arms shipments. They suggest that an unpublished agreement in these years permitted more generous commercial credits for China—perhaps because of the economic strain resulting from the Korean War—than had originally been envisaged. In any case, the heavy Chinese economic dependence upon the Soviet Union at the time of Stalin's death is clear.

When Stalin died in March 1953 all was harmony and cooperation between the Soviet Union and Communist China, at least on the surface. Mao Tse-tung's message to Moscow when he heard the news declared: "The great and profound friendship which Comrade Stalin felt for the Chinese people will forever be remembered with gratitude by the Chinese people." In the funeral procession, Chou En-lai marched with the most distinguished Kremlin personalities in the first rank of the mourners. One of Georgi Malenkov's first steps in trying to build himself up as Stalin's successor was to insert into *Pravda* an altered picture which showed him, Stalin and Mao Tse-tung standing together. Cries of continued unity and friendship went up from both Moscow and Peking.

Yet even then there were circumstances to raise questions about the nature of Sino-Soviet relations. Communist China had not been admitted into either the Communist Information Bureau (Cominform) or the Council for Mutual Economic Assistance (Comecon), the two major international Communist organizations in existence at the time of Stalin's death. Chinese Communist troops were still fighting without openly acknowledged Soviet military support in Korea. The Soviet delegate had returned to the United Nations Security Council and participated in the work of bodies where China was represented by Chiang Kai-shek's delegates and Mao had no direct voice. Moreover, there were signs of differing beliefs about the importance of Mao's teachings and the Chinese example. Liu Shao-chi had declared in Peking in 1949 that the Chinese Communist method of seizing power "is the path that should be taken by the people of the various colonial and semi-colonial countries in their fight for national independence and people's democracy." But in 1951 Soviet scholars in Moscow were declaring that it was "risky to view the Chinese revolution and the ways of her development as an obligatory pattern for people's democratic revolutions in other countries of Asia."[5] The seeds of conflict were visible to those who cared to look.

It seems likely that Mao expected to succeed Stalin as the lawgiver of world Communism. Stalin had had the prestige of almost three decades of Soviet leadership as Lenin's successor. He had led the Soviet Union to victory in World War II and spread Communist rule in Europe and Asia. Compared to him and his achievements, the men who scrambled for power in the Kremlin after Stalin's death were mere pygmies. Mao, who probably thinks of himself as the Chinese Lenin, had brought Communist rule to the world's most populous nation. What comparable claim to world Communist authority could any of the Kremlin rivals—Beria, Malenkov, Molotov and Khrushchev—present? In Chinese eyes, certainly, the answer was none. But events were to show that the men in Moscow had other ideas.

The Malenkov regime which succeeded Stalin in 1953 decided very early after assuming power that to solidify its position it needed relaxation of the high international tension. Shortly after Stalin's death it was campaigning for popularity at home under the equivalent of a "peace and prosperity" theme. China, too, was tired of the Korean War, which had been stalemated for many months. Four days after Stalin's death, Chou En-lai publicly offered concessions on the issue of forced prisoner repatriation, and by the summer of 1953 the war was over. Both Moscow and Peking accepted the fact that their effort to drive American influence from Northeast Asia had failed. Soon afterward both nations extended large amounts of economic aid to North Korea for reconstruction. This could be viewed as unselfish aid for a destitute and ideologically sympathetic neighbor. It could also be viewed as the intensification of Sino-Soviet rivalry for control of North Korea, an area in which the predominant military presence was now China's for the first time in the twentieth century.

In Indo-China, too, the Soviet Union and Communist China worked together to end another key danger spot left over from the Stalin era. With resources freed by the end of Korean fighting, both of the chief Communist powers presumably were in a better position to help Ho Chi-minh's Viet Minh forces, which had been fighting the French for many years. Increased military supplies from these countries presumably played a part in making possible the stunning military victory scored by Ho's army when it captured the French fortified stronghold of Dienbienphu on May 7, 1954. Ho may have wanted to continue the war, confident he could conquer the entire area of French Indo-China. But Moscow and Peking wanted to end this strain on general international relations. Moreover, they feared the United States would replace France in Indo-China and bring American military power close to southern China on the continent. The result was the compromise agreement reached in Geneva, which ended the fighting with the creation of four new states, one of them Communist-ruled North Vietnam.

But the key event of 1954 was a new effort to solve the basic frictions in the Soviet-Chinese relationship, in effect a partial renegotiation of the February 1950 and later accords reached with Stalin. Moscow's desire to soothe Peking's irritations was clear from the high rank of the three party Presidium members who headed the Soviet delegation sent to Peking in October 1954: Nikita Khrushchev, Nikolai Bulganin and Anastas Mikoyan. No Russian delegation of comparable importance had ever visited the capital of China before. Khrushchev went to great lengths to flatter China in the major speech he delivered in Peking. Communist China, he declared, "has emerged as a great power on the international arena." In words whose emptiness he was to demonstrate only a few years later, he asserted that "without the participation of the Chinese Peoples Republic it is now impossible to decide international problems and obtain lessening of tension in international relations and peaceful solution of disputed problems."

The agreements announced at the conclusion of this visit amounted to the final expulsion from Chinese soil of the remnants of the Russian colonialism whose roots went back to the nineteenth century. One agreement called for the removal of all Soviet troops from Port Arthur and for turning over all Soviet property there to the Chinese government. A second provided for the dissolution of the four joint Sino-Soviet companies formed in 1950 and 1951—the non-ferrous metals and oil companies in Sinkiang, the joint civil aviation company and the joint ship-building and ship-repairing company in Dairen—and the transfer of the Soviet share of these companies to the Chinese government, which would pay for them by the exports of Chinese goods to the Soviet Union over a period of years. A third agreement announced plans for building a railroad to connect the Soviet Union and China through Sinkiang on the line Lanchow-Urumchi-Alma-Ata. The Chinese portion of this railroad—after its completion—would greatly improve Chinese access to an area which had long been drawn to Russia because of the greater ease of trading with Soviet Central Asia than with most of China. At the same time, agreement was reached on an additional Soviet credit of 520,000,000 rubles ($130,000,000) to China. The Soviet leaders pledged aid in building 15 additional industrial enterprises in China, as well as promising increased Soviet deliveries for 141 industrial enterprises covered in earlier agreements.

Why did the Soviet Union liquidate its hard-won special positions in Sinkiang, Port Arthur and Dairen? The basic answer must be that the Chinese left the Russians no alternative. They must have made it clear to Moscow that any attempt to preserve positions in China reminiscent of those enjoyed under Tsarist imperialism would create major friction and enmity with the Chinese. Moreover, the major Soviet imperialist foothold in China had been given up at the end of 1952, when the Chinese Changchun Railroad was turned over to Chinese hands. Faced with a unified and increasingly strong China, Moscow must have decided that the tactics and objectives of an earlier day were no longer appropriate. The 1954 Peking visit by Khrushchev and Company must therefore be regarded as the historic occasion on which the Chinese Communists successfully asserted their right to deal with Russia on a basis of genuine equality. Soviet Foreign Minister Molotov in early 1955 went so far in accepting this equality as to suggest that Communist China shared the leadership of the Socialist camp with the Soviet Union.

It seems likely that for a year or so after the Khrushchev-Bulganin-Mikoyan visit to Peking, Soviet-Chinese relations were genuinely cordial. A major factor uniting them then was agreement that international tension had to be reduced. In 1955 the Soviet Union withdrew its troops from Austria, apologized to Yugoslavia for the 1948 split and had its leaders meet at the summit in Geneva with Western leaders. All these major Moscow moves were taken without apparent Chinese objection. Communist China similarly participated in the 1955 Bandung Conference. It presented itself then before Asia and the world as a model of moderation, anxious only to have the best and most amicable relations with its Asian and African neighbors, particularly India. At the height of this era of good feeling, in effect, both Moscow and Peking were operating peace offensives toward the outside world and toward each other. In early 1955, Peking even accepted with relatively good grace Soviet pressure for reduced militancy against Taiwan and the Chiang Kai-shek forces on it. This era of good feeling in Sino-Soviet relations appears to have been closely related to the rise to power in this period of the Bulganin-Khrushchev alliance and the eclipse and defeat of Georgi Malenkov, who resigned as premier in February 1955.

Perhaps as a gesture of Soviet good will, Communist China in 1955 was allowed freer access to Outer Mongolia. The Mongolians agreed that year to permit the immigration of 10,000 Chinese to their country, giving them the option of becoming permanent settlers. Outer Mongolia also accepted Chinese economic aid to build various industrial facilities plus a Chinese grant in aid equivalent to $40,000,000.

Soviet-Chinese trade continued to grow during the middle 1950's, primarily because of the rapid growth of Chinese exports as production within China itself rose sharply. In 1954 and 1955 Peking continued to run trade deficits with the Soviet Union, although the size of these deficits declined sharply. In 1956, for the first time, Communist China exported more to the Soviet Union than it imported from there. Over the years 1950 to 1955, the Soviet Union had permitted Communist China to accumulate a total commercial trade deficit of about $1,000,000,000. Officially announced loans, however—granted under the 1950 and 1954 agreements—amounted to only $430,000,000. There is evidence, too, that in 1954 and 1955 the Chinese Communist government received a good deal of Soviet military equipment on a credit basis which did not enter the trading accounts. In 1957, the Chinese minister of finance put his country's indebtedness to the Soviet Union at about $2,500,000,000, a sum which presumably included the trade deficit, the cost of weapons and military supplies received during and after the Korean War and the value of the Soviet shares of the four joint companies whose dissolution had been agreed on in 1954.[6]

The trade figures for the middle 1950's follow:[7]

Year	Soviet Exports to China	Soviet Imports from China	China's Deficit (−) or Surplus (+) in Trade
		(millions of dollars)	
1953	705.5	474.7	−230.8
1954	759.3	578.3	−181.0
1955	748.3	643.5	−104.8
1956	733.0	764.2	+ 31.2

The years 1956–1958 were a transitional era between the period of most cordial Sino-Soviet relations, 1954 and 1955, and the subsequent years of bitter political struggle between Moscow and Peking. As this transitional period progressed, strains and awkwardnesses in the alliance became ever more visible, though cooperation continued in many fields. We know now that behind the scenes even 1956 was a year of sharp conflict and significant tension, while the temporary improvement that occurred during 1957 gave way to a state of crisis by the end of 1958. But the ability of both powers to keep these realities largely hidden and to act in seeming concert in public suggests that during 1956–1958 both sides felt that the forces keeping them together were more powerful than those driving them apart. The strains that arose during this period originated in both capitals. Peking was growing in strength, becoming more distrustful of Soviet leadership of the Communist world, and increasingly anxious to have its own nuclear weapons. At the same time Mao was beset with difficult internal problems. Moscow was going through twin convulsions: the struggle for power in the Kremlin hierarchy and the effort to exorcise the ghost of Stalin in Soviet life.

At the Twentieth Soviet Communist party Congress in February 1956, Khrushchev delivered two major speeches, one public and one secret. The first was notable for its new line on the issue of war and peace, and for its acceptance of the concept of different roads to Socialism. On the latter issue, Khrushchev pointed out that "much that is unique in socialist construction is being contributed by the Chinese Peoples Republic whose country prior to the victory of the revolution was exceedingly backward, semi-feudal and semi-colonial in character." He praised this contribution of the Chinese as "creative Marxism in action." On the issue of war and peace, Khrushchev put "peaceful coexistence" at the center of Soviet foreign policy. He denied that he expected a Communist world victory to come about "through armed interference by the socialist countries in the internal affairs of the capitalist country." Rather, he asserted, Communist victory would come because the "decisive advantages" of the Socialist system over the capitalist system would succeed in "capturing the minds of the working people in the capitalist countries." His key point was the abandonment of the old Leninist-Stalinist concept of the inevitability of war between the capitalist and Communist worlds. Instead, he asserted "war is not fatalistically inevitable." He justified this on the ground that the forces of Socialism had become so strong as to be able to frustrate the enemy's "adventurist plans." As a corollary of his concept that a new balance of forces existed in the world, one more favorable to Socialism, he advanced the thesis that it was now possible in some capitalist countries to seize power peacefully, using parliamentary means. Khrushchev was cautious in these formulations; he admitted the possibility both of war and of the need in some countries for Communists to seize power "by a sharp class, revolutionary struggle." But it was clear then that he put a markedly different emphasis upon Communist thinking about the future than had existed earlier. As would emerge later, these changes represented an effort to come to grips with the new problems posed by nuclear weapons and their potential for destroying both capitalists and Communists in any war.

Khrushchev's second speech at the Twentieth Communist party Congress in February 1956 was his originally secret denunciation of Stalin. This was the address in which he assailed Stalin as a murdering paranoid who had inflicted injury upon untold numbers of innocent Communists and who had endangered the existence of the Soviet Union by his naïve trust in Hitler on the eve of the German attack in June 1941. Insistent rumor has held that in a portion of this speech unavailable to the West, Khrushchev assailed Stalin for having brought Chinese-Soviet relations to a point of crisis before his death. Whether true or not, it is clear that Khrushchev had not consulted Peking before launching this attack. The Chinese delegate to the Congress spoke highly of Stalin in his speech to his Soviet comrades. Moreover, it seems unlikely that the Chinese would have approved of such a broadside against Stalin. As later developments showed, they feared the impact of this attack upon the entire Communist world, a fear in which they were not alone. Mao Tse-tung had a special reason for disliking an offensive against Stalin and his "cult of personality." There were obvious similarities between Stalin's former role in the Soviet Union and Mao's current role in China. A denunciation of Stalin's dictatorship could lead to skepticism about the virtues of Mao's eminence. Moreover, Khrushchev was clearly trying to present himself as the new lawgiver for international Communism, a role Peking refused to accord him.

Peking's initial public reaction to the Twentieth Congress was cautious. The Chinese public statement issued in April 1956 aimed primarily at limiting the impact of the anti-Stalin movement and protecting Mao against similar charges. But in private the Chinese were more outspoken about their misgivings. That same month of April Mao Tse-tung spoke both to visiting Soviet leader Anastas I. Mikoyan and to the Soviet ambassador about the subject. As Peking revealed in September 1963, Mao then emphasized that Stalin's "merits outweighed his faults." Mao went further later in 1956. On October 23, he told the Soviet ambassador, "Stalin deserved to be criticized, but we do not agree with the method of criticism, and there are some other matters we do not agree with." Five weeks later, on November 30, Mao told the Soviet ambassador that Stalin's basic line and policy were correct. Liu Shao-chi and Chou En-lai also expressed similar views in private to Soviet leaders in October 1956 and January 1957 respectively. They criticized what they called the Soviet leaders' "total lack of an over-all analysis of Stalin," their "lack of self-criticism," and their "failure to consult with the fraternal parties in advance."[8] These were strong objections, but they could not have been put too offensively, for Mikoyan's April 1956 visit resulted in agreement for Chinese purchase of $600,000,000 worth of Soviet goods to help build 55 additional major industrial plants. Three months later the two countries agreed to expand their 1956 trade above earlier agreed levels. In August 1956 they agreed to engage in a cooperative survey of the Amur River Basin with a view to joint exploitation of its power, mineral and other potentials.

This discord was the hidden background for the first direct Chinese challenge to Soviet hegemony elsewhere in the Communist world. The essentials were related to this writer by a high Polish diplomat some months afterward. At the Chinese Communist party Congress in September 1956, the chief Polish delegate, Edward Ochab, was told by Mao Tse-tung and other Chinese leaders that Poland's Communists could expect Peking support if they sought to win greater autonomy. This assurance probably gave the Polish leaders, headed by the national Communist

Wladyslaw Gomulka, the courage to defy Nikita Khrushchev when the latter stormed into Warsaw so dramatically in October 1956. Rumor had it that Mao warned Khrushchev against Soviet military intervention in Poland to remove the new Gomulka leadership. This rumor seems confirmed by Peking's September 1963 charge against the Soviet leadership on this matter, the assertion that "by moving up troops in an attempt to subdue the Polish comrades by armed force, it [the Soviet leadership] committed the error of great power chauvinism."

The Soviet leadership's fury must have been great at this Chinese intervention which forced Moscow to retreat and accord Poland greater autonomy. That fury must have risen a few days later when the successful Polish defiance of Moscow helped ignite the Hungarian Revolution. The Chinese charged in September 1963 that at the critical juncture of the Hungarian Revolution in 1956 the Soviet leaders "intended to adopt a policy of capitulation and abandon Socialist Hungary to counter-revolution." It was Peking, the Chinese declared, that "insisted on the taking of all necessary measures to smash the counter-revolutionary rebellion in Hungary and firmly opposed the abandonment of Socialist Hungary," implying that the Chinese forced the Soviet intervention of November 4, 1956 which crushed the Hungarian Revolution.

If true, this all took place behind the scenes. Publicly the world saw only that Chou En-lai hurried to Eastern Europe late in 1956 and played what appeared to be an influential role in healing the wounds between the Eastern Europeans and the Russians. Peking may have been trying to make amends for its encouragement of the Poles, but it can hardly have escaped either side that these events represented a historic projection—the first in many centuries—of Chinese influence into European affairs. Moreover, it is now clear that this Chinese pressure forced issuance of the Soviet statement of October 30, 1956 admitting "errors" in relations with Eastern Europe and promising their rectification. Moreover, in a public statement during this period, the Chinese declared that "the Polish and Hungarian peoples have advanced demands for strengthening democracy, independence, and equality," demands the Chinese said they considered "fully correct." There must have been more than a little tension when Khrushchev and Chou En-lai conferred in Moscow in

January 1957 and finally issued a statement on correct relations among Socialist countries:

> In the mutual relations between socialist countries there are not and were not fundamental contradictions and collisions of interest. Even if in the past there were some errors and deficiencies, they are being overcome and liquidated at the present time. Moreover these errors and deficiencies can in no manner darken the basic and chief aspect of the relations among socialist countries, mutual aid and cooperation. The facts testify that any questions of the mutual relations of socialist countries can be fully solved on the basis of unity by means of sincere consultations and comradely consideration. It is fully possible to link correctly the unity of socialist countries and the independence of each separate country in their mutual relations.[9]

The Chinese had no interest in pushing the quarrel further. They had made their point about the need for greater independence for each Communist-ruled nation in its relations with Moscow. But they needed a unified bloc because they still feared the United States, they needed help in economic development and they counted on bloc aid in applying pressure to end the Chiang Kai-shek government and incorporate Taiwan into Communist China. The Russians, whose prestige had been so badly battered in late 1956, also wanted to reknit as much as possible of the torn fabric of Communist unity. At the height of the Hungarian disturbances, on October 30, 1956, they had issued a statement suggesting that the Communist-ruled countries form a "commonwealth," with obvious similarity to the British Commonwealth of Nations. But to heal the wounds in Eastern Europe required greater expenditures for additional economic aid to improve the living conditions which had caused such profound discontent. The Soviet Union promised such economic aid, and took advantage of the needs of Eastern Europe to punish the Chinese by cutting down shipments to them. From $733,000,000 in 1956, Soviet exports to Communist China fell to $544,000,000 in 1957 and then rose only to $634,000,000 in 1958. Meanwhile pressure was kept on the Chinese to increase their exports so as to pay off part of the large Chinese debt. As a result, Communist China sent the Soviet Union $441,000,000 worth of goods more than it received during the two years 1957 and 1958. The Chinese, in other words, indirectly provided part of the resources the

Soviet Union needed to meet its increased commitments to Eastern Europe. This took place at a time when the Chinese Communists were under great strain because of their ambitious industrialization program at home and the difficulties they were encountering in meeting that program's needs.[10]

Internal developments in both the Soviet Union and China during 1957 proved of crucial importance to relations between the two nations. In Moscow, June 1957 saw the abortive effort by all of Khrushchev's enemies in the Communist party Presidium to purge him from power, an effort he defeated. The result was that Khrushchev emerged as virtually the one-man leader of the Soviet Union while his key opponents—including Molotov who had appeared ready in 1955 to concede co-leadership of the Communist bloc to China—were purged and disappeared from the Kremlin power center. This was followed in August and October by the two Soviet rocket feats which shook the world: first, the successful testing of a Soviet intercontinental ballistic missile, and then the orbiting of Sputnik I, an event which captured world imagination and raised Soviet prestige throughout the world to a new peak.

In China, the first half of 1957 saw the "hundred flowers" experiment, the effort to relieve internal tension by permitting a period of unprecedented free speech. It seems clear now that the result staggered the Chinese Communist leadership. The flood of bitter criticism of the Chinese Communist party's domestic and foreign policies and of the Soviet Union which arose from many levels of Chinese society revealed profound discontent in the country. As a result, the period of free speech was abruptly terminated and a campaign against "rightists" started. Chinese leaders now had to reckon with the fact that the same kind of ferment which had shaken Eastern Europe in late 1956 existed in their own country. Mao Tse-tung and his colleagues appear to have concluded that this ferment exploded in Eastern Europe because "revisionist" concessions had been made there to the spokesmen for popular dissatisfaction. Their decision was to meet the problem in China by tightening controls and demanding still more intensive efforts and sacrifices from their people for economic development. Thus began a fateful move to the left by the

Chinese Communist party, the party which in 1955 and 1956 had been viewed by many in Eastern Europe as a potential major bulwark of the right wing in the world Communist movement.

— In October 1957 there took place what may well have been the most important single event in Soviet-Chinese relations since at least the end of the Korean War. On October 15, 1957 the two nations reached an agreement on "new technology for national defense," a pact which required the Soviet Union to give China a sample of an atomic bomb and technical data concerning its manufacture. This historic agreement, by which the Soviet Union pledged its help to make China a nuclear power and even to give the Chinese an atomic bomb, was concluded in the deepest secrecy. The world did not learn of this move for almost six years, until August 15, 1963, when a bitter and enraged Chinese Communist regime made the fact of such an agreement public and denounced the Soviet repudiation of this treaty which Peking said had taken place on June 20, 1959.[11] The 20 months between the conclusion and repudiation of this treaty were clearly the crucial period in which the Sino-Soviet alliance met its supreme test and foundered on the shoals of mutual antagonism and distrust.

We can only speculate on why the Khrushchev regime decided to help China become a nuclear power. It seems certain that Moscow had refused to take such a step in earlier years—Russia's first atomic explosion of which we have knowledge took place in September 1949 and its first hydrogen bomb explosion took place in August 1953. Before 1957 Moscow may well have argued that it was too preoccupied with building up its own nuclear resources to be able to spare needed resources for China's nuclear benefit, but such an argument, if offered, must have worn thin by 1957. In August of that year, after all, Soviet scientists had successfully tested the first intercontinental ballistic missile and on October 4, 1957 they had sent the first sputnik into orbit. At a time when it was publicly crowing over having beaten the United States in both missile and space technology, Moscow could hardly plead weakness to the Chinese.

The most likely explanation is that Khrushchev decided to share Soviet atomic secrets and bombs with the Chinese as a desperate move to strengthen the alliance whose weaknesses had begun to show up in 1956. The Soviet leader also wanted Chinese help to insure against further restlessness in Eastern Europe.

Moreover the atomic sharing agreement was reached only four months after Khrushchev had defeated Molotov and the other members of the anti-party group. Molotov had shown by his speech of February 1955 that he was willing to accord the Chinese a higher status than the rest of the Soviet hierarchy, hailing them as partners with the Soviet Union in leading the Communist world. The Chinese may have exhibited nervousness in the summer of 1957 that Molotov's removal was in part a move against them. If so, the atomic agreement would have been aimed at reassuring them. Some credibility is given this hypothesis by the fact that at the end of the same month, October 1957, Moscow took another action whose objective was clearly that of soothing ruffled Chinese feelings. This was the formation in the Soviet Union of a Soviet-Chinese Friendship Society to popularize pro-Chinese feelings among the Soviet people. A Sino-Soviet Friendship Association had been active in China for many years, and the absence of an analogous group in Moscow had been clear evidence of strain and awkwardness in the relationship. Another move in the same direction took place two months later. On December 21, 1957 the two nations signed an agreement on navigation of the Amur River and its tributaries on their common Far Eastern border. This treaty permitted ships of both nations to use the waterways of the border area and their ports freely. In earlier periods, it will be recalled, there had been much Chinese resentment of the unreciprocated Russian freedom to use Manchurian rivers for Russian needs. Now both nations had given each other reciprocal rights.

We know now that Chinese gratitude for the Soviet atomic move was quick to assert itself. Mao Tse-tung—the least-traveled of all major world leaders of the time—personally came to Moscow the very next month, heading the Chinese Communist delegation attending the celebration of the fortieth anniversary of the Bolshevik Revolution. His speech to the jubilee session of the Supreme Soviet on November 6 was ecstatic in its praise of the Moscow regime, declaring: "The path of the Soviet Union, the path of the October Revolution is basically the bright high road of all humanity." He then added a passage which a few years later made very ironic reading:

It is completely clear that if after the October Revolution the proletarian revolutionaries of different countries will ignore or will fail seriously to study the experience of the Russian Revolution, if they will not seriously study the experience of the dictatorship of the proletariat and of socialist construction in the Soviet Union, and also if they will not analytically and creatively apply this experience in correspondence with the concrete conditions of their countries, they cannot master Leninism which is a new stage in the development of Marxism, they cannot correctly solve the problems of revolution and construction in their own countries. . . . In equal measure it is also clear that after the October Revolution if the government of any country refuses to live in friendship with the Soviet Union, then it only brings harm to the real interests of the people of its country.

Mao Tse-tung underlined his seeming new enthusiasm for complete allegiance to the Soviet Union when he spoke at Moscow University on November 17, 1957. He declared there: "The Socialist camp must have a head, and this head is the U.S.S.R. . . . The Communist and workers parties of all countries must have a head and that head is the Communist party of the Soviet Union." The dissidents in Eastern Europe could have no more hope of Chinese help. For the moment, Khrushchev's atomic bribe seemed to have worked.

But behind the scenes the situation was more complex, as became evident to the participants of the international Communist party Congress which met in Moscow in November 1957. There the Chinese vigorously opposed Soviet efforts to have the decisions of the Twentieth (1956) Soviet party Congress taken as the line of the world Communist movement. The fight was particularly bitter, the Chinese claim, over an alleged Soviet attempt to make the peaceful winning of power by Communist parties the only approved method of transition from non-Communist to Communist rule. The Chinese claim they won this battle. Moreover, Mao delivered a speech saying that if necessary—because capitalist nations started it—Communists should not be afraid of fighting a nuclear war which might kill half the world's population. The sounding of this theme could hardly have reassured a Khrushchev now committed to helping China become a nuclear power. Soon the Soviet leader's public speeches began to warn about how much damage both sides—not just the capitalists—would suffer in the event of a nuclear war.

In general Mao Tse-tung appeared at this conference as the advocate of a tough and aggressive policy on the international scene. He justified his position by reference to what he claimed was the impact of the new Soviet weapons advances, as well as what he regarded as the rising tide of revolutionary sentiment throughout the world. He resorted to a meteorological analogy to make his point:

> I am of the opinion that the international situation has now reached a new turning point. There are two winds in the world today: the East wind and the West wind. . . . I think the characteristic of the situation today is the East wind prevailing over the West wind. That is to say, the socialist forces are overwhelmingly superior to the imperialist forces.[12]

Mao was going further than Khrushchev was willing to go. Moreover, the Chinese were calling for a tightly integrated bloc of Communist-ruled countries and parties taking decisions which the Soviet Union, as head of the bloc of nations, and the Soviet Communist party, as head of the world party organization, would be obligated to carry out. Moscow's cautious reaction might have been different if Peking had urged a return to the earlier situation when the Soviet Union under Stalin made policy unilaterally, but this was certainly not the Chinese wish. On the issue of relative power, moreover, the Soviet leaders had a very clear understanding of the enormous military power of the United States. Moscow did not believe that its rocket breakthrough had made it strong enough to run the kind of risk implied in Mao's assessment of the world power situation.

Two statements emerged from the Moscow gathering of Communist parties. One was a general and relatively innocuous peace declaration signed by all the Communist parties represented, including the Yugoslavs. The second was a compromise declaration of policy signed by twelve of the thirteen ruling Communist parties. The exception was Yugoslavia, which refused to accept the reference to the "invincible camp of socialist countries headed by the Soviet Union" or the harsh attack on "revisionism" which the second declaration characterized as the "main danger at present."

Presumably the Soviet Union at least began to take steps that indicated it intended to fulfill its promise to help China become a nuclear power. In September 1958, the Chinese ceremoniously announced the completion of a 10,000 kilowatt nuclear reactor and a 20,000,000 electron-volt cyclotron in a suburb of Peking, both built with Soviet help and Soviet equipment. This concrete help explains the good relations that appeared to prevail between Moscow and Peking in early 1958. In February, for example, Peking announced it would evacuate its troops from North Korea by the end of the year, terminating a seven-year occupation. A few weeks later both the Chinese and the Soviet press were in the forefront of the general Communist attack on the new Yugoslav Communist program. The Chinese broadsides were verbally more bitter against the Yugoslav "revisionists," but the Soviet Union took more effective practical steps. It postponed extension of almost $300,000,000 in credits promised Yugoslavia and cancelled the scheduled visit to Belgrade of Klimenti Voroshilov, then titular head of the Soviet state. But that there was not complete identity of views was glaringly revealed by the Middle East crisis which followed the Iraqi revolt of July 1958. The movement of Anglo-American troops into Lebanon and Jordan provoked a thinly veiled Chinese Communist demand for counter military action by the Communist bloc, while Khrushchev in Moscow busied himself trying to get a summit meeting on the issue in the United Nations Security Council. The crisis itself faded, but before the Soviet and Chinese positions were fully coordinated Khrushchev had to make an extraordinary flying visit to Peking. It was now clearly evident that something less than full identity existed between the foreign policies of the two countries. But in September 1958 when the Chinese Communists began artillery bombardment of the Nationalist-held islands of Quemoy and Matsu, the Soviet press quickly came to Peking's support, and Khrushchev warned President Eisenhower that an American attack on the Chinese Communists would mean war with Russia. Moscow was trying hard to present a picture of a faithful ally, but the Chinese Communist failure to mount an invasion of these islands may have been the result of Soviet restraining influence.

Developments within China itself during middle and late 1958 made clear the wide gulf that was opening up behind the scenes.

This was the early stage of the Chinese "great leap forward," when Peking confidently asserted that it could accomplish economic miracles and was doing so. Hundreds of thousands of primitive, small iron and steel furnaces sprouted in Chinese backyards as part of the policy of "walking on two legs," i.e., using both the modern complex metallurgical factories built with Soviet help and the primitive furnaces which could be manned by millions of inexperienced workers everywhere in the country. Most important, this was the period of the revolutionary transformation of the Chinese countryside and collective farms into the system of people's communes.

The people's communes into which some 500,000,000 Chinese peasants were herded in 1958 represented the extreme of Chinese Communist leftist domestic policy. They were an attempt to solve all of China's internal problems at one stroke by an organizational revolution of a scope and magnitude hitherto unknown. We may suspect that the radical nature of the people's commune program was partially inspired by difficulties in China's relations with Russia, particularly the refusal of Moscow to give Peking any large-scale economic aid. The emphasis in the communes upon giving their adult male members military training and forming them into a vast militia armed with primitive weapons may also have reflected the increasing tensions developing between the two countries over implementation of the 1957 atomic aid agreement. China, in short, may have sought to find in the people's communes and their extreme measures an alternative means of achieving economic and military strength, a means which if successful would make China less dependent upon the Soviet Union.

At the extreme—and by no means all communes reached the extreme—the communes abolished all private property, instituted a system of free supply of food and other goods on an equal basis without regard to work, wiped out normal family life by housing all members in separate men's and women's dormitories, and established a system of militarized labor combining intensive farm and other work with military instruction and drill. For a few months in the autumn of 1958, the Chinese Communist leaders apparently believed they had found the magic key for raising production at a tempo never before known in history and for bringing perfect Communism to China very quickly, well before the Soviet Union achieved it. In the words of the Chinese Communist party Central Committee resolution adopted August 29, 1958: "It seems that the attainment of communism in China is no longer a remote future event. We should actively use the form of the people's communes to explore the practical road of transition to communism."[13]

By December 1958, cooler heads began to prevail and a partial retreat from the most extreme aspects of the commune system was ordered. But as late as April 1959 the Chinese Communists still believed that by means of the "great leap forward" in industry and the people's communes in agriculture they were making unprecedentedly rapid progress in production and economic strength. Premier Chou En-lai told Communist China's legislature in April 1959 that steel output had jumped from 5,350,000 tons in 1957 to 11,080,000 tons in 1958, and that grain output had also more than doubled from about 185,000,000 tons in 1957 to 375,000,000 tons in 1958. He forecast similar major and rapid gains in output in 1959.

In the late summer and early fall of 1958, it quickly became apparent to foreign observers that the Soviet Union was not happy about what was going on in China and had doubts about both the backyard furnaces and the people's communes. This became clear from the nearly complete blackout of news about these Chinese developments in the Soviet press. While the Chinese press and radio crowed incessantly about great revolutionary advances, *Pravda* and *Izvestiya* kept their readers almost—but not entirely—uninformed on these changes.

At least three reasons could be seen even then for Soviet displeasure. First, the Chinese move to the left in agriculture contrasted sharply with—and therefore was implicitly critical of—Khrushchev's move to the right in Soviet agricultural policy early in 1958, when he had permitted the collective farms to buy the state-owned tractors and other farm machinery which for three decades had been monopolized by the machine-tractor stations of Russia. Second, the Chinese claims to have discovered a shortcut to Communism and to have achieved fantastically high rates of production increase were implicit rebukes to the Russians and implicit claims that the Chinese Communist leaders—not the men in Moscow—deserved to be the ideological leaders of world Communism. Why had not the Soviet Union, with its more than three-decade headstart on China, discovered these techniques itself and traversed the full road to perfect Communism? This was the question clearly posed by the Chinese propaganda fusillade. Finally, Khrushchev and his colleagues feared that the radical moves in China would lead to disaster and endanger Communist rule there. In a remarkable conversation with Senator Hubert Humphrey in December 1958, Khrushchev attacked the whole commune idea, calling the communes "reactionary" and "old fashioned." The Soviet Union had tried such radical measures at the very beginning of its history and had found they did not work, he said, adding that any effort to remove wage inequalities and the incentives they provided must inevitably damage efforts to raise production. These critical remarks to the American senator were not made generally known in the Soviet Union. But two months earlier, in October 1958, a Soviet philosopher had made plain the Soviet skepticism about the Chinese claims of having achieved a short cut to Communism. In an article published in the magazine *Voprosy Filosofi* (Problems of Philosophy), T. A. Stepanyan had declared that the Soviet Union and its Eastern European allies would reach the goal of perfect Communism together first, and only later would the Asian Communist-ruled countries arrive at the same ideal state.

Faced with this challenge to his primacy as chief theoretician of the Communist world, Khrushchev struck back in January 1959 by enunciating his own version of the road to the Communist Utopia. He did not mention the Chinese Communists in his speech to the Twenty-first Soviet Communist party Congress, but his target could not be missed when he declared: "Society cannot leap from capitalism to communism." He centered his fire on the idea that it was possible to shift from pay according to work to a policy of distribution according to need. Russia had indeed done this in the early civil war years, but, he explained, "this was not due to abundance, but to a stringent shortage of food and consumer goods." He abandoned Stepanyan's theory of the two-phased achievement of Communism, but even while doing so he managed to get in an implied dig at the Chinese. It was improbable, he asserted, that one country would achieve Communism while others were left trailing behind (as the Chinese had implied they would do). Rather, he argued, "the socialist countries will enter the higher phase of communist society more or less simultaneously" because they would cooperate and there

would be "mutual assistance." Here he seemed to be implying
that if the Chinese Communists behaved themselves they could
get more Soviet economic aid.[14]

In retrospect, it seems likely that the debate over the communes
and their ideological implications was the decisive turning point
in the Soviet-Chinese relationship of the 1950's. The Chinese had
shown publicly an arrogance, a self-confidence and a contempt
for the Khrushchev leadership which must have profoundly
shocked Moscow. How deep the wound must have been we can
judge from Khrushchev's action in communicating his adverse
reaction to a United States senator. All this must have been related to the circumstances, still not fully known in the West,
surrounding what the Chinese Communists charged in September
1963 was a Soviet misdeed during the period discussed here: "In
1958 the leadership of the Soviet Communist party put forward
unreasonable demands designed to bring China under Soviet
military control. These unreasonable demands were rightly and
firmly rejected by the Chinese Government." We may speculate
that this was the Chinese reaction to Soviet demands that Moscow
control directly any nuclear weapons given to or produced by
Communist China.

The events of late 1958, it is now clear, left incurable wounds.
The Chinese began to suspect Khrushchev wanted to improve
his relations with the United States. Khrushchev clearly viewed
the Chinese ideological claims of late 1958 as an outright attempt
to seize the leadership of the world Communist movement, a
continuation of the trouble-making the Chinese had pioneered
in 1956 when they encouraged the Polish defiance of Moscow.
His misgivings must have been increased by signs that in Bulgaria,
Albania and elsewhere there were important figures attracted to
the idea of the Chinese communes as well as to Chinese extremism.
Sino-Soviet hostility developed swiftly after 1958.

Yet neither side could afford, in early 1959, to carry the dispute too far publicly. The Soviet Union at that point was engaged in a major confrontation with the United States, demanding that Western troops leave West Berlin and conversion of
that area into a "free city." Moscow might need Chinese aid if
this resulted in war. The men in Peking knew they might need
Soviet help to win back Taiwan. Moreover, Communist China's
frantic industrialization program needed more Soviet goods than

ever. Thus, rather contradictory trends developed in early 1959. On the one hand, Khrushchev sent Mikoyan to the United States to begin the soundings and wooing of American public opinion that were to lead to the Soviet Premier's visit to the United States. On the other hand, Soviet-Chinese trade was increased. Soviet exports to China mounted 50 per cent in 1959, reaching almost a billion dollars. But the Chinese raised their shipments to the Soviet Union to $1,100,000,000 worth of goods, thus attaining a trade surplus which further reduced the Chinese debt. Peking, it was clear, was determined to wipe out its commercial obligations to the Soviet Union as soon as possible. Though this trade involved no Soviet aid or credits to China, there was much propaganda in the Soviet press on the "brotherly help" being given to China.

The events described above as productive of Soviet-Chinese tension in late 1958 reached their climax in June 1959 when the Soviet Union took a fateful step. It cancelled the agreement to help China become a nuclear power. No hint of this action, taken on June 20, 1959, reached the outside world at the time, but it clearly created a crisis of major proportions. Premier Khrushchev could not know then what the cancellation of the treaty would mean, though he must have known that it raised possibilities of troublesome developments on the Asian borders of the Soviet Union. In this situation, while nominally continuing to threaten a showdown over Berlin, he may actually have been most anxious to improve his relations with the United States. It was probably to explore the possibilities of such a development that he sent Anastas Mikoyan to the United States at the beginning of 1959. Mikoyan's report, on his return, must have been favorable. Then, almost at the same time as the cancellation of the treaty with China, First Deputy Premier and party Presidium member Frol R. Kozlov arrived in the United States. His nominal mission was to open the Soviet Exposition in New York City's Coliseum. His actual main purpose was to arrange with President Eisenhower for the Khrushchev visit to the United States in September 1959. This sequence of events is undoubtedly what the Chinese had in mind when they charged in August 1963 that the treaty was cancelled "as a presentation gift at the time the Soviet leader went to the United States for talks with Eisenhower in September." The Chinese have also charged that the Soviet Union secretly revealed the existence and subsequent renunciation of the Sino-Soviet atomic aid agreement to the United States. The possibility that they are correct raises interesting questions. Did President Eisenhower invite Khrushchev to the United States because Frol Kozlov told him Russia had just repudiated its agreement to make Peking a nuclear power? Or was the sudden sprouting of the "Spirit of Camp David" in September 1959 and the subsequent extraordinary, if short-lived, Soviet-American cordiality the result of a revelation of this matter by Premier Khrushchev to President Eisenhower during their private talks at Camp David, Maryland in September 1959? There is much we still do not know about these events.

Related to all this was the serious worsening of China's relations with India in 1959. Peking was furious when the Indians gave sanctuary to the Dalai Lama and other refugees from Tibet. This tension, plus disagreements on the border between the two countries, created the situation which produced the Sino-Indian frontier clash in the latter half of 1959. But Moscow pointedly refused to let these developments harm its links to India and continued its massive flow of economic aid to New Delhi despite China's displeasure. The first climax in this triangular relationship was reached in September 1959, when a TASS announcement stated official Soviet neutrality in the Indian-Chinese dispute. To the Chinese, this appeared to be an unprecedented refusal by one Communist-ruled state to support another Communist-ruled state in a dispute with a bourgeois government. As the Chinese later indicated, they considered this Soviet move an act of treachery, one fully in line with the attitude revealed by the cancellation of the atomic aid agreement.

The matters reviewed above would have been sufficient to present the Chinese Communist party Central Committee with a crisis when it met at Lushan in August 1959 to review the developments of the past tempestuous year. But in addition the Central Committee was faced with the grave problems arising from the economic difficulties which had begun to be widely felt throughout China. A re-examination had shown that the 1958 production figures announced earlier had been grossly exaggerated. Grain output in 1958, the Central Committee was told, had been only 250,000,000 tons, not the 375,000,000 tons originally claimed. The 1958 production of steel usable in industry had been only 8,000,000 tons, and the remaining 3,080,000 tons claimed for that year were only useful for "the requirements of rural areas." The original goals for 1959, announced earlier that year, were unrealistic and would have to be scaled down substantially. Accompanying this bitter news was what seems to have been a revolt by a portion of the Peking leadership, an effort by a group of rightists to secure a complete reversal of economic policy, including abandonment of both the "great leap forward" and the people's communes. There is some evidence suggesting that this revolt was led by a group of military men under the Chinese Politburo member and Minister of Defense, Marshal Peng Teh-huai. Marshal Peng is reported to have opposed Mao's policy of basing much of China's defense upon a poorly trained militia armed only with conventional weapons. Marshal Peng reportedly wanted China to obtain nuclear weapons. He is supposed to have won Soviet support by writing Premier Khrushchev a secret letter explaining his views. Some support for these reports is given by a Chinese revelation in September 1963. This states that in conversation with the Chinese delegation to the Twenty-second Soviet Communist party Congress in 1961, Khrushchev "even expressed undisguised support for anti-party elements in the Chinese Communist party." If these reports are true, Khrushchev may have encouraged Marshal Peng by promising reinstatement of the Soviet agreement to help China become a nuclear power if Mao were overthrown as leader of Chinese Communism.

If there was such a struggle for power at the Lushan meeting, it was won by Mao. Certainly there was a stress on Chinese independence and on the need for China's course to be decided in China in an important article published at that time in the Chinese Communists' official party organ, *Red Flag:*

> In the course of our country's building of socialism, the construction experiences accumulated by the Soviet Union and other fraternal countries have been studied and utilized as reference material by us. This is an important factor in helping our country to develop her undertakings smoothly. However, what we intend to do is to build socialism in a country of more than 600,000,000 people where the original economic foundation is extremely backward; in the course of our building of socialism, the question of how to combine the general

principles of Marxism-Leninism with the actual conditions of China must be solved by ourselves. This question has been solved by our Party and Comrade Mao Tse-tung.[15]

Soviet-Chinese tension increased further at the conclusion of Khrushchev's visit to the United States. The aura of good fellowship and friendship between the United States and the Soviet Union, lauded by Khrushchev as the "Spirit of Camp David," appalled the leaders in Peking. To them it seemed like nothing less than betrayal for the leader of the Soviet Union to be hobnobbing with the President of the United States, hailing him as a lover of peace and as a friend. Coming so soon after the cancellation of the atomic aid agreement, this spectacle must have suggested to Mao that a Soviet-American alliance against China was in the making. All these developments must have contributed to a growing conviction in Peking that Khrushchev was a revisionist, a traitor to Marxism.

The atmosphere was icy indeed when Khrushchev arrived in Peking early in October to help celebrate Communist China's tenth anniversary. It became icier still when he lectured the Chinese leaders, warning them that it "would be wrong" to "test the stability of the capitalist system by force" and praising President Eisenhower as one who "understands the need to relax international tension." But Khrushchev's most provoking action on this occasion, the Chinese charged on August 31, 1963, was to hint very broadly that Communist China should agree to end its quarrel with Chiang Kai-shek on Taiwan. This Khrushchev espousal of a "two Chinas" solution, the Chinese said, was an "absurd view" which "was of course rebutted and rejected by China." The Chinese were also disturbed in this period by Khrushchev's speech before the United Nations in which he urged general and total disarmament. Many in the West regarded this speech as a mere propaganda gambit. The Chinese soon showed they believed the Soviet leader advanced the idea seriously; they feared this meant a Khrushchev effort to disarm the world's revolutionary forces. Peking also, no doubt, felt China had become the first victim of Khrushchev's zeal for disarmament.

At the beginning of 1960, the differences between Moscow and Peking in evaluating the United States and its intentions emerged unmistakably. In January 1960, for example, Khrushchev announced that the Soviet armed forces would be reduced by a third, from 3,600,000 to 2,400,000 men. This move was a consequence both of the improved international situation and of Khrushchev's conclusion that the advent of nuclear weapons and rockets had ended the era of mass armies. The Soviet press maintained its friendly attitude toward President Eisenhower, and extensive preparations began in Moscow for receiving him on his scheduled spring 1960 visit. Khrushchev's plan was to welcome the American President in a fashion surpassing any reception ever before given to a foreign visitor.

Chinese distrust of the United States was made clear in February 1960 in a speech delivered at the meeting of the Warsaw Treaty powers by the Chinese observer, Kang Sheng. For obvious reasons the speech was not published in the Soviet Union, though it was extensively publicized in Peking's propaganda media. Kang charged:

> The new tricks of the United States are designed to gain precisely what it failed to obtain by its old tricks. The actions of the United States prove fully that its imperialist nature will not change. American imperialism still remains the arch-enemy of world peace. All those throughout the world who are working sincerely for peace must maintain their vigilance against United States double dealing.[16]

Elsewhere the Chinese made clear their conviction that President Eisenhower was talking of peace only as a trick to gain time while the United States sought frantically to overcome the Soviet missile advantage.

Concurrently with these exchanges about the United States, the Soviet Union and Communist China were taking different positions toward the underdeveloped non-Communist countries. At issue was the proper attitude toward the governments of such countries as Iraq, India and Egypt, which are governed by what Communists call the national bourgeoisie. Moscow believed that the rulers of these countries should be wooed by economic aid, by personal visits of Soviet leaders and similar means, and that the Communist parties in these countries should adopt relatively cautious tactics. Peking, on the other hand, favored much more vigorous tactics and a harsher attitude. Peking asked, in effect, why should a leader such as Egypt's Nasser get Soviet economic aid when he ruthlessly repressed his local Communists? The Chinese approved of the attempted Communist armed revolution in Iraq in mid-1959, while the Russians regarded it as an "adventure" whose debacle proved the soundness of their own stand. The Chinese attitude, it seems likely, was influenced by memories of the high price they had paid in the 1920's for collaborating with Chiang Kai-shek's national bourgeois Kuomintang. To them it seemed Khrushchev was encouraging mistakes similar to those made three decades earlier by Stalin. They were increasingly convinced that Khrushchev's dislike for militant revolutionary activities in these countries was linked with his general attitude of "appeasing" the West. They felt that this appeasement policy was being cloaked by a specious claim that an overly militant strategy in these countries could provide the spark that would touch off nuclear world war.

In the pages that follow we shall be very much concerned with the great debate that has raged between the Soviet Union and China since early 1960. Until July 1963 this war of words was conducted in Aesopian language designed to baffle the uninformed reader but to be crystal clear to initiates. Both sides used the phrases "certain persons," "some comrades," "some persons claiming to be Marxist-Leninists" and the like to denote their opponents. The Chinese often employed the phrases "revisionists" or "modern revisionists" to attack their Soviet opponents or, when they wanted to imply that it was Premier Khrushchev they were denouncing, would name Yugoslav Marshal Tito, Italian Communist leader Palmiro Togliatti, or French Communist leader Maurice Thorez as the nominal object of their ire. Correspondingly, the Russians attacked "dogmatists," "sectarians" and "Trotskyites" when they meant the Chinese.

Some of these phrases have ideological significance in the argument as well as being devices for thinly hiding the target for attack. Revisionism is a current in Marxism going back to the writings of the French Socialist Eduard Bernstein and his followers before World War I. The original revisionists sought to modify classical Marxist ideas to take account of the changes, particularly the reforms and improvements, which had taken place in capitalism since Marx died. They believed in an evolutionary movement toward Socialism, one based on democracy, rather than supporting revolution and dictatorship. In 1956 the Polish and Hungarian dissenters from Moscow's rule were dubbed revisionists, too, implying they wished to depart from true Marxism toward compromise with capitalism. By calling their Soviet and Yugoslav opponents "modern revisionists," the Chinese imply that Khrushchev and Tito are really intellectual and political heirs of Bernstein and not of Lenin. Conversely, by "dogmatists" Communists mean persons who stick to the literal letter of Marxist ideas regardless of the latter's appropriateness. Both Premier Khrushchev and Mao Tse-tung have tried to depict themselves as men of the center, as leaders who have successfully avoided both revisionism and dogmatism. In reality this amounts to the claim by each man that he represents the correct Marxism-Leninism of the present day and that the only legitimate and required changes in that ideology are those he sponsors. Each man considers as revisionists those who want to make more changes than the leader does, and as dogmatists those who refuse to accept the changes the leader has endorsed. The official position of the world Communist movement in the late 1950's and early 1960's was that revisionism was the greatest and most dangerous heresy of that time.

Though, as we have seen, there were earlier differences, the great public debate within modern Communism broke out in April 1960. Its first expression took the form of major statements both sides issued on the occasion of the anniversary of Lenin's birth, a major Communist occasion annually. Peking began the attack with a long editorial entitled "Long Live Leninism" published in the Chinese Communist theoretical organ, the magazine *Red Flag*. The nominal target of the editorial was Yugoslav President Tito. The editorial's essence was the claim that nothing fundamental had changed in the nature of imperialism so that the militant tactics Lenin had prescribed were still appropriate for world Communism. The Chinese stated the matter this way:

> We believe in the absolute correctness of Lenin's thinking: War is an inevitable outcome of systems of exploitation and the source of modern wars is the imperialist system. Until the imperialist system and the exploiting classes come to an end, wars of one kind or another will always occur. They may be wars among the imperialists for redivision of the world, or wars of aggression and anti-aggression between the imperial-

ists and the oppressed nations, or civil wars of revolution and counter-revolution between the exploited and exploiting classes in the imperialist countries, or, of course, wars in which the imperialists attack the socialist countries and the socialist countries are forced to defend themselves. All these kinds of wars represent the continuation of the policies of definite classes. Marxist-Leninists absolutely must not sink into the mire of bourgeois pacifism, and can only appraise all these kinds of wars and thus draw conclusions for proletarian policy by adopting the method of concrete class analysis.[17]

This implied accusation that Khrushchev was a bourgeois pacifist who had abandoned the path of true Leninism was published on April 16. Less than a week later a member of the Soviet Communist party Presidium, Otto V. Kuusinen, answered it vigorously in his Lenin anniversary speech in Moscow. The essence of his reply was that Khrushchev's tactics represented an application of creative Leninism. He quoted Lenin's wife as recalling that Lenin had foreseen that "the time will come when war will become so destructive as to be impossible." The implication clearly was that nuclear weapons had brought that time already. Kuusinen added: "In order to be loyal to Marxism-Leninism today it is not sufficient to repeat the old truth that imperialism is aggressive. The task is to make full use of the new factors operating for peace in order to save humanity from the catastrophe of another war. A dogmatic position is a backward position."[18] The Chinese obviously held a "dogmatic position."

Almost immediately upon the heels of this exchange came the Soviet downing of the United States U-2 reconnaissance plane over Siberia and Khrushchev's explosion at President Eisenhower when they met at the abortive summit meeting in Paris in May 1960. Khrushchev's hopes of obtaining major concessions from the United States on Berlin had obviously failed. World tension rose. Peking could scarcely contain its glee at these developments. Mao saw them as fully confirming his suspicious evaluation of the United States and President Eisenhower. The Chinese press taunted Khrushchev almost openly, saying in effect "we told you so." President Eisenhower was hailed as a "teacher by negative example," a phrase implying that Khrushchev was the dull pupil who had had to be taught by the U-2 incident that his evaluation of the American President was unrealistic. The Chinese also began to step up their efforts to increase their influence in other Communist parties. A pamphlet containing "Long Live Leninism" and similar polemical articles was translated into many languages, published in large quantities and distributed as widely as possible throughout the world.

Thus emboldened, the Chinese went on the offensive when the Communist-dominated World Federation of Trade Unions met in Peking, June 5–9, 1960. Here was a forum in which they could make their views known—and try to make converts—among influential Communists and left wingers of many nations. The ferocity of the attack that was mounted against Khrushchev's idea is shown by this treatment—in the Chinese representative's speech—of the Soviet total disarmament proposal:

> We support the disarmament proposals put forward by the Soviet Union. It is of course inconceivable that imperialism will accept proposals for general and complete disarmament. The purpose of putting forward such proposals is to arouse the people throughout the world to unite and oppose the imperialist scheme for arms drive and war preparations, to unmask the aggressive and bellicose nature of imperialism. . . . But there are people who believe that such proposals can be realized when imperialism still exists and that the 'danger of war can be eliminated' by relying on such proposals. This is an unrealistic illusion. As to the view that after disarmament, imperialism would use the funds earmarked for war purposes for the 'welfare of the laboring masses' and for 'assisting underdeveloped countries' and that this would 'bring general progress to people as a whole without exception'—this is downright whitewashing and embellishing imperialism, and indeed this is helping imperialism headed by the United States to dupe the people throughout the world.[19]

This was indeed a savage attack. It not only denied the validity of the basic theses Khrushchev had presented to the United Nations in September 1959 but it accused him almost directly of "helping imperialism headed by the United States to dupe the people throughout the world." The Soviet response came quickly on June 10 and 12 in articles in the Moscow press. Here is an extract from one of these answers:

> The policy of achieving peaceful coexistence, of ending the armament race and establishing peace and friendship between

peoples of capitalist and socialist countries is interpreted by contemporary leftists as a 'deviation' from Marxism-Leninism. They take the slightest aggravation of the international situation as proof of their sectarian ideas. Though they seem very 'revolutionary' from the outside, they harm the cause of rallying the working class to the fight against the aggressive plans of the imperialists, for the end of the 'cold war' and the strengthening of international peace.[20]

It was against this background that a wrathful Khrushchev came to the Bucharest congress of the Rumanian Communist party late in June 1960. He was apparently determined to have a showdown with the Chinese and, reportedly, brought with him and circulated a long secret attack on the Peking position. Some accounts indicate that the meeting saw a bitter personal exchange of accusations and epithets between Khrushchev and the Chinese delegate, Peng Chen. It was also at this meeting, apparently, that the Albanian Communists openly sided with Peking and in effect broke with the Soviet Union. The bitterness of the exchanges was suggested by the direct way in which Khrushchev defended himself in his public speech against the Chinese charge that he had deserted Leninism. On the contrary, Khrushchev declared, Lenin's words on the inevitability of war could not be mechanically repeated in very different historical circumstances. "If Lenin could rise from his grave," Khrushchev declared, he would take such dogmatists who repeated old formulas by rote and reprove them. Here is his answer to the Chinese quotation of Lenin against his own ideas:

> We live in a time when we have neither Marx, nor Engels, nor Lenin with us. If we act like children who, studying the alphabet, compile words from letters, we shall not go very far. . . . One must be able not only to read, but also to understand correctly what one has read, and apply it in the specific circumstances of the time in which we live, taking into consideration the existing situation and the real balance of forces. A political leader acting in this manner shows that he not only can read but can also creatively apply the revolutionary teaching. If he does not do this, he resembles a man about whom people say: "He looks into a book, but sees nothing!"

Not only was this a rude gibe at Mao, it was also a claim by Khrushchev that he was Lenin's successor, entitled to be sole judge of what portion of Lenin's heritage was still appropriate and what portion was out of date.

The Chinese fury at Khrushchev's conduct in Bucharest was embodied in a bitter document they circulated to the parties in attendance at the meeting, a document first published in September 1963. It declared in part:

> The Central Committee of the Communist party of China maintains that at this meeting Comrade Khrushchev . . . has completely violated the long-standing principle in the international Communist movement that questions of common concern should be settled by consultation among fraternal parties, and has completely broken the agreement made prior to the meeting to confine it to an exchange of views and not make any decision; this he has done by his surprise attack of putting forward a draft communique of the meeting without having consulted the fraternal parties on its contents beforehand and without permitting full and moral discussion. . . .
>
> This is an abuse of the prestige enjoyed by the Communist party of the Soviet Union in the international Communist movement . . . it is moreover, an extremely crude act of imposing one's own will on other people . . . this attitude and this way of doing things on the part of Comrade Khrushchev will have extraordinarily grave consequences for the international Communist movement.[21]

This was the declaration of political war by both sides. Events moved quickly thereafter. Albania, China's ally, found Soviet and Eastern European economic aid cut sharply and had to turn to Peking for help. The Chinese soon became Tirana's chief source of economic and technical aid. Even more important, in August 1960 the Soviet Union withdrew its technicians, over 1,300 of them, from China, thus worsening the already difficult Chinese economic situation. About this time, too, China's mounting agricultural difficulties forced it to start reducing the food and other farm raw materials it could ship to the Soviet Union. Moscow retaliated by cutting its exports to China, making sure that the Chinese did not run up new commercial debts such as they had incurred in the early 1950's. For 1960 as a whole, Soviet exports to China fell to $816,000,000, about 15 per cent below the 1959 mark. The Chinese exports to the Soviet Union fell even more sharply to $847,000,000, a decline of more than 20 per cent. An article widely printed in the Soviet provincial press during the summer of 1960 warned the Chinese not too subtly of the consequences to them if they let the dispute go too far. The article asked: "Is it possible to imagine the successful building of socialism under modern conditions even in such a great country as, let us say, China, if that country were in an isolated position, not depending on the cooperation and mutual aid of all other socialist countries?"[22]

The bitterness the Chinese felt at these and other Soviet pressures was indicated by both Premier Chou En-lai and Deputy Premier and Foreign Minister Chen Yi in interviews they gave in late 1960. Chou told Edgar Snow that there were differences between the Soviet Union and Communist China because of their different situations and called attention to the fact that Moscow participated in the United Nations along with delegates from Nationalist China, while Communist China "will not participate in any meeting and organization in which the Chiang Kai-shek clique is included." Chen admitted there were differences and debates between the Chinese and the Russians, and then made this disparaging comment on Soviet economic aid:

> I take exception to the view that without Soviet aid, China would not have developed to the present stage. Our rehabilitation and construction depend on our own efforts. Of course we received aid from the USSR, East Europe, Vietnam and Korea. Soviet aid was especially great. Aid is not a cure-all, however. When a man is alive, a drug may prove effective, but once he is dead, no doctor can do anything for him. Soviet aid thus far extended to China is roughly equivalent to China's aid extended to Southeast Asian nations.

Chen then went on to reveal that about 20,000 Soviet technicians had come to China, and declared: "It is a normal phenomenon that the number of Soviet specialists dispatched to China is on the decrease, since the Chinese themselves have mastered technical know-how." For the Chinese to make such statements to non-Communists was clear proof of their bitterness.[23] Three years later the Chinese were to discuss this issue more candidly. Even scholarly exchanges between the two countries were affected by this growing anger. A particularly vivid example was afforded by the World Conference of Orientalists held in Moscow in the summer of 1960. About 500 Chinese scholars had been expected. Not a single one came.

It was against this background that the second world conference of Communist parties was held in Moscow in November 1960. Though its proceedings were secret, enough information leaked out afterward to make clear that this was a vituperative, no-holds-barred fight between the Soviet and Chinese representatives and their respective supporters. The Peking representatives denounced the attitude of the Soviet government toward their country and the Soviet support of India. They accused the Soviet Communist party of fostering a political line that encouraged surrender to the imperialists. They demanded greater militancy and greater willingness to take risks, arguing that talk of peaceful coexistence was useful only to secure the moral disarmament of the capitalist peoples and the material disarmament of their governments. The Chinese struck out at Khrushchev's criticism of Stalin's "cult of personality" and accused him and his followers of revisionism and opportunism. Khrushchev and his supporters gave as good as they got. Khrushchev called Mao Tse-tung a "megalomaniac warmonger" and accused the Chinese of failing completely to understand the nature of modern war and its dangerous consequences. The Soviet representatives accused the Chinese of trying to disrupt various Communist parties and of slandering Khrushchev and seeking to have him purged from his posts in Moscow. This was clearly the bitterest and stormiest meeting in the history of the world Communist movement. The document that emerged from it as the platform of world Communism was a compromise so worded that each side could point to it and claim that its own position had been vindicated and supported. This document was a device aimed at avoiding an open break, not a means for healing the chasm that had opened.[24]

By the beginning of 1961 it was clear that China was in the midst of a major economic crisis born of grossly inadequate food production. The forced internal readjustments were great, including the movement of millions of people from the hungry cities to rural areas, sharp reduction of capital investment in industry and a precipitous decline in industrial output. To the Russians it must have seemed that their earlier warnings had been more than fully justified. Peking, of course, could admit no such thing and blamed "natural catastrophes" for its troubles. The strain in the Soviet-Chinese relationship was soon obvious in these economic difficulties, too. For one thing, Peking conspicuously turned to the West—not to the Soviet Union—for several hundred million dollars worth of grain it bought to supplement its domestic production. In this hour of Chinese need, Soviet aid was conspicuously absent. Moscow did give the Peking regime an interest-free loan of 500,000 tons of sugar—worth about $40,000,000—in April 1961, but this did not even begin to scratch the surface of China's needs. The only other gesture of Soviet friendship was an agreement to extend a five-year loan of $320,-000,000 to cover the unpaid balance of China's existing indebtedness. So far as current trade went, Moscow's position was that Peking could have what it could pay for, and nothing—aside from the sugar—more. The result was a catastrophic drop in Soviet-Chinese trade in 1961, when the Soviet Union sent to China a smaller amount of goods than in any earlier full year since the Chinese Peoples Republic was proclaimed in late 1949. The 1961 Soviet exports of $367,000,000 were less than half the 1960 value, and little more than one-third the 1959 amount. Chinese exports to the Soviet Union dropped, too, but not nearly so precipitously. Amounting to $551,000,000, they exceeded Soviet exports by $184,000,000. At the height of China's economic crisis, in short, it paid the Soviet Union almost $200,000,000 on its past debts. Could there be more eloquent testimony of how sour the once "brotherly friendship" had become? The one positive aspect of the matter for Peking was the fact that the Soviet Union continued to ship the oil and oil products China needed.

To add fuel to the controversy, the Soviet leadership in mid-1961 took a bold step to reassert its ideological primacy among Communists. It released the Third Program of the Soviet Communist party, a document hailed as the blueprint for bringing the Soviet Union to the threshold of Communist abundance and perfection by 1980. At a time when hundreds of millions were hungry in China and when Chinese dreams of rapid industrialization had been shattered, the Soviet regime presented its people with dazzling promises and statistics of a glorious future in which food, clothing, durable consumer goods and housing would be abundant, when the hard toil and great sacrifice of the past would be entirely gone. This was the real answer to the Chinese impudence of 1958 when Peking had dared to suggest that it would achieve Communism long before the Soviet Union because it had invented forms and methods of progress far superior to anything Moscow had been able to devise.

It seems safe to assume that behind the scenes the Chinese denounced this program as a vicious example of national selfishness. If the Soviet Union was so rich as to be able to look forward to Communist abundance within a comparatively short time, why did it not give massive aid to the poorer Communist-ruled countries, particularly China, so they could catch up? Probably this question was asked by many, not only Chinese. A Soviet writer gave the sanctimonious answer to this question in early 1962. "It is difficult to imagine a situation in which a socialist country would accomplish its economic plans by relying solely or chiefly on aid from other socialist countries," he wrote, and then added: "It is just as impossible to build socialist society with the labor of other people as it is to become a good swimmer without once plunging into a river." And, indicating complete abandonment of Khrushchev's 1959 line about the simultaneous entry into the Communist Utopia of all the bloc members, the Soviet writer declared: "It would be strange, to say the least, if the Soviet Union, having completed the building of socialism ahead of the other countries, were to wait for the levelling up of the general economic development of the socialist countries before starting on the construction of communism."[25] The moral was plain: the Chinese would have to get along as best they could. The Soviet Union would not delay giving its people the fruits of their long and costly development in order to share large amounts of its growing production with the Chinese or others of the poorest Communist-ruled states. This was Soviet national Communism with a vengeance.

The Soviet Communist party's Third Program—a document which may be said to incorporate the essence of Khrushchev's revisionism and anti-Chinese, Soviet-First ideology—was adopted at the Twenty-second Congress of the Soviet Communist party in October 1961. This meeting marks one of the great historic divides in the history of the world Communist movement as well as in the saga of Soviet-Chinese relations. Three factors besides the adoption of the program make this meeting memorable for our purposes. One was the public onslaught against Stalin and the public revelation of many of his crimes, a process that culminated rather gruesomely with the removal of Stalin's embalmed corpse from the side of Lenin's preserved cadaver in the Mausoleum in Red Square. It seems almost certain that the Chinese had no advance warning that this was intended. When Premier Chou En-lai laid a wreath to Stalin at the Mausoleum just before the party congress began, he can hardly have known that a few days later the man whose memory he was honoring would be publicly reviled so that his corpse could no longer remain in this place of honor.*

A second feature of this Congress was the assault on former Premier Vyacheslav Molotov—purged in mid-1957—and the discussion by *Pravda* Editor Pavel Satyukov, and others, of the letter Molotov circulated to the Central Committee before the Twenty-second Congress began. Read against the background of what became known afterward, it is clear that the points Molotov was attacked on—his opposition to the Third Program, his insistence on the inevitability of war and the like—are remarkably close to or perhaps even identical with the Chinese position enunciated clearly in 1962–1963. Otto Kuusinen's speech hinted in fact that Molotov had or was trying to get foreign allies. Kuusinen used this allegory:

> In fact, Molotov is trying to cook up a certain sectarian platform for his further anti-party speculations. It appears that he decided to muddy the waters so that later on he could try to catch fish in there. Who knows, some bony ruff might take a bite. If it is not in the domestic reservoirs, then perhaps in some foreign waters.

The known facts strongly imply, in short, a link between the Chinese and Molotov, suggesting he acted as Peking's spokesman

---

* The onslaught against Stalin had been begun in February 1956 in Khrushchev's secret speech at the Twentieth Communist party Congress. But that speech has never been published in the Soviet Union, and the anti-Stalin publicity between 1956 and 1961 was sufficiently vague so that many millions of Soviet citizens were genuinely shocked and astonished when delegates to the Twenty-second party Congress in October 1961 finally spoke publicly about the old tyrant's misdeeds.

in Moscow in a vain effort to regain power by challenging Khrushchev with a platform made in Peking. We noted earlier that in 1955 Molotov had spoken out publicly as willing to regard China as co-leader with the Soviet Union of the Communist world. The evidence of a Molotov-Mao alliance seems compelling.

Finally, and most important, the Twenty-second Congress was the occasion on which Premier Khrushchev astounded the world by publicly denouncing the leaders of Albania—a country which was a complete Chinese satellite by then—as murderers and criminals unworthy of being called Communists. To this public attack —unprecedented since the Cominform denunciation of the Yugoslavs in the late 1940's—the chief Chinese delegate, Premier Chou En-lai, replied with these seemingly mild, but actually knife-sharp, words spoken in the Kremlin before Khrushchev and the assembled Soviet and foreign delegates:

> We hold that if a dispute or difference unfortunately arises between fraternal parties or fraternal countries, it should be resolved patiently in the spirit of proletarian internationalism and on the principles of equality and unanimity through consultations. Any public, one-sided censure of any fraternal party does not help unity and is not helpful in resolving problems. To lay bare a dispute between fraternal parties of fraternal countries openly in the face of the enemy cannot be regarded as a serious Marxist-Leninist attitude. Such an attitude will only grieve those near and dear to us and gladden our enemies.[26]

Chou En-lai left the conference shortly thereafter, before its end, and returned to Peking where he was ostentatiously greeted at the airport by the highest Chinese leaders, including Mao Tse-tung. Khrushchev's reply came a few days later, and it, too, was knife-sharp, implying that the Chinese were at fault and that they could have avoided public airing of the dispute if they had chosen to put pressure on the Albanians. Khrushchev declared on October 27, 1961:

> The leader of the delegation of the Communist party of China, Comrade Chou En-lai, in his speech expressed anxiety over the matter of openly raising at our congress the question of Albanian-Soviet relations. As far as we understand it, the main thing in his speech was alarm that the present state of our relations with the Albanian Workers party might influence the

cohesion of the socialist camp. We share the anxiety of our Chinese friends and appreciate their concern for the strengthening of unity. If the Chinese comrades desire to apply their efforts to normalization of relations on the part of the Albanian Workers party with the fraternal parties, then hardly anyone can make a better contribution to the solution of the problem than the Communist party of China. This would really benefit the Albanian Workers party and would correspond to the interest of the whole commonwealth of socialist countries.[27]

The struggle was now fully in the open. China and the Soviet Union stood publicly opposed to each other, each espousing a different concept of Communist strategy and seeking to win as much support for itself as possible among and within the Communist parties of the world. Moreover, it seems likely that both Khrushchev and Mao probed for support within each other's ranks as each sought for means to destroy his opponent's primacy at home.

In the first nine months of 1962 political warfare of varying intensity raged publicly between the Khrushchev and Mao camps and their supporters throughout the world. The most vocal and direct assailants of Khrushchev were the Albanians who used direct language to accuse him of treachery and other crimes at which the Peking fusillades only hinted. The Albanians had nothing to lose. Khrushchev was pledged to the political extermination of the Tirana leaders, had broken diplomatic relations with them and had ended economic ties with their country. The Chinese had stepped in to supply the commodities and skilled personnel that Enver Hoxha, the Albanian leader, needed to maintain his economy. The dispute spread to the Communist front organizations, threatening to produce splits in such groups as the World Peace Council. Most of the world's Communist parties lined up with Moscow, but the Chinese won support not only from the Albanians but in Indonesia, North Korea and elsewhere in Asia, as well as sympathy from factions within many Communist parties whose leaders backed Khrushchev.

The loudest explosion in the dispute up to that time was touched off in October 1962 when two events occurred almost simultaneously: the Soviet-American confrontation over Cuba which ended with Soviet withdrawal of its missiles and jet bombers from that island, and the short-lived but militarily successful Chinese attack on India. In the months that followed, almost all restraints were dropped by both sides in a furious debate that stretched throughout the late fall of 1962 and the following winter.

In touching off both disputes, the Chinese were clearly provocative and intended to be so. On the issue of Cuba, the Chinese press—using only thinly veiled language—accused Khrushchev of the twin crimes of "adventurism and capitulationism." He was an adventurer, Peking argued, because he had put his missiles into Cuba, hoping to deceive the United States and pull off a risky *coup*. He was a coward and capitulated, Peking then added, because he had bowed to President Kennedy's ultimatum and withdrawn his missiles. The fact that Khrushchev had agreed—without consulting Cuban Premier Castro—that Cuba should be subject to international inspection to verify the removal of the missiles was seized upon by the Chinese as new evidence of Moscow's disregard of small nations and its readiness to sacrifice those nations' interests for the Soviet Union's. In all this the Chinese were clearly appealing to the most revolutionary and leftist elements in the world Communist movement. They were also apparently hoping to win over to Peking's side Premier Castro himself. He made no secret at the time of his unhappiness with the Soviet-American agreement that ended the crisis. Castro's high prestige in the underdeveloped countries would have been a major Chinese asset, had he been won over.

As regards India, the Chinese attack, which swiftly rolled the Indian forces back in October 1962 and brought Peking's forces over the Himalayas almost to the plains of Assam, clearly shocked and dismayed the Soviet Union and its Eastern European allies. The Peking move—later evidence showed—had been made without advance consultation with Moscow and the Eastern Europeans, who would certainly have opposed it, if given the opportunity. The Chinese attack threatened to throw India completely into the Western camp, negating all the influence and prestige Moscow, Prague and other Communist capitals had won in almost a decade of industriously wooing Prime Minister Nehru with hundreds of millions of dollars of economic aid.

The Soviet retreat on Cuba had shown the primacy of Soviet security for Moscow. Similarly the Chinese attack on India—the result of a border quarrel—indicated how deeply nationalistic

Peking was, how it was willing to give its conception of its own national interests priority over any concept of the overall interest of the Communist world as a whole.

The acrimonious debate which followed took place at the congresses of the Italian, Bulgarian, Czechoslovak, Hungarian and East German Communist parties and also filled many pages in the press of the Communist-ruled nations. Intensifying the debate in these months of late 1962 and early 1963 was the fact of a new Soviet-Yugoslav *rapprochement,* while Peking kept to its line that the Yugoslavs were imperialist agents who had restored capitalism in their own country and were seeking to betray the class struggle, world revolution and the colonial peoples. The Chinese attacks were nominally directed at "modern revisionists" and upon Yugoslav President Tito as one who sought to achieve an alliance with the West against the oppressed peoples of the world. The real target, visible behind this Aesopian language, was Premier Khrushchev, who stood accused of seeking a deal to put the world under a Soviet-American co-dominion.

Hundreds of thousands, perhaps millions, of words were written and spoken during the bitter exchanges between late 1962 and June 1963. All that we can do here is indicate some of the high points of the Soviet-Chinese verbal battle and their significance for the overall dispute.

Premier Khrushchev's speech to the Supreme Soviet in Moscow on December 12, 1962 was one of the broadest Soviet statements during this period and his key points are well worth examining. Like the Chinese, he used Aesopian language most of the time, but his targets were clear.

First, he denied the Chinese charges that the Soviet Union had suffered a defeat in the Cuban crisis. The missiles had been installed only to defend Cuba, he argued, and they had been removed only in exchange for a pledge that the United States would not invade Cuba, thus achieving the original purpose.

Second, he asserted, "some dogmatists have taken to Trotskyite positions and are trying to push the Soviet Union and other socialist countries onto the path of unleashing a world war." This came close to an accusation that the Chinese were seeking to provoke a Soviet-American war and regretted this had not happened in the Cuban crisis.

Third, he accused the Chinese of bribing the Albanians to denounce the Soviet Union. He declared that "someone" had taught the Albanians "to pronounce foul words, and they walk under windows and shout hooligan curses at the Communist party of the Soviet Union. . . . For their swearing they get the promised three kopeks. And when they begin to swear more violently and colorfully, they get another five kopeks and are praised."

Fourth, he denounced Mao Tse-tung's concept of imperialism as a "paper tiger." Khrushchev declared that "those who claim this know that this 'paper tiger' has atomic teeth. It can put them to work; and it cannot be regarded frivolously."

Fifth, counterattacking on the Chinese charge that the Soviet Union was not militant enough, he pointed out that two pieces of Chinese territory, Hong Kong and Macao, were held by Britain and Portugal respectively. If the Chinese wanted to be militant, they could take these territories back as India had seized Goa; their failure to do so, he implied, indicated they, too, knew that in some situations maximum militancy was unwise.

Sixth, he lumped together the "dogmatists"—that is, the Chinese—"who do not believe in the possibility of the victory of socialism . . . in peaceful competition with capitalism" and the "aggressive adventurist forces of imperialism" who want war because they do not believe capitalism can win the peaceful competition with socialism. Then he declared: "Both want to push history toward the launching of a war, to decide the question of the victory of communism or capitalism by war, by killing millions and millions of people." In effect he declared that the extreme right in the West and the extreme left in the Communist world were really allied warmongers. By implication he appeared to be arguing, too, that there was a common cause between the moderate elements in both ideological parts of the world since both sought to prevent war.

Seventh, Khrushchev praised the Chinese for pulling back over the Himalayas after their military victory, but he made clear his distress that the fighting against India had taken place at all. He called for peace between the two governments.

Finally he came to the nub of the matter. "The left-sectarian disorder is fed by nationalism, and in turn it feeds nationalism."[28] By this statement he really accused the Chinese of serving their own national interests under the guise of being ultra-revolutionary Communists.

The Chinese point of view was expressed in a number of lengthy statements. Here we shall present only the key points made by Peking in these declarations.

First, Peking made clear that it regarded the struggle in the underdeveloped countries of Asia, Africa and Latin America as the center of all revolutionary activity in the world, declaring that to further this struggle it was necessary to be prepared to take risks of a spark setting off a general conflagration. The Soviet effort to curb the militancy of revolutionaries in these countries was denounced bitterly. Later Moscow was to charge that by this line the Chinese were trying to make themselves the heads of an Asian-African-Latin American bloc based on racism —on a struggle of non-whites against whites—rather than on Marxist principles of class struggle between workers and employers.

Without naming the Chinese directly, a Soviet commentator writing in the spring of 1963 described the Chinese policy at the Afro-Asian Peoples Conference held in Moshi, Tanganyika in February 1963, a meeting where the right of Soviet delegates to participate was contested on the ground they came from Europe not Asia:

> Some of the more chauvinistically-inclined leaders would like to direct the solidarity movement not against imperialism, colonialism and its agents, but against all white people. They are ready to sacrifice the truth, as they did, so far cautiously, in Moshi, and to shrug their shoulders at the participation (even though only partial) of international organizations such as the World Council of Peace. . . . They sacrifice the truth because they pretend that the liberation of Asia, Africa and Latin America is possible even without the participation of progressive organizations throughout the world, without those white people who because of their views actively fight against imperialism and its colonial attributes.[29]

Second, the Chinese blamed the origin of the dispute and its public airing upon the Soviet Union. The Soviet Communists had attempted to put the resolutions of their party above the agreed position of the 1957 Moscow conference, the Chinese charged, and about the time of the Khrushchev-Eisenhower Camp David talks in September 1959 the Russians "put forward a series of erroneous views on many important issues relating to the international situation and the international communist movement, views which departed from Marxism-Leninism and violated the Moscow declaration." The public exposure of the differences, the Chinese declared, began on September 9, 1959 when the TASS agency put out the Soviet statement on the Sino-Indian dispute. The Chinese then added:

Making no distinction between right and wrong, the statement expressed 'regret' over the border clash and in reality condemned China's correct stand. They even said that it was 'tragic' and 'deplorable.' Here is the first instance in history in which a socialist country, instead of condemning the armed provocations of the reactionaries of a capitalist country, condemned another fraternal socialist country when it was confronted with such armed provocation.[30]

Third, the Chinese attacked the Russians for withdrawing their technical experts from China and otherwise cutting their aid to that country in 1960 after the Bucharest meeting. Here is the way the Chinese put the matter:

After the Bucharest meeting, some comrades who had attacked the Chinese Communist party lost no time in taking a series of grave steps applying economic and political pressure against China. Disregarding international practice, they perfidiously and unilaterally tore agreements and contracts they had concluded with a fraternal country. These agreements and contracts are to be counted not in twos or threes or in scores, but in hundreds. These malicious acts, which extended ideological differences to state relations, were out and out violations of proletarian internationalism and of the principles guiding relations among fraternal socialist countries. Instead of criticizing their own errors of great nation chauvinism, these comrades charged the Chinese Communist party with the errors of 'going it alone,' sectarianism, splitting, national communism and so forth.[31]

Fourth, the Chinese made plain they would not bow to any majority vote of the world Communist movement. They argued: "Anyone with some common sense knows that such questions as who is right and who is wrong, and who has truth on his side, cannot be determined by who is in the majority or the minority at a given moment. . . . History abounds with instances in which in a certain period, under certain circumstances, truth is not on the side of the majority, but on the side of the minority."[32]

Fifth, the Chinese denied they want nuclear wars or fail to recognize the "unprecedentedly destructive power of nuclear weapons." But they insisted this did not wipe out the Marxist-Leninist idea that there are just wars which deserve Communist support, and they argued that "if imperialism should nevertheless unleash imperialist war, without regard to any of the consequences, it would only result in the extinction of imperialism and definitely not in the extinction of mankind."[33] Thus the Chinese argued that a nuclear war could be won, and therefore was not entirely intolerable. Further, the Chinese declared:

> In the eyes of the modern revisionists [i.e., the Russians] any revolution and any action that supports revolution runs counter to the 'logic of survival' now that nuclear weapons and similar military techniques exist. In fact, what they call the 'logic of survival' is the logic of slaves, a logic that would paralyze the revolutionary will of the people of all countries, bind them hand and foot and make them the submissive slaves of imperialism and the reactionaries of various countries.[34]

Sixth, the Chinese reacted to Khrushchev's gibes about their failure to retake Hong Kong and Macao by reminding Moscow about China's victimization at the hands of Tsarist Russia and the possibility Peking might yet insist on trying to undo those depredations. The issues raised here are so explosive in their possibilities for the future that the Chinese statement deserves extensive quotation:

> In the hundred years or so prior to the victory of the Chinese revolution, the imperialist and colonial powers—the United States, Britain, France, Tsarist Russia . . . carried out unbridled aggression against China. They compelled the governments of old China to sign a large number of unequal treaties —the Treaty of Nanking of 1842, the Treaty of Aigun of 1858, the Treaty of Tientsin of 1858, the Treaty of Peking of 1860, the Treaty of Ili of 1881. . . . By virtue of these unequal treaties, they annexed Chinese territory in the north, south,

east and west and held leased territories on the seaboard and
in the hinterland of China. . . .

At the time the Peoples Republic of China was inaugurated, our
Government declared that it would examine the treaties concluded by previous Chinese governments with foreign governments, treaties that had been left over by history, and would
recognize, abrogate, revise or renegotiate them according to
their respective contents. In this respect, our policy towards
the socialist countries is fundamentally different from our
policy towards the imperialist countries. . . . With regard to
the outstanding issues, which are a legacy from the past, we
have always held that, when conditions are ripe, they should
be settled peacefully through negotiations and that, pending
a settlement, the status quo should be maintained. . . .

Why is it that after the Caribbean crisis this correct policy of
ours suddenly became a topic of discussion among certain persons and a theme for their anti-China campaign?

These heroes are apparently very pleased with themselves for
having picked up a stone from a cesspool, with which they
believe they can instantly fell the Chinese. But whom has this
filthy stone really hit?

You are not unaware that such questions as those of Hong
Kong and Macao relate to the category of unequal treaties left
over by history, treaties which the imperialists imposed on
China. In raising questions of this kind, do you intend to raise
all the questions of unequal treaties and have a general settlement? Has it ever entered your heads what the consequences
would be? Can you seriously believe that this will do you any
good?[35]

These were the bluntest words of the debate. The Chinese
were directly threatening to demand revision of the Soviet-Chinese borders. At the time these words appeared, the issue seemed
to be theoretical, merely another expression of Soviet-Chinese
verbal struggle. Six months later, in September 1963, both sides
revealed the tension along the Sino-Soviet border. The Chinese
accused the Soviet Union of carrying on "subversive activities"
in the Ili region of Sinkiang, and of having in April and May,
1962 "enticed and coerced several tens of thousands of Chinese
citizens into going to the Soviet Union." The Russians replied
with accusations that, beginning in 1960, there had been thou-

sands of violations of the Soviet border by Chinese civilians and military personnel, and that the Chinese had tried repeatedly to seize Soviet territory. Behind the words quoted above, in short, were the raw materials for a possible border war along the Sino-Soviet frontier.

Seventh, the Chinese made clear their disagreement with the extent of the Soviet attack on Stalin, by quoting him at key points in their case.

Eighth, the Chinese dismissed Soviet talk about the possibility of a peaceful victory for the proletariat, asserting, "History records no case of an oppressed class becoming the ruling class through the vote. . . . It is even less likely for the proletariat to become the ruling class through elections."[36]

Ninth, the Chinese reached the height of abuse against the Russians when they compared their own practice of printing in the Chinese press the attacks by Moscow on them with the complete blackout of the Chinese position in the Soviet press. The Chinese declared:

Dear friends and comrades who claim to possess the whole truth! Since you are quite definite that our articles are wrong, why don't you publish all these erroneous articles and then refute them point by point, so as to inculcate hatred among your people against the 'heresies' you call dogmatism, sectarianism, and anti-Marxism-Leninism? Why do you lack the courage to do this? Why such a stringent embargo? You fear the truth. The huge spectre you call 'dogmatism,' i.e., genuine Marxism-Leninism, is haunting the world, and it threatens you. You have no faith in the people, and the people have no faith in you. You are divorced from the masses. That is why you fear the truth and carry your fear to such absurd lengths. . . . We are not afraid to publish everything of yours in full. We publish all the 'masterpieces' in which you rail at us. Then, in reply we either refute them point by point, or refute their main points. Sometimes we publish your articles without a word in answer, leaving the readers to judge for themselves. Isn't that fair and reasonable? You modern revisionist masters! Do you dare to do the same? If you are men enough, you will. But having a guilty conscience and an unjust case, being fierce of visage but faint of heart, outwardly as tough as bulls but inwardly as timid as mice, you will not dare. We are sure you will not dare.[37]

CHAPTER X

The War of Words

In his novel *Nineteen Eighty-Four*, George Orwell describes how some of the inhabitants of the mythical land of Oceania learn that their world's political situation has changed. It is the sixth day of Hate Week. The novel's protagonist is in the middle of a crowd being harangued by a speaker who is denouncing the barbarous atrocities and other iniquities committed by the enemy, Eurasia. The square in which the meeting is being held is jammed with people, many of them carrying banners denouncing the foe. Suddenly the speaker is handed a note informing him that Eurasia has become Oceania's ally and Eastasia is now the enemy. The speaker does not even interrupt his speech, nor does he alter its basic content. All he does is change the name of the enemy, referring to Eastasia where he had formerly talked of Eurasia. The crowd immediately understands and gets to work quickly to destroy the offending posters and banners attacking Eurasia. Hate Week continues with only one minor change: the nation to be hated becomes Eastasia.

Life never imitates art exactly. Even in 1963 the people of the Soviet Union were not so completely conditioned as the inhabitants of Orwell's Oceania, and their reactions to a change of line were not nearly so automatic and so quick. Yet no observer of the Soviet Union who had read *Nineteen Eighty-Four* and also lived through the late spring and summer of 1963 could avoid the eerie feeling that Orwell, dead many years by that time, had foreseen, if only dimly, what was happening. One had only to substitute Russia for Oceania, the United States for Eurasia and China for Eastasia. The resemblance between what actually happened and what the novel described was only approximate, but still uncanny.

197

The essentials of the historic change we must now describe were compressed into a period of less than seven weeks, from June 10, 1963, to shortly after July 25, 1963. On the morning of the first day of this period, the average unsophisticated Soviet citizen knew that the political line was clear: the United States was the great enemy, the center of the aggressive imperialists; China was the great brotherly Communist nation, a trifle difficult and argumentative at times but still the true comrade at the side of the Soviet Union. When this period ended, this same Soviet citizen knew that the United States, for all its capitalist faults and sins, was joined with the Soviet Union to save the world from thermonuclear disaster but China was an enemy, ruled by men who had betrayed Marxism-Leninism and who were determined to use all their power to provoke a nuclear conflict that would claim hundreds of millions of victims. The reader is assured that for millions of ordinary Soviet citizens— the great mass of people who had neither the background nor the time to probe behind the earlier Aesopian attacks on "dogmatism" and "sectarians"—this picture is only slightly exaggerated. The politically sophisticated in the Soviet Union, of course, were far better prepared for the change.

Yet even the sophisticates had reason for surprise when the split finally took place between the Soviet Union and China. During much of the first half of 1963 an effort to achieve Soviet-Chinese reconciliation had appeared to be under way. In his January speech in East Berlin, Premier Khrushchev took a relatively conciliatory tone and suggested that public polemics among Communist parties be discontinued. On February 21, 1963, the Soviet Communist party Central Committee sent a letter to its Chinese counterpart suggesting that representatives of both parties meet to discuss and try to settle or minimize their differences. The letter was courteous. It stressed the forces uniting the two groups, declaring: "No matter how serious our differences might seem today, one cannot forget that in the great historical struggle of the forces of socialism against capitalism, we are standing with you on the same side of the barricade." The Chinese replied with an equally polite letter dated March 9, 1963, declaring: "We welcome your letter. We welcome the desire for unity expressed in it; we welcome the normal attitude of equality towards fraternal parties as shown in it." The Chinese promised to stop their public polemics. They announced they had invited Premier Khrushchev to visit Peking for an "exchange of views." If he could not come, the Chinese said, they would welcome a Soviet delegation in Peking or they would send one to Moscow. But there was a subdued vein of iron in both letters, revealed in the careful way both sides indicated they maintained their old positions. Moreover, the Chinese letter revealed that in April 1962 Peking had sent a letter to Moscow suggesting five steps for improving the situation. They had suggested then that Soviet leaders call another world Communist conference and that the latter "take the initiative" in improving relations with the Albanians. The implication of the Chinese letter was that the Russians had failed to follow these suggestions.

The Russian reply of March 30, 1963 was a lengthy and mildly worded exposition of the Soviet ideological position. It expressed gratitude for the invitation to Premier Khrushchev but said he could not come. Noting that Khrushchev had been in Peking three times while Mao had only been in Moscow twice, the letter suggested Mao come to Moscow. The Soviet message said Mao could thus realize an earlier-expressed ambition to tour the Soviet Union and that high Soviet leaders would accompany him "for an exchange of opinion on different questions." If Mao could not come, the letter suggested that delegations of the two parties meet in Moscow around May 15, 1963. This letter was written after the Afro-Asian Solidarity meeting in Moshi, Tanganyika at which the Chinese had shown they looked on the Russians as whites having no place in Asia. Hence, in one of the most significant sentences of the Soviet letter, the men in Moscow warned: "The militant call 'Workers of all countries, unite!' formulated by Marx and Engels means that at the basis of this unity lies anti-imperialist class solidarity and not any principle of nationality, color or geographical location." The German magazine, *Christ und Welt*, reported on July 5, 1963 that Chinese delegates at the Afro-Asian Journalists Congress in Djakarta in the spring of 1963 declared that Russia would have to return the former Chinese areas of Siberia if it wished to be welcomed at Afro-Asian meetings. The Chinese called the delegates from Soviet areas in Asia "marionettes of a white imperialist power."

Sometime in the spring of 1963, it now seems clear, the Chinese Communist leaders in Peking decided that the breach with

Moscow was irreparable and that they had nothing to lose by dropping all caution. Why did they reach this decision? This is the still-unresolved problem facing the historian.

None of the known events occurring in the spring of 1963 provides an obvious explanation. The fighting in Laos, for example, must have involved rival Soviet and Chinese pressures on the pro-Communist Pathet Lao forces, but Laos seems much too insignificant to have been the major *casus belli*. That same spring the Soviet regime brought Fidel Castro to Moscow, gave him a triumphant reception and bribed him with a substantial increase in the price paid for Cuban sugar by the Soviet Union. The clear motivation for this was the Kremlin desire to win Castro's backing for Moscow in the fight with Peking, or at least to win his neutrality. But again, this seems too trivial a factor to have weighted the Chinese scales decisively. Finally, too, it should be noted that in this fateful spring the Soviet-American-British negotiations on a nuclear test ban were going badly. Premier Khrushchev was telling visitors he felt betrayed by the United States' refusal to accept his December 1962 offer of two or three on-site inspections as adequate to justify a comprehensive test-ban treaty banning all nuclear explosions. This situation cannot have worsened the Soviet-Chinese relationship. Clearly the determining causes must have been factors behind the scenes.

One possibility is that the Chinese stated their price for reconciliation to the Soviet Union and were turned down. In the late spring of 1963 a Communist diplomat from a Warsaw Pact member country in Eastern Europe told this writer that the Chinese had asked the Soviet Union to deliver nuclear weapons to Peking's forces and had been refused. If this actually happened, it would go far to explain the Chinese decision to break with Moscow by forcing the ideological battle beyond all bounds tolerable to the Kremlin leaders. It is not unlikely that Peking asked Moscow to reinstate and implement the 1957 atomic aid agreement as a condition for peace.

A second possibility is that the Chinese tried unsuccessfully to unseat Premier Khrushchev by means of a cabal organized among key figures in the Soviet hierarchy. The evidence for this is flimsy, but the possibility cannot be disregarded. In March, April and May of 1963 there were signs of strain in the Kremlin hierarchy. A slogan for May Day 1963 dealing with Yugoslavia had to be changed publicly because it implied Yugoslavia was not a full-fledged member of the Socialist camp as Premier Khrushchev maintained. Khrushchev himself made an unusual speech referring to the fact that he was 69 years old and could not remain in office forever. A surprise reorganization of the Soviet economic hierarchy in this same period put Dmitry Ustinov, who had built his career directing Soviet weapons production, at the head of the economy. Finally, and most important, the Soviet Communist party's apparent second secretary, Frol R. Kozlov, disappeared from public view and was said to be suffering from an illness. Observers wondered whether his ailment was not more political than organic, recalling he had long been rumored to be a leading Stalinist opposed to Khrushchev's liberalizing reforms. These and other events in this period may have been mere coincidences. Or there may have been a bitter pitched political battle between pro- and anti-Khrushchev forces in Moscow. If such a battle took place, it was won by the Premier and doomed Peking's hopes that the dispute could be resolved by Khrushchev's downfall.

Both the above possibilities, singly or together, are consistent with a suspicion that the United States government knew much more about what was going on in Moscow's inner circles than it let on publicly, and that it acted decisively at a crucial moment to bolster Khrushchev's position. What raises this suspicion is the remarkable speech President Kennedy made at American University on June 10, 1963, the address in which the President called for a re-examination of American ideas toward the Soviet Union and toward the Cold War. No President of the United States since Franklin D. Roosevelt had so clearly and warmly held out the hand of friendship to the Soviet Union. Was this an effort to provide Khrushchev with evidence that he could do business with the United States? Did Khrushchev ask for such action in one of the secret letters he exchanged with President Kennedy during this period? Did the speech convince the men in Peking that a Soviet-American deal at their expense had been all but made? We do not know. But the probability seems strong that this speech, delivered at a most delicate moment in Sino-Soviet relations, played a significant role in subsequent events. The rapidity with which *Pravda* printed the full text of this speech made clear the Kennedy remarks were welcome in Moscow.

The generosity of spirit with which President Kennedy spoke and the vividness with which he extended the hand of friendship to the Soviet Union are best indicated by a few excerpts from this remarkable address:

No government or social system is so evil that its people must be considered as lacking in virtue. As Americans, we find Communism profoundly repugnant as a negation of personal freedom and dignity. But we can still hail the Russian people for their many achievements—in science and space, in economic and industrial growth, in culture and in acts of courage.

Among the many traits the peoples of our two countries have in common, none is stronger than our mutual abhorrence of war. Almost unique among the major world powers, we have never been at war with each other. And no nation in the history of battle ever suffered more than the Soviet Union in the Second World War. At least 20,000,000 lost their lives. Countless millions of homes and families were burned or sacked. A third of the nation's territory, including two-thirds of its industrial base, were turned into a wasteland—a loss equivalent to the destruction of this country east of Chicago.

Today, should total war ever break out again—no matter how —our two countries will be the primary targets. It is an ironic but accurate fact that the two strongest powers are the two in the most danger of devastation. All we have built, all we have worked for, would be destroyed in the first 24 hours. And even in the cold war . . . our two countries bear the heaviest burdens. For we are both devoting massive sums of money to weapons that could be better devoted to combat ignorance, poverty and disease.

We are both caught up in a vicious and dangerous cycle with suspicion on one side breeding suspicion on the other, and new weapons begetting counter-weapons.[1]

Four days after the President's speech, the Chinese took the decisive step. On June 14, 1963 they sent the Soviet leaders their answer to Moscow's March 30 letter. This reply had been promised a few weeks earlier when it had been publicly announced that the Russians and Chinese had agreed their delegations would meet in Moscow on July 5. But there had been nothing in that announcement to prepare the world for the provocative and inflammatory contents of the Chinese letter. That document abandoned almost all restraint; its tone showed none of the calm politeness which had marked the exchange of correspondence the previous March. The Chinese letter's contents made clear its authors had abandoned all hope of reconciliation with Moscow and regarded the negotiations scheduled to begin on July 5 as doomed before they began. We may theorize that Peking stated its arguments boldly in this letter because the Soviet leaders would be under great pressure to publish this official reply to Moscow's earlier missive. Mao Tse-tung presumably expected his theses could win many converts in the Soviet Communist party if its members could finally get to read an unvarnished statement of the Chinese views. Whatever interpretation one takes, the central point is clear: the Chinese letter of June 14 was a declaration of political war against the Soviet Communist party, one from which there could be no turning back.

The fury this letter aroused in Moscow quickly became evident. In an unprecedented action, the Soviet party authorities announced they would not publish the letter at least for the time being, arguing that the Chinese document would require a public answer which would darken the prospects for the bilateral negotiations scheduled to begin on July 5. Even a politically unsophisticated Soviet citizen may have grasped that something very important was happening at this point. The contrast between the rapid publication of President Kennedy's speech and the public refusal to print the Chinese letter had a significance few could miss.

The Chinese had apparently anticipated that this might be the Soviet reaction and put their resources into circulating their letter as widely as possible in the Soviet Union and Eastern Europe. Translated copies of the letter were distributed in these countries by Chinese diplomats, correspondents and students. The Chinese crew on the Moscow-Peking Express distributed copies of the Russian translation at every stop in the Soviet Union and utilized the time spent at each station to broadcast portions of the letter in Russian over the train's loudspeaker. Moscow's rage at these efforts exceeded all previous bounds. The Soviet foreign ministry protested to Peking, charging the Chinese with gross violation of Soviet national sovereignty; the Chinese answered that they were doing nothing the Russians had not been permitted to do routinely within China. To show their anger, the

Soviet authorities in Moscow deported five Chinese, including three diplomats, for their activities in distributing translations of the letter. The expelled Chinese were greeted as heroes in Peking. A public meeting was held in their honor, a demonstration at which high Chinese officials assailed the Soviet regime for keeping the Chinese letter from its people. The mutual recriminations even extended into the area of the farcical. Some Russian youths, apparently drunk, broke a glass display case in front of the Chinese embassy in Moscow. Peking publicized the incident widely as a typical example of Soviet anti-Chinese sentiment; the Chinese diplomats in Moscow ostentatiously left the case unrepaired. The rancor spilled over into the meeting in Moscow of the pro-Communist World Women's Congress. Chinese delegates there clashed publicly and bitterly with the pro-Soviet majority, adding more fuel to the flame. Amidst all this uproar, the meeting of the Chinese and Soviet party delegations in Moscow lasted for two weeks and, apparently, accomplished absolutely nothing toward reconciling the two points of view. But even before that meeting broke up, the Soviet leaders had broken the impasse created by their earlier refusal to publish the Chinese letter. On July 14, 1963, they published the Chinese statement, accompanying it with an acrimonious and lengthy reply, one in which all of Moscow's pent-up hatred for Peking was at last clearly and publicly expressed. The split between the two great Communist powers was at last fully out in the open. The enmity between China and Russia was no longer hidden by Aesopian language.

What was in this Peking letter to produce such an explosive and historic effect? Its essential content was nothing less than a comprehensive political program offered to Communists everywhere as an alternative to Moscow's policy of peaceful coexistence. Titled "A Proposal Concerning the General Line of the International Communist Movement," the missive was a general restatement of the Chinese Communist position, including many points which had been made in the Chinese statements issued after the 1962 Cuban crisis. But now these points were made directly and bluntly to the Soviet Central Committee in a letter whose arrogant tone was unmistakable. And while the discussion was still in Aesopian language, the target of the letter's sharpest gibes was unmistakably Premier Khrushchev. Here, for example, are some typical passages:[2]

There are certain persons who assert that they have made the greatest creative contributions to revolutionary theory since Lenin and that they alone are correct. But it is very dubious whether they have ever really given consideration to the extensive experience of the entire world communist movement, whether they have ever really considered the interests, the goal and tasks of the international proletarian movement as a whole, and whether they really have a general line for the international communist movement which conforms with Marxism-Leninism. . . .

Moreover, certain persons have concocted the strange tale that China and some other socialist countries want to 'unleash wars' and to spread socialism by 'wars between states.' . . . To put it bluntly, the purpose of those who repeat these slanders is to hide the fact that they are opposed to revolutions by the oppressed peoples and nations of the world and opposed to others supporting such revolutions. . . .

However, a few years ago certain persons suddenly claimed Lenin's policy of peaceful coexistence as their own 'great discovery.' They maintain that they have a monopoly on the interpretation of this policy. They treat 'peaceful coexistence' as if it were an all-inclusive, mystical book from heaven and attribute to it every success the people of the world achieve by struggle. What is more, they label all who disagree with their distortions of Lenin's views as opponents of peaceful coexistence, as people completely ignorant of Lenin and Leninism, and as heretics deserving to be burnt at the stake. . . .

Errors of dogmatism will be committed if one . . . mechanically copies the policies and tactics of another Communist Party, submits blindly to the will of others or accepts without analysis the program and resolutions of another Communist Party as one's own line. Some people are now violating this basic principle. . . . On the pretext of 'creatively developing Marxism-Leninism,' they cast aside the universal truth of Marxism-Leninism. Moreover, they describe as 'universal Marxist-Leninist truths' their own prescriptions which are based on nothing but subjective conjecture and are divorced from reality and from the masses, and they force others to accept these prescriptions unconditionally.

The target of these and similar gibes was clearly Premier Khrushchev. But the Chinese went further. For the first time, they attacked publicly the Third Program of the Soviet Communist party adopted at the Twenty-second Congress in October 1961, a document which the Soviet leader regarded as his quintessential contribution to Marxist-Leninist theory. This program predicted that the Soviet Union would achieve full Communism and Communist abundance within the lifetime of the present generation. It declared that there was no more need in the Soviet Union for a dictatorship of the proletariat and that therefore the Soviet state could turn into a state of the whole people and the Soviet Communist party into a party of the whole people. The problem raised by all this, the Chinese insisted, was not a question affecting only the internal affairs of one state "but a fundamental problem involving the universal truth of Marxism-Leninism." The dictatorship of the proletariat must remain for the entire transition period to Communism, they declared, and all Socialist countries have both classes and class struggles. Moreover, they denied that the Soviet Union was anywhere near a level of Communist abundance:

> In their present level of economic development all socialist countries are still far, far removed from the higher stage of communism in which 'from each according to his ability, to each according to his needs' is put into practice. Therefore it will take a long, long time to eliminate the class difference between worker and peasant. And until this difference is eliminated, it is impossible to say that society is classless or that there is no longer any need for the dictatorship of the proletariat.

Khrushchev, the Chinese hinted bluntly, was trying to "replace the Marxist-Leninist theory of the state by the bourgeois theory of the state" and was engaged in "nothing but a great historical regression."

From Premier Khrushchev's point of view, this whole theoretical discussion could be seen as nothing but an unforgivable Chinese intrusion into Soviet internal affairs, an open effort to discredit the correctness—and therefore the legitimacy—of Khrushchev's rule over the Soviet Union. But even worse was the Chinese attack on his doctrine of the new nature of the Soviet Communist party:

> What will happen if it is announced halfway before entering the higher stage of communist society that the party of the

proletariat has become a 'party of the entire people' and if its proletarian class character is repudiated? . . . Does this not disarm the proletariat and all the working people, organizationally and ideologically, and is it not tantamount to helping restore capitalism?

Khrushchev was really a traitor, the Chinese charged in this passage, implying that he must be overthrown to save Socialism in the Soviet Union.

There were many other points in this document to infuriate Moscow. The Chinese suggested that Premier Khrushchev's proposal to integrate the Communist bloc and secure greater efficiency through international division of labor and specialization was really an expression of "national egoism" aimed at "gaining profit for oneself at the expense of others." This encouragement of economic nationalism was clearly aimed at winning the Rumanians who were clashing with Russia on this issue in the Council for Mutual Economic Assistance, the Communist analogue of the Common Market. The Chinese asked sneeringly: "Is it possible that the leading comrades of the Communist party of the Soviet Union do not really feel their responsibility for the fact that Soviet-Albanian relations have so seriously deteriorated?" And most serious of all, perhaps, the Chinese presented a set of criteria and a position which could only mean that they were appealing to their sympathizers all over the world in Communist parties allied with the Soviet Union to leave those parties and form new parties—in short to help create a pro-Chinese Communist International. Here is the way the Chinese put it:

If a party is not a proletarian revolutionary party but a bourgeois reformist party; if it is not a Marxist-Leninist party but a revisionist party; . . . if it is not a party representing the interests of the proletariat and all the working people but a party representing the interests of the labor aristocracy; . . . if it is not a party that can use its brains to think for itself and acquire an accurate knowledge of the trends of the different classes in its own country through serious investigation and study, and knows how to apply the universal truth of Marxism-Leninism and integrate it with the concrete practice of its own country, but instead is a party that parrots the words of others, copies foreign experience without analysis, runs hither and thither in response to the baton of certain persons abroad, and has become a hodgepodge of revisionism, dogmatism, and everything but Marxism-Leninism principle; then such a party is absolutely incapable of leading the proletariat and the masses in revolutionary struggle, absolutely incapable of winning the revolution and absolutely incapable of fulfilling the great historical mission of the proletariat.

The line of action for foreign Communists sympathetic to Peking but belonging to parties siding with Moscow was plain from this passage.

On the major policy issues dividing the two sides, the Chinese broadside repeated the customary demands for greater militancy, the old skepticism of peaceful transition from capitalism to socialism, the usual advocacy of reliance on armed revolution and the like. But it was on the issue of the struggle in Asia, Africa and Latin America that the Chinese laid down their harshest dictum, one which came close to accusing Premier Khrushchev of being an advocate of continued colonialism and white supremacy. The passage merits quotation:

The various types of contradictions in the contemporary world are concentrated in the vast areas of Asia, Africa and Latin America; these are the most vulnerable areas under imperialist rule and the storm centers of world revolution dealing direct blows at imperialism. . . .

The anti-imperialist revolutionary struggles of the people in Asia, Africa and Latin America are pounding and undermining the foundations of the rule of imperialism and colonialism, old and new, and are now a mighty force in defense of world peace. In a sense, therefore, the whole cause of the international proletarian revolution hinges on the outcome of the revolutionary struggles of the peoples in these areas who constitute the overwhelming majority of the world's population. Therefore, the anti-imperialist revolutionary struggle of the people in Asia, Africa and Latin America is definitely not merely a matter of regional significance but one of overall importance for the whole cause of proletarian revolution.

Certain persons now go so far as to deny the great international significance of the anti-imperialist revolutionary struggles of the Asian, African and Latin American peoples and on the pretext of breaking down the barriers of nationality, color and geographical location, are trying their best to efface the line of demarcation between oppressed and oppressor nations and between oppressed and oppressor countries and to hold down the revolutionary struggles of the peoples in these areas. In fact, they cater to the needs of imperialism and create a new 'theory' to justify the rule of imperialism in these areas and the promotion of its policies of old and new colonialism. Actually, this 'theory' seeks not to break down the barriers of nationality, color and geographical location but to maintain the rule of the 'superior nations' over the oppressed nations. It is only natural that this fraudulent 'theory' is rejected by the people in these areas.

Here the Chinese were hitting the Soviet leaders at an extremely important and sensitive point. The Chinese demand could be read as urging that the Communist movement concentrate not only against Western imperialism but also against the Russian position in Asia, against rule by the "superior" Russian nation over the Uzbeks, the Turkmens, the Bashkirs, the Yakuts and the numerous other Asian nations incorporated in the Soviet Union.

At one point in the Chinese letter, Peking's national bitterness at its treatment by the Soviet Union came through vividly:

The comrades of the Communist party of the Soviet Union state in their letter that 'the Communist party of the Soviet Union has never taken and will never take a single step that could sow hostility among the peoples of our country towards the fraternal Chinese people or other peoples.' Here we do not desire to go back and enumerate the many unpleasant events that have occurred in the past, and we only wish that the comrades of the C.P.S.U. will strictly abide by this statement in their future actions. During the past few years, our party members and our people have exercised the greatest restraint in the face of a series of grave incidents which were in violation of the principles guiding relations among fraternal parties and countries and despite the many difficulties and losses which have been imposed on us. The spirit of proletarian internationalism of the Chinese Communists and the Chinese people has stood a severe test.

The Chinese letter of June 14 arrived in Moscow as the Central Committee of the Soviet Communist party assembled for a meeting that had been scheduled some weeks earlier. The timing could not have been accidental. The Chinese had planned their move in a way that would force Khrushchev for the first time to discuss the dispute formally before the entire Central Committee. In this the Chinese hopes were not disappointed. Even while Peking's letter was being kept from the mass of the Soviet people, the Central Committee members received copies and settled back to listen to a parade of high-ranking speakers, headed by Premier Khrushchev and Mikhail Suslov, a Communist party secretary, discuss the letter and explain the issues. Were pro-Chinese voices heard in these Moscow deliberations? We do not know, for the proceedings were kept secret. At the end of the Central Committee meeting an official announcement claimed that the meeting had unanimously condemned the Chinese letter as "groundless and slanderous" and supported the activities and policies of Nikita Khrushchev. It was this meeting which must have decided to accept the Chinese declaration of political war and to respond so vigorously on July 14, when the Soviet answer appeared.

But the decision to engage in open political war with the Chinese could not be confined to matters of party affairs and ideology. The men who ruled the Chinese Communist party also ruled China, a country which borders the Soviet Union for thousands of miles. The whole issue of the security of the Soviet state's Asian borders against possible Chinese encroachment was immediately raised in the wake of the decision to fight Mao politically with no holds barred. It was a familiar problem in Russian and Soviet foreign policy and an old rule still held good: the Soviet Union must not face the threat of attack simultaneously in Europe and Asia; if tension rises in one sector, steps must be taken to lower tension in the other. The logical strategic corollary of the situation now arisen with China was the imperative necessity of improving relations with the West.

Khrushchev acted swiftly. On July 2, 1963, he made a historic speech in East Berlin. The Soviet Union, he announced, was prepared to sign a partial nuclear test-ban treaty with the United States and Great Britain, a pact that would prohibit nuclear testing in the atmosphere, under water and in outer space. This was a complete reversal of position, since such a treaty had been rejected often before by the Premier on the ground that the Soviet Union could only sign a treaty banning all tests, including those conducted underground. But to detect

underground explosions on-site inspections were needed and
these the Soviet government had often denounced as "espionage."
In late December 1962 Khrushchev had reinstated his old offer
to permit two or three on-site inspections annually in the Soviet
Union, but this had been rejected by the West as inadequate to
guard against underground nuclear tests. But on July 2, Khrushchev announced he was willing to forget about prohibiting underground tests for the time being. He wanted an agreement with
the West, and the improved relations such an agreement would
bring. Khrushchev's July 2 speech coupled this concession with
a call for conclusion of a non-aggression pact between the NATO
and Warsaw Pact powers, but later developments showed that
this demand was not a condition for the test-ban treaty. Events
moved swiftly thereafter. The Soviet reply to the Chinese was
published on July 14 as British and American negotiators gathered
in Moscow to begin the nuclear treaty talks. On July 25, the first
formal international treaty banning nuclear tests of any kind was
initialed in Moscow.

We shall have to treat later the storm that rose between the
Soviet Union and China over the test-ban treaty, but first let us
look at the points made in the July 14 Soviet reply to the vitriolic
message Peking had sent a month earlier, a reply printed as an
open letter to Soviet Communists.[3]

Very early in the reply, the theme is set that the Chinese attack is aimed at the Soviet people and the Soviet nation, a theme
that moves to enlist Soviet nationalism on Premier Khrushchev's
side:

> Everyone who reads the Chinese Communist party Central
> Committee letter will see behind its ringing phrases about
> unity and solidarity, unfriendly, slanderous attacks on our
> party and the Soviet country, a desire to belittle the historical
> importance of our people's struggle for the victory of com-
> munism in the USSR. . . . How the tongue does twist to say
> such things about the party of the great Lenin, about the
> motherland of socialism, about the people who were the first
> in the world to carry out a socialist revolution.

The statement goes on to accuse the Chinese of base ingratitude
for Soviet aid, to recite some of the statistics of this aid and to

complain that the Chinese leaders "have recently tried to belittle the importance of Soviet aid." In June 1960, the document asserts, the Chinese began plotting behind the Soviet Communist party's back, criticizing the Soviet party at a secret meeting held in Peking during a conference of the World Federation of Trade Unions. Thus the picture is drawn of the treacherous Chinese leaders conniving and scheming against the Soviet Union and the Soviet people, heedless of the generous aid given the Chinese in earlier years.

The next section seeks to show the great lengths to which Soviet leaders went, in vain, to prevent a split. It tells of secret meetings in October 1961 and in the fall of 1962. At the latter, the letter declares, Khrushchev sent the following proposal to Mao Tse-tung: "Let us cast aside all disputes and differences and not decide who is right and who is wrong, not stir up the past, but rather begin our relations on a fresh page." The letter then adds, "We did not even receive any answer to this sincere appeal."

The Soviet statement goes on to accuse the Chinese of carrying the party dispute over into state relations: "Chinese agencies began curtailing economic and trade relations with the Soviet Union and other socialist countries . . . the volume of China's trade was reduced almost two-thirds over the past three years. . . . This reduction was made at the initiative of the Chinese leaders." The letter continues: "The Chinese leaders have not told their people the truth about whose fault it was that these ties were curtailed. There was broad propaganda among the Chinese Communists, and even among the population, directed toward discrediting the foreign and domestic policies of the Communist party of the Soviet Union and toward inflaming anti-Soviet feelings." In all this discussion there is no mention of China's serious economic difficulties and setbacks as a factor in the curtailment of trade.

Then the Soviet reply turns to matters of ideological substance, to the question of war and peace:

The Chinese Communist party Central Committee's letter of June 14 has much to say about 'inevitable sacrifices' allegedly in the name of revolution. Some responsible Chinese leaders have also mentioned the possibility of sacrificing hundreds of millions of people in war. In the anthology 'Long Live Lenin-ism!' that was approved by the Chinese Communist party Central Committee, it is asserted that 'the victorious people will create rapidly on the ruins of dead imperialism a civiliza-tion a thousand times higher than that under the capitalist system, will build their own truly beautiful future.' One might ask the Chinese comrades if they are aware of what sort of ruins would be left behind by a nuclear-missile war? The Cen-tral Committee of the Communist party of the Soviet Union . . . cannot share the views of the Chinese leadership about the creation of 'a civilization a thousand times higher' on the corpses of hundreds of millions of people. These views are in fundamental contradiction to the ideas of Marxism-Leninism.

Turning next to the Chinese criticism of Soviet conduct in the Cuban crisis, the letter repeats the Soviet position noted in the last chapter. It asks whether the Chinese "really seriously think that all bourgeois governments are completely devoid of reason in all their affairs?" And then it asks an even more bitter question about the Chinese attitude toward the Cuban crisis and its reso-lution: "What are the Chinese leaders dissatisfied with? Can it be with the fact that it was possible to avert an invasion of Cuba and the outbreak of a world war?" Then the letter declares:

At the most difficult moment the Chinese Communist party leadership, which before this had pointed out that imperialism might at any time unleash a world war, took the stand of a critic instead of acting as a militant ally and a comrade. Dur-ing those days no one heard the Chinese leaders making any statements about their practical actions in defense of the Cuban revolution. Instead the Chinese leaders openly tried to aggravate what was already a tense situation in the Caribbean, threw tinder on the smoldering fire of conflict.

Next the Soviet letter assails the Chinese attitude on disarm-ament, putting forward this stern indictment of Peking:

The Chinese comrades have put forward the slogan of 'blade against blade,' counterposing it to the policy of other socialist countries directed toward easing the international situation and halting the 'cold war.' Essentially this slogan is water for the mill of the imperialist 'brink of war' policy and aids the partisans of the arms race. One gets the impression that the leaders of the Chinese Communist party think it to their advantage to maintain and intensify international tension, especially in the relations between the USSR and the USA.

No less indignantly, the Soviet letter denies that the Soviet party has renounced revolution and supplanted class struggle with peaceful coexistence. "The principle of peaceful coexistence, naturally, cannot in the slightest degree extend to relations between antagonistic classes within the capitalist states; it is impermissible to extend it to the struggle of the working class against the bourgeoisie for its class interests, to the struggle of oppressed people against the colonialists."

Then the Soviet statement assails the Chinese as defenders of Stalin, attacking them also for their denunciation of the Soviet party's Third Program:

> The leaders of the Chinese Communist party have assumed the role of defenders of the cult of the individual, disseminators of the mistaken ideas of Stalin. They are trying to impose upon the other parties the order, the ideology and morals, the forms and methods of leadership that flourished during the cult of the individual. We shall say bluntly that this is an unenviable role that will bring neither honor nor glory. . . .

> The Soviet people find it strange and outrageous that the Chinese comrades are trying to belittle the program of the Communist party of the Soviet Union, the majestic plan for creating a Communist society.

> Alluding to the fact that our party proclaims as its task the struggle for a better life for the people, the Chinese Communist party leaders hint at some sort of "bourgeoisification" and "degeneration" of Soviet society. According to their logic, if people walk about in bast sandals and drink thin cabbage soup from a common bowl, this is communism, but if a working person lives well today and wants to live better tomorrow, this is all but a restoration of capitalism!

The Chinese arguments about the continued existence of class struggle in the Soviet Union are dismissed as nonsensical, and the Chinese are accused of opposing "the development of socialist democracy. . . . It is no accident that nowhere in all their verbose letter was a place found for even a mention of the development of democracy in conditions of socialism." The Soviet letter professes bafflement as to why the Chinese support the cult of the individual, but charges: "In essence, for the first time in the

history of the international Communist movement we encounter
the open extolling of the cult of the individual." Even Stalin,
the letter declares, never dared to go so far. The implication is
plain: Peking supported Stalin and his cult because Mao Tse-
tung still maintains his own cult of the individual more than a
decade after Stalin's death.

From internal Soviet problems, the Soviet letter moves on to
assail the Chinese demand for revolution and Peking's scorn for
the Communist parties in Western industrialized countries who
are trying to use parliamentary means to advance their cause.
The Soviet rebuttal sums up the argument in these words:

> Having come out against everything the Communist parties
> of the developed capitalist countries are engaged in at the
> present time, the Chinese comrades have shown neither an ele-
> mentary feeling of solidarity with the Communists who are
> joining battle with capital on the front lines of the class
> struggle nor an understanding of the concrete conditions in
> these countries. . . . In essence they 'repudiate in the name
> of revolution' precisely those paths that lead toward the revo-
> lution, they impose a course that would lead to the isolation of
> the Communist parties from the masses. . . .

> The Chinese comrades consider the basic criterion of revo-
> lutionary spirit to be the recognition of armed uprising always,
> in everything and everywhere. Thus the Chinese comrades
> actually deny the possibility of employing peaceful forms of
> struggle for the victory of the socialist revolution, whereas
> Marxism-Leninism teaches that Communists must master all
> forms of revolutionary class struggle, both violent and non-
> violent.

The next long section of the letter deals with the Chinese
demand for primacy of revolution in Asia, Africa and Latin
America. Before taking up this issue, the Soviet statement had
already thrown out broad hints that the Chinese were really anti-
white racists, declaring, for example, that the Chinese

> . . . came out against the participation of the representatives
> . . . of the European socialist countries in the Third Afro-
> Asian Solidarity Conference in Moshi [Tanganyika]. The
> leader of the Chinese delegation told the Soviet representatives
> that 'there was nothing there for whites to do.' At the journal-
> ists' conference in Jakarta, the Chinese representatives followed

a line against allowing Soviet journalists full participation on the ground that the Soviet Union is not an Asian country!

The Soviet letter also points to the racist implications of the favorite Chinese slogan, "The wind from the East will prevail over the wind from the West," noting that slogan was one "lacking all class content." But it is in the refutation of the Chinese demand for a special position for Asia, Africa and Latin America that the Soviet statement makes the sharpest accusations that the Chinese have deserted Marxism-Leninism for a racist approach. Peking, the Soviet letter charges, is trying "to win popularity among the peoples of Asia, Africa and Latin America in the easiest way." The Chinese, by insisting on the national liberation movement as the decisive force in the struggle against imperialism, are actually "isolating the national-liberation movement from the international working class and its offspring, the world system of socialism." The Chinese are violating the Leninist injunction that the working class must head the struggle against imperialism, the Soviet letter charges, and "the Chinese comrades want to 'correct' Lenin and prove that it is not the working class but the petty bourgeoisie or the national bourgeoisie, or even 'certain patriotic-minded kings, princes and aristocrats,' who should be the leaders of the world struggle against imperialism." And after thus hinting that racism rather than Marxism animates the Chinese, the Soviet letter asks darkly:

> What is the explanation for the false tenets of the Chinese Communist party leadership on the vital problems of our times? Either the complete estrangement of the Chinese comrades from actual reality, a dogmatic bookish approach to the problems of war, peace, and revolution, a lack of understanding of the concrete conditions of the modern epoch: Or do other goals, having nothing in common with revolution, hide behind the deafening noise about 'world revolution'?

The rest of the Soviet letter covers relatively secondary and familiar issues. It accuses the Chinese Communists of seeking to split the world Communist movement by backing opposition groups to existing Communist parties in many countries. It charges the Chinese with cutting in half their trade with all other Communist-ruled countries together and with seeking a minimum of economic ties with other socialist countries. Placing the basic blame for the dispute with Albania on the Chinese, the Soviet letter declares that the Chinese leaders "did everything to use the Albanian leaders as their mouthpiece." It adds that "it is now known that the Chinese comrades directly pushed them [the Albanians] onto the road of open warfare against the Soviet Union and the other socialist countries and fraternal parties."

With this exchange of verbal broadsides, both sides dropped all pretense and a historic war of words began. For weeks thereafter the press, radio and other communications media of each country hurled daily propaganda salvos at the other. The object in each case was plain. For years each government had sedulously indoctrinated its people in the spirit of Sino-Soviet friendship; now each population had to be re-indoctrinated, this time to regard the other country's leaders (and by implication the other country as well) as enemies.

The Chinese used interesting tactics. Not only did they carefully print the Soviet letter of July 14 in their own press but for a time they gave their people daily, detailed summaries of the bitter attacks on Peking appearing in the Soviet press. The appeal to Chinese nationalism in all this was evident. In reprinting the Soviet letter, *Jenmin Jih Pao*, the Chinese Communist party official organ, moved to nail several Moscow assertions it indicated were lies. Thus, it denied that Chinese leaders would have no scruples about attaining socialism through a world nuclear war that would sacrifice millions of persons. In November 1957, at the Moscow international Communist party meeting, the paper said, Mao's position had been the following:

Since World War II, Comrade Mao Tse-tung has consistently and relentlessly laid bare the U.S. imperialists' policy of nuclear blackmail and shown that their criminal purpose in publicizing the horrors of nuclear weapons is to terrorize the people of all countries in the attempt to enslave the whole world.

Comrade Mao Tse-tung also said that we should consider another possibility: If the imperialists dare to launch nuclear war and plunge mankind into such an unprecedented disaster, what should the international proletariat and the people of all countries do? It is perfectly clear that there are two alternatives, either to resist imperialism firmly and bury it, or to be afraid of sacrifice and to capitulate. But some people believe that if nuclear war breaks out all mankind will perish. In reality such talk amounts to saying that there is no alternative to capitulation in the face of imperialist nuclear blackmail. Directing himself to this pessimistic and capitulationist talk, Comrade Mao Tse-tung pointed out that mankind will definitely not be destroyed even if the imperialists insist on a nuclear war with the possible sacrifice of hundreds of millions of people and impose it on mankind. The future of mankind will nevertheless be a bright one. The imperialists cannot succeed in their attempt to destroy humanity and civilization.

Jenmin Jih Pao then turned to denying that the Chinese had fluctuated in their attitude toward Soviet de-Stalinization. On four occasions between May and November 1956, it revealed, Mao spoke to Soviet Communists and made clear the Chinese position. "We repeatedly pointed out that Stalin's merits outweighed his faults and that an all-round analysis was needed. We held that the leaders of the C.P.S.U. were in error in failing to make an all-round analysis, in failing to make self-criticism and in failing to consult with fraternal parties." Then the Chinese newspaper gave its version of why Soviet-Chinese trade had fallen so precipitously:

The fact is that on July 16, 1960, the Soviet side suddenly notified China of its decision to withdraw all the 1,300 and more Soviet experts in China within a month, to scrap the hundreds of agreements and contracts it had signed and to discontinue supplies of many important items of equipment and materials. This inflicted incalculable difficulties and losses on China's economy, national defense and scientific research and was the main reason for the reduction in the economic and commercial links between China and the Soviet Union. China is the victim.

Jenmin Jih Pao completed its introductory remarks by saying the Soviet letter was full of such misstatements, "no less than 70 to 80 of them," and promised to "provide the necessary material to clear these matters up in future articles."[4]

Going beyond such refutation, Peking began to present a new image of Soviet internal life to the Chinese people. Peking's press broke out in a rash of articles drawing on the Soviet reporting of speculators, swindlers and similar anti-Socialist ele-

ments in the Soviet Union. All the negative aspects of Soviet
life, so long suppressed in the Chinese press, now occupied the
center of the stage so as to form a picture of a Soviet Union in
which capitalist activities and capitalist tendencies were rampant.
At the extreme, the Chinese press juggled statistics to suggest
that prices were much higher in the Soviet Union than in China,
implying that the Soviet living standard was poorer than China's.[5]
In late July and early August of 1963 reports began to spread of
new promises of Soviet military aid to India. The Chinese Communist party official organ leaped to take advantage of this opportunity:

> It became obvious around the time of the signing of the Mos-
> cow tripartite [nuclear test-ban] treaty that Soviet-Indian re-
> lations had become extraordinarily intimate. One after another,
> Nehru's personal envoy, his daughter, Madame Indira Ghandhi,
> the Indian national defense delegation, and others went to
> Moscow. The Indian reactionaries' intention to ally with the
> Soviet Union to oppose China was all too clear. And from the
> fervor and cordiality shown by Khrushchev and other Soviet
> leaders to the 'distinguished guests' from India, it is not diffi-
> cult to fathom the subtle significance of it all.

> It is reported that the Soviet government has agreed to in-
> crease its military aid to the Indian reactionaries, to ship more
> weapons of still newer types to the anti-communist and anti-
> popular Nehru government which has become the spearhead
> of the United States in its campaign against China. . . . No
> wonder the Indian press could not refrain from acclaiming
> the 'opening of a new and brighter chapter of cooperation' in
> Indian-Soviet relations.

> Indeed, this is not just a 'new chapter' in Indian-Soviet rela-
> tions. It is also a new chapter of collaboration between the
> Soviet leaders and U.S. imperialism to ally with India against
> China.[6]

The passionate anger which the Chinese brought to this quarrel
was perhaps best demonstrated in early August 1963 in Hiro-
shima, Japan when Soviet and Chinese delegations clashed at the
observance of the eighteenth anniversary of the atom bombing
of that city. Here are the words the Chinese delegation leader
Chu Tzu-chi addressed to the Soviet group:

In the Cuban crisis, you committed both the error of adventurism and the error of capitulationism. You and U.S. imperialism have been helping a third country [India] with arms to attack socialist China. You said that by possessing nuclear weapons the Soviet Union has protected the socialist camp. But how can we have any trust in you? What you do has entirely violated Lenin's teachings and the interests of the Chinese people, the socialist camp, and the people of the world. You have also betrayed the interests of the Soviet people. By your vote in the United Nations in favor of the dispatch of U.N. forces to the Congo, you helped United States imperialism in the murder of Patrice Lumumba. We can list 100 cases of your capitulation to imperialism. But can you give a single case of the Chinese people's capitulation to imperialism? No, you cannot and will never.[7]

Soviet propaganda organs were by no means backward or shy in maintaining their side of this mud-slinging match, though the Soviet statements tended to be less strident and shrill than the Chinese blasts. The Soviet press concentrated on trying to convince its readers that the dispute was between the Kremlin advocates of peace and the Chinese warmongers, that the overwhelming majority of the world's people and also of the world's Communists supported the Soviet Union, and that the Chinese were not only maligning the Soviet Union but also substituting anti-white racism for Marxist class struggle ideology. As the debate continued, it widened and grew even more acrimonious. Outraged at what it called the Chinese distortion of Soviet reality, the Soviet press began to tell its readers more about China's great economic difficulties and failures. Soviet criticism of the Chinese military actions on the Indian border became more pointed and less tactful. The sharper character of Soviet polemics published during August may be indicated by these excerpts from a comprehensive review of the dispute in *Kommunist*, the Soviet Communist party's theoretical journal:

The leadership of the CPC [Communist party of China] has begun to transfer the ideological differences to the area of politics, worsening its relations with Marxist-Leninist parties and socialist states. It has carried out in China a broad propaganda campaign, which . . . carries a clear anti-Soviet character and is calculated also to arouse in the Chinese people a feeling of dislike and even enmity to other socialist countries. . . .

Evidently, the current line of the Chinese comrades is connected with those difficulties which arose in China as a result of the realization of a series of erroneous propositions of the CPC. The CPC leaders try to distract the masses' attention from the actual causes which brought failure to China's internal life. In this connection the central committee of the CPC tries to assure the people that escape from this situation lies in quickening, in nudging the world revolution. By such maneuvers, utilizing 'leftist' ultra-revolutionary phrases, the Chinese comrades try to hide their disbelief in the internal forces of the socialist structure. For these goals, there has begun in China the inflaming of nationalism, the teaching of national, and then of racial exclusiveness. . . .

The Chinese comrades have a different point of view: 'The atomic bomb is a paper tiger,' it is 'not terrible at all.' The question of sacrifices which humanity would suffer in a world war for the liquidation of imperialism, they consider a secondary problem. It is no accident that in articles and in the letter of the CPC central committee so much is said of 'inevitable sacrifices,' it is not accidental that some responsible Chinese leaders talk about the possibility of sacrificing half the Chinese people and even half of humanity in a world war for destroying imperialism. . . .

Whether the Chinese comrades want it or not, their position is objectively close in many respects to that of the 'madmen'— the representatives of the extremely aggressive imperialist circles. The assertion that disarmament is an 'unsalable illusion' and that the mass struggle for it is hopeless provides grist in the nature of things for the mills of the imperialist apologists of the policy of 'balancing on the brink of war,' of the supporters of the ceaseless arms race. The impression is gained that the leaders of the CPC consider advantageous the maintenance and strengthening of international tension, especially between the USSR and the USA. . . .

The CPC leadership is carrying on subversive work against the Marxist-Leninist parties of the capitalist countries. The goal of the campaign may be understood from the following words of an article in *Jenmin Jih Pao*. It is said there: 'We are confident that both in the ranks of the American Communist party and outside it will be found real Marxist-Leninists who will lead this party on the correct path.' In the June 14 letter this thought is developed still more broadly as applied to the Communist parties of the capitalist world. . . . There is the nub of the matter. An effort is being made under guise of the struggle with reformists to split the Communist parties, to create in them and about them fractions which will obediently follow the guiding finger of Peking. . . . [The Chinese position on the national-liberation struggle and the alleged opposition of some Communists to it is] an effort to replace the Leninist proposition of the inseparable connection of the socialist countries and the socialist revolution with the national-liberation movement . . . by the anti-Marxist, thoroughly demagogic 'theory' about the special geopolitical and racial closeness of the peoples of Asia, Africa and Latin America. . . . In this connection there is of interest the statement of the noted figure of the Japanese Liberal-Democratic party, Kendzo Matsumura who, referring to his conversations with the leaders of the CPC, expressed their opinion thusly: '. . . East still is East. We Asians must change world history. We must firmly unite and strengthen connections between our people of one skin color and one system of writing.' This statement was published in *Jenmin Jih Pao* without any commentary. It was not disavowed by the Chinese leaders. . . .

In recent years the Chinese press has said nothing about the defense and development of Marxist-Leninist theory by other Communist and Workers parties, except for the Albanian Labor party whose activities are praised in every way. Posing in the role of the sole interpreters of Marxist-Leninist teachings, the leaders of the CPC excommunicate from Marxism all that which does not agree with their views. The entire propaganda apparatus of the CPC tries to portray matters as though in our epoch the sole creative theoreticians of Marxism-Leninism are the Chinese leaders. . . . One of the figures of the Chinese Communist party has said: 'The experience of China and the international Communist movement confirms that revolution and the matter of construction obtains victory only when it is directed by the ideas of Mao Tse-tung. . . .' After this and many analogous assertions, it already does not arouse surprise that even generally known propositions of Marxism are presented as though they were first discovered in China. . . .

Everyone understood—and this was said not once by the Chinese comrades themselves—that the 'peoples communes' and the 'great leap' were experiments. However the CPC leaders did not await the checking of these experiments. The Chinese press affirmed that in China it had been found that 'the best

organizational form for hastening the construction of socialism
and the shift in the future to communism is the peoples commune.' When life showed that too much haste had been shown
in advertising the commune, the Chinese leaders did not find
in themselves the strength openly to analyze their errors.
Changing the policy in the countryside, they continue to maintain and publicly proclaim the slogans which have been shown
to be anachronistic.[8]

In midsummer 1963, the main field in the propaganda battle
shifted from the two Communist parties to the two governments.
This was touched off by Chinese fury at the Soviet signing, with
the United States and Great Britain, of the partial nuclear test-
ban treaty. An official Chinese government note declared: "This
treaty signed in Moscow is a big fraud to fool the people of the
world." It went on to assail the treaty as capitulation by Khrushchev to the United States and to claim that the treaty "actually
strengthens the position of the nuclear powers for nuclear blackmail and increases the danger of imperialism launching a nuclear
war and a world war." Declaring that the Chinese government
"is firmly opposed to nuclear war and a world war," the statement proposed destruction of all nuclear weapons, dismantling of
all foreign military bases, an end to all nuclear tests and the
establishment of nuclear weapon-free zones in the Asian and
Pacific region "including the United States, the Soviet Union,
China and Japan" as well as in Africa, Latin America and Central
Europe. Finally the statement proposed a summit meeting of all
heads of government to discuss the prohibition and destruction
of nuclear weapons. The Chinese strategy was clear. Peking now
presented itself as even more peace-loving and even more opposed to nuclear weapons than Moscow.

But the key paragraph of this official Chinese government document was this:

The indisputable facts prove that the policy pursued by the
Soviet government is one of allying with the forces of war
to oppose the forces of peace, allying with imperialism to oppose socialism, allying with the United States to oppose China,
and allying with the reactionaries of all countries to oppose
the peoples of the world.[9]

This was by far the strongest statement ever made by the
Chinese. It was an official proclamation of the Soviet Union as

the enemy of China, a charge incompatible with the treaty of alliance and mutual defense existing between the two countries. Stung by this attack, the Soviet government moved quickly to reply. The official answer attacked the Chinese as pursuing an "all or nothing" policy devoid of all realism. The substantive arguments this statement gave for the treaty parallelled to a large extent those used for the same purpose by the Kennedy Administration. But for its purposes, the Soviet government went further, reminding the Chinese in particular of the role of Soviet nuclear weapons in defending Communist-ruled countries, including China. It accused the Chinese of following a policy intended to increase international tension and speed up the arms race. Finally, as a last blow, the Soviet leaders had *Pravda* and *Izvestiya* publish the full text of the Chinese statement, preceding it with a statement saying that while the document did not deserve to be printed it was being presented to show Soviet citizens the extreme that had been reached by the Chinese leaders.[10]

Peking's answer was a bombshell. It came on August 15 in a note which revealed for the first time that the Soviet Union had agreed in 1957 to help China become a nuclear power and that Moscow had repudiated that agreement in June 1959. In this statement, the Chinese government finally discussed openly what had probably been the central issue in the Sino-Soviet debate for a half decade: China's desire to have its own atomic and hydrogen bombs and Russia's reluctance and then refusal to aid its brother Communist nation to achieve that end. "The real aim of the Soviet leaders is to compromise with the United States in order to seek momentary ease and to maintain a monopoly of nuclear weapons and lord it over the socialist camp," the Chinese statement declared. It then gave this justification for its position that China must have its own nuclear weapons and can not be willing to depend on Soviet nuclear weapons for its defense:

In fighting imperialist aggression and defending its security, every socialist country has to rely in the first place on its own defense capability—and only then—on assistance from fraternal countries and the people of the world. For the Soviet statement to describe all the socialist countries as depending on the nuclear weapons of the Soviet Union for their survival is to strike an out-and-out great power chauvinistic note and to fly in the face of the facts.

The Chinese government has always fully appreciated the importance of the Soviet Union's possession of nuclear weapons. However, such possession must in no way be made a justification for preventing other socialist countries from increasing their own defense capabilities. . . .

With regard to preventing nuclear proliferation, the Chinese government has always maintained that the arguments of the U.S. imperialists must not be echoed, but that a class analysis must be made. Whether or not nuclear weapons help peace depends on who possesses them. It is detrimental to peace if they are in the hands of imperialist countries; it helps peace if they are in the hands of socialist countries. It must not be said undiscriminatingly that the danger of nuclear war increases along with the increase in the number of nuclear powers.

Nuclear weapons in the possession of a socialist country are always a means of defense against nuclear blackmail and nuclear war. So long as the imperialists refuse to ban nuclear weapons, the greater the number of socialist countries possessing them, the better the guarantee of world peace.

For all its talk about "socialist countries," this passage made clear that Chinese nationalism was at the root of this issue. With a few minor changes in wording, Peking's justification for wanting to have its own nuclear weapons could have been issued in Paris as a statement of De Gaulle's reasoning as to why France must become a major nuclear power. But the Chinese could not be satisfied with a statement that appealed only to their own people's nationalism. They continued, after all, to seek support within the Soviet Communist party for a reversal of the Khrushchev position. Hence they included in their statement this striking passage on Russia's need for help from others:

It should be understood that the relationship between the Soviet people and the other peoples of the world is one of mutual reliance, like that between lips and teeth. The existence and development of the Soviet Union are a support to the revolutionary struggles of other peoples, while in turn these peoples' revolutionary struggles and victories support the Soviet Union. There is no reason whatsoever to think that the Soviet Union no longer needs others' support. In fact this is not the case. If the lips are gone, the teeth are exposed. If U.S. imperialism should be given a free hand to put down the revolutionary struggles of other peoples and if the Soviet leaders should ally

themselves with U.S. imperialism against the fraternal countries, eventually it will not be possible for the Soviet Union
itself to be preserved.[11]

Once again the Soviet government responded quickly, and
once again *Pravda* and *Izvestiya* printed the full text of the
Chinese government statement simultaneously. On the issue of
whether or not the Soviet Union should help the Chinese have
nuclear weapons, clearly the Soviet leaders had no fears about
the Soviet people knowing Peking's full position.

The answering Soviet note of August 21, 1963 covered much
the same ground as before but also took account of the new
elements in the latest Chinese statement. The anger in Moscow
at the Chinese disclosure of their previously secret agreement
was made clear in a very cold paragraph indeed:

> The government of the Chinese Peoples Republic, disregard-
> ing its duty as an ally, abusing relations of trust existing among
> the socialist countries, has embarked upon the road of making
> public classified documents and information relating to the
> defenses of the countries of the socialist commonwealth, and,
> what is more, of presenting the facts tendentiously, in a dis-
> torted light. Of course the Soviet government will not fall as
> low as to embark upon the road of divulging information relat-
> ing to the defenses of the socialist nations. The Soviet govern-
> ment is compelled to state that after these actions of the
> government of the Chinese Peoples Republic there is hardly
> anyone who will believe the sincerity of its assurances and
> trust it with information of defensive importance. It is natural
> that the Soviet government will draw its conclusions on this
> score.

The heart of this Soviet reply was an argument trying to
justify the Soviet refusal to help China become a nuclear power.
Since the Soviet regime was also trying to influence people in
China and win supporters against Mao's line there, it could not
talk about Soviet fears that Chinese atomic or hydrogen bombs
might be used against Russia, or might be employed to start a
general world thermonuclear war. Hence the argument was put
in terms of China's problems and China's self-interest—as seen in
Moscow, of course:

> The position of the government of the Chinese Peoples Re-
> public, set forth in the statement of August 15, can be under-

stood only in the sense that the Chinese leaders do not care how the nuclear weapons spread among the capitalist countries as long as the Chinese Peoples Republic leaders get a chance to lay their hands on a nuclear bomb and see what it is like.

It must be admitted that, being at a definite stage of its economic development, possessing a definite economic potential, the Chinese Peoples Republic is yet unprepared to produce nuclear arms in quantity. Even if the Chinese Peoples Republic were to produce two or three bombs, this would not solve its problem but would bring about a great exhaustion of the Chinese Peoples Republic economy. We know from our experience what it costs for a country, for a people, to produce nuclear arms on a large scale, at a level meeting modern military techniques, modern defense requirements.

But we were compelled to do this in order to stand up against the imperialist camp, which possessed such arms. And the Chinese Peoples Republic can now rely on the means of defense which have been developed through the efforts of the Soviet people and which reliably serve the purposes of defending the countries of the socialist commonwealth.

This is why the most reasonable policy for the Chinese Peoples Republic in the present conditions—if, of course, its desires and potential are to be commensurate—would be to devote its efforts to the development of the national economy, science, technology and agriculture, devoting them to raising the welfare of the Chinese people, to meeting their vital needs. The Chinese people are experiencing many privations, and this is why such a course in the policy of the Chinese leaders would be more beneficial to the Chinese people, would be more appreciated by them and correctly understood throughout the world.

Let us grant that by overstraining its economy the Chinese Peoples Republic will finally be able to produce a few atomic bombs. But how many such bombs would in this case be aimed by the imperialists at the Chinese Peoples Republic? Would the Chinese leaders then feel themselves more secure, even though sitting on their own atomic bomb?[12]

Here was a clear Soviet appeal to the Chinese people over the heads of the Chinese leaders. China's people needed more attention to "meeting their vital needs," Moscow argued, but China's megalomaniacal leaders thought only of useless and dangerous atomic bombs. This was a clear call for removal of the Chinese leaders if they did not change their ways.

That Peking would respond explosively to such a challenge was predictable. The answer came at the end of August: "Even if we Chinese people are unable to produce an atomic bomb for a hundred years, we will neither crawl to the baton of the Soviet leaders nor kneel before the nuclear blackmail of the U.S. imperialists." The statement added: "The Soviet government is insolent enough to say that we are able to criticize it only because China enjoys the protection of Soviet nuclear weapons. Well, then, leaders of the Soviet Union, please continue to protect us awhile with your nuclear weapons. We shall continue to criticize you, and we hope you will have the courage to argue the matter with us." Perhaps the most cutting passage of the reply, however, was this: "The Soviet leaders insist on exaggerating the role of nuclear weapons and trust blindly in them, despise the masses and have forgotten that the masses are the makers of history, and so they have degenerated into worshippers of nuclear weapons."[13]

In September and October 1963, the Soviet-Chinese war of words continued unceasingly, becoming even sharper in some respects than it had been during the bitter exchanges of July and August. But even while the struggle continued, there were signs in the mid-autumn of 1963 that efforts were being made to reduce the fury of the struggle, and perhaps even to effect a reconciliation. Thus, in an interview with the head of Reuters news agency in mid-October, Premier Chou En-lai minimized the significance of Soviet-Chinese friction in Sinkiang, declared that disappointment awaited anyone trying to take advantage of the dispute between the Soviet and Chinese Communist parties, and indicated his belief that if either the Soviet Union or China were the victim of aggression, the other would come to its support.[14] Two weeks later, Premier Khrushchev appealed publicly once again for an end to open polemics between Moscow and Peking, declaring that such exchanges helped only the enemies of Communism.[15] In early November it became known that the Polish Communist leadership was seeking to bring the two sides together and persuade them at least to moderate their anger at each other.[16] But whatever the future results of these efforts to restore Communist harmony, the attacks exchanged during September and October 1963 remain an indelible portion of the historical record, and it is to these we now turn.

On September 6, 1963, the Chinese issued a comprehensive document which gave their version of the secret history of the dispute. Most of the key points of this statement—notably the accusations made about the Soviet attitude on Poland and Hungary in 1956, the revelation of the Soviet encouragement of the flight of Chinese citizens from Sinkiang in 1962, and the Chinese view of what happened at the secret international Communist meetings in Bucharest and Moscow in 1960—have already been mentioned in Chapter IX. Here we may note that this statement charged the Soviet leadership with acting "in flagrant violation of the Sino-Soviet Treaty of Friendship, Alliance, and Mutual Assistance," and declared that "Moscow, Washington, New Delhi and Belgrade are joined in a love feast and the Soviet press is running an endless assortment of fantastic stories and theories attacking China."[17]

A week later, September 13, the Chinese delivered the sharpest single blow yet directed personally against Khrushchev. The historic importance of this article, which was devoted to examining the question of Stalin, and of its revelations about past Soviet-Chinese friction, is best indicated by these quotations:[18]

Stalin's life was that of a great Marxist-Leninist, a great proletarian revolutionary . . . Stalin . . . also made certain mistakes. . . . In the work led by Stalin of suppressing the counter-revolution, many counter-revolutionaries deserving punishment were duly punished, but at the same time there were innocent people who were wrongly convicted. . . . In handling relations with fraternal parties and countries he made some mistakes. He also gave some bad counsel in the international communist movement. These mistakes caused some losses to the Soviet Union and the international communist movement. . . .

While defending Stalin, we do not defend his mistakes. Long ago the Chinese communists had first hand experience of some of his mistakes. Of the erroneous 'left' and right opportunist lines which emerged in the CCP at one time or another, some arose under the influence of certain mistakes of Stalin's. . . . In the late twenties, the thirties and the early and middle forties, the Chinese Marxist-Leninists represented by Comrades Mao Tse-tung and Liu Shao-chi resisted the influence of Stalin's mistakes; they gradually overcame the erroneous lines of 'left' and right opportunism, and finally led the Chinese revolution to victory. But since some of the wrong ideas put forward by

Stalin were accepted and applied by certain Chinese comrades, we Chinese should bear the responsibility. . . .

In what position does Khrushchev, who participated in the leadership of the party and the state during Stalin's period, place himself when he beats his breast, pounds the table, and shouts abuse of Stalin at the top of his voice? In the position of an accomplice to a 'murderer' or a 'bandit'? Or in the same position as a 'fool' or an 'idiot'? . . .

In abasing Stalin, Khrushchev is in fact wildly denouncing the Soviet system and state. His language in this connection is by no means weaker but is actually stronger than that of such renegades as Kautsky, Trotsky, Tito and Djilas. . . .

Why does Khrushchev, who was in the leadership of the party and the state in Stalin's period and who actively supported and firmly executed the policy for suppressing counter-revolutionaries, repudiate everything done during this period and shift the blame for all errors on to Stalin alone, while altogether whitewashing himself?

When Stalin did something wrong, he was capable of criticizing himself. For instance, he had given some bad counsel with regard to the Chinese revolution. After the victory of the Chinese revolution, he admitted his mistake. . . . But what about Khrushchev? He simply does not know what self-criticism is; all he does is to shift the entire blame on to others and claim the entire credit for himself. . . .

The 'combat against the personality cult' launched by Khrushchev is a despicable political intrigue. Like someone described by Marx, he is in his element as an intriguer, while a nonentity as a theorist.

On October 21, 1963, another bitter Chinese article assailed the Soviet leaders as "apologists of neocolonialism." It accused them of having failed in their obligations to the Algerian revolution and of working with the United States to use the United Nations to put down the Congolese people's armed struggle against colonialism. The Soviet leaders' policy and purposes in giving aid to newly independent nations was declared "open to suspicion" since these leaders "often take an attitude of great power chauvinism and national egoism in matters concerning aid to newly independent countries, harm the economic and political interests of the receiving countries, and as a result discredit the socialist countries." But the most serious attack came on the subject of racism. The Soviet leaders were accused of emulating German Kaiser Wilhelm II in his strictures a half century ago about the "yellow peril." The motives of Soviet leaders in attacking alleged Chinese racism were described in these terms:

When they peddle the 'theory of racism,' describing the national liberation movement in Asia, Africa and Latin America as one of the colored against the white race, the leaders of the Communist party of the Soviet Union are clearly aiming at inciting racial hatred among the white people in Europe and North America, at diverting the people of the world from the struggle against imperialism, and at turning the international working class movement away from the struggle against modern revisionism.[19]

The Chinese summed up their case in October by declaring Khrushchev had joined in a new "Holy Alliance" with President Kennedy against the people of the world, hinting broadly that the goal is a Soviet-American condominium over all mankind.[20]

The magnitude of the Soviet propaganda offensive in this quarrel is suggested by an incomplete Chinese count showing that between July 15 and October 27, 1963 well over 700 anti-Peking articles appeared in the Soviet press, of which some 430 appeared between September 1 and October 27.[21] Here it is possible only to indicate some of the key new points raised by Soviet spokesmen during the latter period.

The most virulent attack appeared in the Soviet party magazine *Kommunist* in late October, clearly reflecting Moscow's rage at the anti-Khrushchev barbs the Chinese had loosed in their discussion of Stalin a month earlier. "The political and ideological conceptions of the Chinese Communist party theoreticians coincide in large measure with those of the Trotskyites," *Kommunist* declared. It accused Peking of trying to form an international bloc composed mainly of unprincipled people in many lands who had been expelled from their national Communist parties. The Chinese were seeking to win "cheap popularity" among the peoples of Asia, Africa and Latin America in order "to establish over them their [*i.e.*, Chinese] hegemony and to utilize them for egoistical, great power goals." "Great harm is being caused to socialism and the entire revolutionary movement," *Kommunist* warned, "and each Communist, no matter in what country he lives or in what situation he fights for his ideals must do everything possible in order to stop the development of events in the direction Peking desires." But the sharpest attack was on Mao Tse-tung:

> The statements of the Chinese directors against overcoming the cult of Stalin's personality are a crusade against the method of collective leadership, an appeal to support the conversion of Mao Tse-tung into a god, a cause Chinese propaganda has been intensively occupied with. For several years such preaching of the cult of Mao Tse-tung's personality has been actively carried on in the ranks of the Chinese Communist party and among the broadest groups of the Chinese people. With full definiteness it may be said that the Communist movement has collided with an effort to replace Leninism with 'Mao Tse-tungism.' . . . We are witnesses to a crusade against Marxism-Leninism such as has not been seen since the time of Trotsky.

But the most somber portion of this statement was a passage warning the Chinese that by whipping up the passions of nationalism they were sowing the seeds of possible bloody future conflicts:

> It is impossible to ignore the slander and misinformation in relation to the Communist party of the Soviet Union, the Soviet Government, the leaders of brotherly parties, in relation to their policies in the decisive problems of the life of contemporary society; these slanders and misinformation are seeds of dissension which are being energetically disseminated now by Chinese propaganda through the entire world. These seeds can give the most harmful and, in their consequences, far reaching sprouts. They can give an abundant harvest for the renaissance of the most nationalistic reactionary tendencies. And then it will be too late for the Chinese leaders to say they did not want this. Communists cannot and do not have the right to stand on nationalist positions and occupy themselves with anti-Soviet, anti-Communist propaganda.[22]

These words sounded sanctimonious, however, to those aware of how often the Soviet leaders moved to mobilize Soviet and Russian nationalism on their own behalf. In the Soviet government's statement of September 20, 1963, for example, the picture of China threatening the Soviet borders was put before the Soviet people in these words:

> Beginning with 1960, Chinese servicemen and civilians have been systematically violating the Soviet border. In the single year of 1962, more than 5,000 violations of the Soviet border from the Chinese side were registered. Attempts are also being made to 'utilize' some parts of Soviet territory without permission.

> A Chinese citizen who crossed the border had the directive of the peoples committee of Heilungkiang Province which said: 'In catching fish on the disputed Amur and Ussuri River islands, our fishermen are often faced by demands of Soviet border guards that they leave these islands. We propose that fishing on the disputed islands be continued and the Soviet border guards be told the islands belong to China and that they are violating the border and not we.' . . .

> The Soviet Government has more than once proposed to the Chinese Government that consultations be held on the question of making more exact the different parts of the border line in order to avoid any possibility for misunderstanding. However the Chinese side has declined such consultations, while at the same time violating the border.

> This cannot but make us wary, especially in view of the fact that Chinese propaganda is making definite hints about the past injustice of some parts of the border.

> However, the artificial creation in our times of any territorial problems, especially between socialist countries, would be tantamount to embarking on a very dangerous path. If at present states begin to make territorial claims on one another using as arguments some ancient data and the graves of their forefathers, if they start fighting for the revision of the historically developed frontiers, this will lead to no good, merely creating feuds among all the peoples to the joy of the enemies of peace.[23]

In Kazakhstan, where much of the population consists of the same peoples as inhabit Sinkiang, a public drive was conducted in September 1963 to paint a picture of Chinese persecution of the non-Chinese inhabitants of Sinkiang. The tone of this campaign is suggested by this extract of an article by a Soviet citizen who had returned from Sinkiang after serving as a Chinese major general:

> How bitter it is to know that thousands of my brothers, Uigurs and Kazakhs, Kirghiz and Mongols, have remained there, beyond the barricade, and are being subjected today to incredible persecution and repression. . . . I saw how the Chinese leaders were treating the national minorities in an increasingly harsh way. Peking does not hide its goal of 'Sinifying' Sinkiang, of fencing it off from its northern neighbor, the Soviet Union, with a blank wall. . . .

> With what can one compare the monstrous, unprecedented incident that occurred in May 1962, after my departure! Forty dwellers of the Ili-Kazakh Province went to the local party committee, seeking permission to leave for the Soviet Union. But the officials there did not even want to listen to them. And when more than 300 persons gathered before the party committee building, bursts of machine gun fire from the windows scoured the crowd. From the military district headquarters across the street fire was also opened and people were shot in the back. Ordinary people—shepherds and farmers—fell, mowed down by a scythe of lead, and as they fell they cursed the maniacs driven mad by a thirst for power.[24]

Many more such examples of Soviet vitriol directed against China during the late summer and early fall of 1963 could be cited here, as could other similar examples of anti-Soviet Chinese prose. But the quality of mutual bitterness, nationalistic hatred, and—between Mao Tse-tung and Nikita Khrushchev—personal enmity which dominated these exchanges should be clear enough from the examples given above. Whatever the future might bring, the Sino-Soviet war of words during June-October 1963 had proved that as November 1963 began the two largest and most powerful Communist-ruled nations on earth were deadly enemies engaged in as bitter and potentially explosive a struggle as any witnessed during the more than 300 years which had elapsed since Russian and Chinese subjects first met—and exchanged shots—on the Amur River in the 1650's.

CHAPTER XI

The Past as Prologue

THE SUMMER of 1900 was a bad one for white men in China. The Boxer Rebellion was in full swing. While the legation quarter fought off the famous siege in Peking, Boxer forces in the provinces were killing such missionaries and other whites as they could find. The rampant Chinese xenophobia had a field day in Manchuria where thousands of Russians had come in connection with the building of the Chinese Eastern Railroad. Those Russians who could, fled to safety across the Amur or to Port Arthur; many of those who did not flee in time were murdered. But horrible as the atrocities committed by the Boxers were, the height of barbarism in that period was reached by the Russians. Here is a contemporary account of what happened that bloody summer to the Chinese population of the Russian city of Blago-veshchensk:

> The entire Chinese population of 5,000 souls was escorted out of town to a spot five miles up the Amur, and then, being led in batches of a few hundreds to the river bank, was ordered to cross over to the Chinese side. No boats were provided and the river is a mile wide.

> The Chinese were flung alive into the stream, and were stabbed or shot at the least resistance, while Russian volunteers who lined the bank, clubbed or shot any who attempted to land. Not one escaped alive. The river bank for miles was strewn with corpses.[1]

During the 1950's and early 1960's, most Americans were deceived by the notion that Communism had united Russia and China and made them virtually one in presenting a menace to this

235

country and the rest of the non-Communist world. The historical record—of which the horrible story recounted above is but one small part—revealing the elemental passions and the deep fears which divide Russia and China was disregarded by both American policy makers and American public opinion. As late as January 1963—when it took no great discernment to see the fundamental fissures reappearing in the Sino-Soviet relationship—President Kennedy still expressed predominant American thinking when he declared in his State of the Union Message that "the Soviet-Chinese disagreement is over means, not ends. A dispute over how best to bury the Free World is no ground for Western rejoicing."

On the contrary, the historical record suggests that the reverse is much more nearly true, that the present Soviet-Chinese dispute —like Russian-Chinese conflicts earlier—is far more about ends than about means. At the heart of the struggle is Lenin's old but still fundamental question, "*kto-kogo?*" which in this context may be translated as "who shall rule whom?" Shall Russia dictate to China or China to Russia? Shall Khrushchev or Mao Tse-tung be the ruler of the world Communist movement? Shall Communism be, as in Stalin's time, an instrument of Russian imperial policy or of Chinese imperial policy? This is what the struggle is all about; the rest is propaganda to deceive the innocent and credulous. Behind the Marxist-Leninist doubletalk of both sides, the discerning eye perceives the conflict of national ambitions and the play of national fears. And the conflict is exacerbated in this case because Russians are white-skinned and now relatively rich, while Chinese are yellow-skinned and, in the mass, among the most desperately poor people on this planet.

Both sides, of course, are trying to misrepresent each other's position. It is no more true that the Chinese Communist regime is ruled by madmen who look forward to blowing up the world— as Moscow claims—than it is that the Soviet Union has entered into an alliance with the United States to keep down the peoples of Asia, Africa and Latin America as Peking would have the world believe. On the first issue, the real difference between Moscow and Peking is the degree of risk which each is willing to accept in seeking to make gains at United States or free world expense. That Khrushchev is willing to take a calculated risk was shown when he put his rockets into Cuba; what he was not willing to do was to take the greater risk that President Kennedy might carry out his threats if those rockets were not removed. The Chinese argument comes down to asserting that at the point of crisis, the United States would not dare use its nuclear weapons, having too much to lose itself in the event of thermonuclear war. On the second issue, Peking chooses to interpret Moscow's relatively cautious policy as betrayal, but no American should need to be persuaded that there is no Soviet-American alliance. The kernel of truth in all this, of course, is that the United States and the Soviet Union have a common interest in retaining as much of their primacy in atomic weapons as possible, and therefore in trying to hinder not only China but all other nations from acquiring nuclear weapons. It was the realization of that common interest which finally secured the limited nuclear test-ban treaty initialed on July 25, 1963. But it is indicative of the strength of the continuing suspicion between the two countries that they have not agreed on a total nuclear test-ban, one omitting the possibilities which the permitted underground tests leave open for present non-nuclear powers.

For many Americans, no doubt, Moscow's most persuasive and attractive argument against the Chinese is that dealing with racism. A reverse racism has long resulted in widespread American and Western European speculation about a Soviet-American alliance against China. Yet it is important to realize that here, too, Moscow goes too far and that it would be dangerous to accept the Soviet view of China. Clearly the Chinese use the slogan "Colored Peoples Unite" as an argument in some situations, but that is only one weapon in their armory. They are as ready to accept the allegiance of militant leftist whites—such as the group which controls the pro-Peking New Zealand Communist party— as they are of non-whites. Moreover, a view of a racist China intent upon organizing the colored peoples of the world in a color war clashes sharply with the reality of Chinese border demands on India, the second largest non-white nation on earth. Finally it was all too little noted that when Mao Tse-tung spoke out to take advantage of the 1963 Negro ferment in the United States, he took a position that was essentially Marxist, not racist. His words are worth quoting:

> In the United States, it is only the reactionary ruling circles among the whites who are oppressing the Negro people. They

can in no way represent the workers, farmers, revolutionary intellectuals and other enlightened persons who comprise the overwhelming majority of the white people.[2]

This is a far cry from the position of the Black Muslims or other racist groups among American Negroes. The point is worth repeating: the Chinese will use racism when it suits their purposes; they will eschew racism when such action better suits their needs. And even if the Chinese should in the future go over to a completely racist line, they will have no easy time convincing millions of Asians that Peking stands for the welfare of all non-whites, rather than for the welfare of China. In many parts of Asia, it is worth remembering, the Chinese are the merchants, the money lenders and the industrialists whose prosperity and exactions make them objects of envy and hatred among other Asians. The anti-Chinese campaigns in rural Indonesia in recent years are a case in point.

We could go on analyzing the fallacies and misrepresentations which abound in each side's arguments, but the above should at least indicate how critically each side's propaganda is most wisely received.

What of the future? Is a reconciliation between China and the Soviet Union likely in the foreseeable period ahead?

So long as both Khrushchev and Mao Tse-tung are alive, a genuine reconciliation seems unlikely. Too much bitterness has welled up in the two men's relationships to permit peace short of one capitulating to the other, which each is determined never to do. The probability that one or both of these old men will die or be removed from the scene by severe illness during the next decade is high. Then some easing of the present high tension between the two countries is conceivable, and we have the example of the post-Stalinist easing of relations between the Soviet Union and Yugoslavia as an example. But even between Moscow and Belgrade the much improved situation as of September 1963 is still a far cry from the subordination Yugoslavia was subjected to in 1946 and 1947. Similar considerations apply in the case of Russia and China. An improvement of relations in the future is certainly conceivable, but the lessons both sides learned about each other in the years 1949–1963 and the bitterness of the present period will not be forgotten for a long time to come. For the years immediately ahead, the likelihood is that the two countries will be on unfriendly terms and that the two Communist parties will head what may be equivalent to separate and competing international Communist movements.

But future Soviet-Chinese relations do not depend only upon what happens in those two countries; they will also be profoundly influenced by United States policy. With the wisdom of hindsight, we may wonder if the tension-racked alliance of the past would have survived as long as it did if the United States had given the Chinese any alternative to the Soviet tie. Should the United States in this new period continue its policy of undeviating hostility to Peking, its almost complete ban upon political, economic, cultural and other relations between the United States and China? Moscow would obviously like us to do so, and much of its current anti-Chinese propaganda is designed to encourage and inflame American fear and dislike of China. But what is in Soviet interest is not necessarily in United States interest.

The essence of the matter here is that it is in the American interest to help sustain Chinese independence of the Soviet Union. For the time being the facts of geography and of Chinese weakness in long-range modern weapons delivery systems make China far more of a problem for the Soviet Union than it is for the United States. The United States has sought to discourage Chinese aggression against the American client states in Southeast Asia by the threat of armed force. Is there not also a case for trying to discourage such aggression through diplomacy, through the use of the economic weapons at our command? Communist China today is the only important underdeveloped country receiving no economic aid from any source. Might it not be worthwhile to explore what easing of political tensions with China we might obtain by agreeing to normalize trade or even, if Peking is willing to pay the price, to extend economic aid? Those who share the Soviet-painted image of a China ruled by madmen hell-bent for war will dismiss such ideas immediately. Those who have watched the careful and clever way in which China has mended its relations with Ceylon, Burma, Nepal and Pakistan may feel more charitably inclined toward such explorations.

The point is that the Soviet-Chinese split has shattered the image of a world divided into two ideological camps between whom compromise or normal diplomatic maneuver are impossible. Instead, we face the reality of a world divided into many nations, each pursuing its own interests, and some—like the Russians and the Chinese—using ideology as a weapon to serve those interests, as well, of course, as having their image of their own interests also molded to some extent by that ideology. If we now view China as a national state serving its national interests rather than as part of an implacable conspiracy dedicated solely to our extermination, the possibility of accommodation for mutual advantage cannot be excluded. We have already granted such possibility in the case of the Soviet Union. Why must China be regarded as so much more evil than its former partner and ally?

This point of view is by no means intended to suggest an American-Chinese alliance against Russia. Rather it seeks to point out that if international tension is to be decisively reduced, Chinese-American as well as Soviet-American relations must be improved. We are not parties to the Soviet-Chinese dispute, but we would be negligent of our interests if we did not try to take advantage of that dispute to improve our own position relative to both powers. President Kennedy spoke grimly at his press conference on August 1, 1963 of the perspectives posed for the 1970's by a Stalinist China with nuclear weapons. Such prospects are not reassuring but they should be even more disturbing for the Russians than for us. We do not know how strong China may be in the 1970's, but there is every reason to suppose that the Soviet Union will be even stronger then than it is now. For an equilibrium in the Eurasian continent is there not merit in thinking of a stronger China as a counterweight to Russia? Suppose the Soviet Union of the 1970's is Stalinist? Would it not be useful to have that state concerned about the security of its Asian borders as a means of discouraging possible aggression? These are elementary considerations of balance of power politics. Moreover, we should not forget that however strong China may be in the 1970's, it is unlikely to be the military equal of either the Soviet Union or the United States. It is China today which is a "paper tiger" and it will be a long time before China can have the hydrogen bombs, the intercontinental ballistic missiles and the military capabilities in space which are likely to be the hallmarks of major military powers in the 1970's.

These reflections deal mainly with policy for the near future and the medium future. Any attempt to think of long-range American policy must start from the premise that in a world of terrible weapons such as humanity now possesses there is no viable alternative to real peace and genuine coexistence. We must aim to live in peace and friendship with the Soviet Union and China and with all the other countries of the world. The goal will clearly not be easy to gain. The Soviet Union has by no means given up its ambitions and Khrushchev still dreams of a Moscow-dominated world Communist community. Fortunately the break with China almost guarantees that these ideas are fantasies. In China, the frustrations, hatreds, pressures and xenophobia born of a century of exploitation at foreign hands, of abysmal mass poverty in an era when abundance has for the first time been realized over a significant portion of the world and of unceasing population growth pose even more explosive possibilities than those inherent in Moscow's dreams of glory.

The years since 1945 have shown that all the great nations of the world have been willing to exert immense efforts and to spend almost incredible sums to prosecute the struggle we call the Cold War. That struggle, as we have known it since 1945, was ended by the Soviet-Chinese split. It remains to be seen whether the people and nations of the world are able and willing to apply the same kinds and amounts of effort, resources and imagination to creating the only kind of world in which peace and human survival are assured: a world in which the vast sums now being spent on instruments of destruction are diverted to the nobler and wiser goal of helping raise all humanity to the levels of health and prosperity which today are enjoyed only in North America, Europe, Japan, Australia and New Zealand.

Notes

CHAPTER I

[1] These statements were broadcast respectively by Radio Peking on July 31, 1963, and by Radio Moscow on August 3, 1963.

[2] The quotation is from President de Gaulle's press conference on July 29, 1963, as translated into English by the French Press and Information Service in the United States.

[3] Harry Schwartz, *Russia Enters the 1960's*. Philadelphia: Lippincott, 1962, p. 33.

[4] Mao Tse-tung, *Selected Works*. Peking: Foreign Languages Press, 1956, vol. III, pp. 73–74.

[5] Immanuel C. Y. Hsü, *China's Entrance into the Family of Nations*. Cambridge: Harvard University Press, 1960, pp. 3–8.

[6] G. F. Hudson, *Europe and China*. Boston: Beacon Press, 1961, p. 9.

[7] William Theodore de Bary *et al.*, compilers, *Sources of Chinese Tradition*. New York: Columbia University Press, 1960, pp. 708–709.

[8] Hans Kohn, ed., *The Mind of Modern Russia*. New Brunswick: Rutgers University Press, 1955, pp. 256–257.

CHAPTER II

[1] Olga Andreyev Carlisle, *Voices in the Snow*. New York: Random House, 1962, pp. 135–136.

[2] From *The Diary of a Writer*, vol. II.

[3] Abram Tertz, *On Socialist Realism*. New York: Pantheon, 1960, pp. 72–73.

[4] Michel N. Pavlovsky, *Chinese-Russian Relations*. New York: Philosophical Library, 1949, pp. 4–5.

[5] M. I. Sladkovsky, *Ocherki Ekonomicheskikh Otnosheni SSSR s Kitaem*. Moscow: Vneshtorgizdat, 1957, p. 16.

[6] Cheng Tien-fong, *A History of Sino-Russian Relations*. Washington: Public Affairs Press, 1957, p. 21.

[7] Pavlovsky, *op. cit.*, p. 127.

[8] Sladkovsky, *op. cit.*, p. 21.

[9] Pavlovsky, *op. cit.*, p. 114.

[10] Cf. a translation of the treaty in Victor A. Yakhontoff, *Russia and the Soviet Union in the Far East*. New York: Coward-McCann, 1931, pp. 351–352.

[11] *Bolshaya Sovetskaya Entsiklopediya*, 2nd ed., vol. XXIX, p. 488.

CHAPTER III

[1] Michel N. Pavlovsky, *Chinese-Russian Relations*. New York: Philosophical Library, 1949, p. 29.

[2] *Ibid.*, pp. 29–30.

[3] *Ibid.*, pp. 31-32.

[4] David J. Dallin, *The Rise of Russia in Asia*. New Haven: Yale University Press, 1949, p. 18.

[5] *Ibid.*, pp. 18, 20.

[6] Peter S. H. Tang, *Russian and Soviet Policy in Manchuria and Outer Mongolia 1911–1931*. Durham: Duke University Press, 1959, p. 24.

[7] Immanuel C. Y. Hsü, *China's Entrance into the Family of Nations*. Cambridge: Harvard University Press, 1960, pp. 103–105.

[8] *Diplomaticbesky Slovar*. Moscow: Gosudarstvennoye Izdatelstvo Politicheskoy Literatury, 1960, vol. I, p. 25.

[9] Owen Lattimore, *Pivot of Asia*. Boston: Little, Brown and Company, 1950, p. 28.

[10] Cheng Tien-fong, *A History of Sino-Russian Relations*. Washington: Public Affairs Press, 1957, p. 47.

[11] Lattimore, *op. cit.*, p. 42.

CHAPTER IV

[1] Teng Ssu-yü and John K. Fairbank, *China's Response to the West*. Cambridge: Harvard University Press, 1954, p. 48.

[2] A. Lobanov-Rostovsky, *Russia and Asia*. Ann Arbor: George Wahr, 1951, p. 223.

[3] Edward H. Zabriskie, *American-Russian Rivalry in the Far East*. Philadelphia: University of Pennsylvania Press, 1946, p. 26.

[4] David J. Dallin, *The Rise of Russia in Asia*. New Haven: Yale University Press, 1949, p. 35.

[5] Zabriskie, *op. cit.*, p. 27.

[6] *Ibid.*, p. 35.

[7] Victor A. Yakhontoff, *Russia and the Soviet Union in the Far East*. New York: Coward-McCann, 1931, p. 366.

[8] Zabriskie, *op. cit.*, pp. 88–89.

[9] Peter Fleming, *The Siege at Peking*. New York: Harper & Brothers, 1959, pp. 242–243.

[10] Michael T. Florinsky, *Russia, A History and an Interpretation*. New York: Macmillan, 1953, vol. II, pp. 1267–1268.

[11] William L. Langer, *The Diplomacy of Imperialism*. New York: Knopf, 1960, pp. 714–715.

[12] Zabriskie, *op. cit.*, p. 95.

CHAPTER V

[1] Edward H. Zabriskie, *American-Russian Rivalry in the Far East*. Philadelphia: University of Pennsylvania Press, 1946, p. 144.

[2] Peter S. H. Tang, *Russian and Soviet Policy in Manchuria and Outer Mongolia 1911–1931*. Durham: Duke University Press, 1959, p. 53.

[3] *Ibid.*, pp. 290–291.

CHAPTER VI

[1] Conrad Brandt, *Stalin's Failure in China*. Cambridge: Harvard University Press, 1958, p. 153.

[2] Allen S. Whiting, *Soviet Policies in China 1917–1924*. New York: Columbia University Press, 1954, pp. 270–271.

³ X. J. Eudin and Robert C. North, *Soviet Russia and the East 1920–1927*. Stanford: Stanford University Press, 1957, p. 200.

⁴ David J. Dallin, *The Rise of Russia in Asia*. New Haven: Yale University Press, 1949, p. 192.

⁵ Whiting, *op. cit.*, p. 105. Quoted from *Pravda*, March 4, 1923.

⁶ *Ibid.*, p. 104.

⁷ Peter S. H. Tang, *Russian and Soviet Policy in Manchuria and Outer Mongolia 1911–1931*. Durham: Duke University Press, 1959, p. 154.

⁸ Eudin and North, *op. cit.*, p. 65.

⁹ Whiting, *op. cit.*, p. 51.

¹⁰ Benjamin I. Schwartz, *Chinese Communism and the Rise of Mao*. Cambridge: Harvard University Press, 1951, p. 37.

¹¹ Brandt, *op. cit.*, pp. 26–27.

¹² *Ibid.*, pp. 32–33.

¹³ Cheng Tien-fong, *A History of Sino-Russian Relations*. Washington: Public Affairs Press, 1957, pp. 124–125.

CHAPTER VII

¹ Henry Wei, *China and Soviet Russia*. Princeton: D. Van Nostrand, 1956, p. 109.

² Owen Lattimore, *Pivot of Asia*. Boston: Little, Brown and Company, 1950, p. 63. Quotation is from *Izvestiya*, January 8, 1928.

³ Alexander Barmine, *One Who Survived*. New York: G. P. Putnam's Sons, 1945, p. 231.

⁴ Charles B. McLane, *Soviet Policy and the Chinese Communists 1931–1946*. New York: Columbia University Press, 1958, p. 9.

⁵ Benjamin I. Schwartz, *Chinese Communism and the Rise of Mao*. Cambridge: Harvard University Press, 1951, p. 136.

CHAPTER VIII

¹ Charles B. McLane, *Soviet Policy and the Chinese Communists 1931–1946*. New York: Columbia University Press, 1958, p. 160.

² Department of State, *United States Relations with China*. Washington: Government Printing Office, 1949, pp. 113–114.

³ McLane, *op. cit.*, pp. 162–163.

⁴ *Ibid.*, p. 165.

⁵ *Ibid.*, p. 1.

⁶ Cheng Tien-fong, *A History of Sino-Russian Relations*. Washington: Public Affairs Press, 1957, p. 243.

⁷ Milovan Djilas, *Conversations with Stalin*. New York: Harcourt, Brace and World, 1962, p. 182.

⁸ Harry Schwartz, *Russia's Postwar Economy*. Syracuse: Syracuse University Press, 1947, p. 106.

⁹ Allen S. Whiting and General Sheng Shih-tsai, *Sinkiang: Pawn or Pivot?* East Lansing: Michigan State University Press, 1958, p. 117.

CHAPTER IX

¹ Harry Schwartz, *The Red Phoenix*. New York: Praeger, 1961, p. 402.

² Russian texts of these documents will be found in *Sovetsko-Kitaiskie Otnosheniya 1917–1957*. Moscow: Izdatelstvo Vostochnoi Literatury, 1959, pp. 217–226.

[3] Allen S. Whiting, "'Contradictions' in the Moscow-Peking Axis," in John H. Hallowell, ed., *Soviet Satellite Nations: A Study of the New Imperialism*. Gainesville: Kallman Publishing Company, 1958, p. 130. Mr. Whiting cites a New China News Agency release from Peking dated June 18, 1957.

[4] All data in this paragraph from M. I. Sladkovsky, *Ocherki Ekonomicheskikh Otnosheni SSSR s Kitaem*. Moscow: Vneshtorgizdat, 1957, pp. 310, 360.

[5] David J. Dallin, *Soviet Foreign Policy After Stalin*. Philadelphia: Lippincott, 1961, pp. 78, 92.

[6] Whiting, "'Contradictions' in the Moscow-Peking Axis," *op. cit.*, p. 129.

[7] Data from Sladkovsky, *op. cit.*, p. 332 and *Vneshnyaya Torgovlya SSSR za 1956 god*. Moscow: Vneshtorgizdat, 1958, p. 9.

[8] These and other materials from the Chinese Communist party statement of September 1963 are taken from the text in the *New York Times*, September 14, 1963.

[9] *Izvestiya*, January 19, 1957.

[10] Marshall I. Goldman, "Sino-Soviet Trade: A Barometer." *Problems of Communism*, November–December 1962, p. 48.

[11] The revelation was made in the official statement of the Chinese government dated August 15, 1963, and transmitted by the New China News Agency on that date. The text appeared in *Pravda*, August 21, 1963.

[12] This past section based on *Sovetsko-Kitaiskiye Otnosheniya*. Moscow: Izdatelstvo Vostochnoi Literatury, 1959, p. 365. *Pravda*, August 12, 1963. Donald S. Zagoria, *The Sino-Soviet Conflict 1956–1961*. Princeton: Princeton University Press, 1962, pp. 146, 160.

[13] *Communist China 1955–1959*. Cambridge: Harvard University Press, 1962, p. 456.

[14] The full text of Khrushchev's speech is in *Pravda*, January 28, 1959.

[15] *Communist China 1955–1959, op. cit.*, pp. 559–560.

[16] *Peking Review*, No. 6, 1960, p. 31.

[17] *Peking Review*, No. 17, 1960, p. 26.

[18] *Pravda*, April 23, 1960.

[19] *Peking Review*, No. 24, 1960, p. 35.

[20] *Sovetskaya Rossiya*, June 10, 1960.

[21] Khrushchev quotation is from *Pravda*, June 22, 1960. Chinese statement is from the *New York Times*, September 14, 1963.

[22] *Sovetskaya Latviya*, August 16, 1960.

[23] Harry Schwartz, *op. cit.*, pp. 401–403.

[24] *Ibid.*, pp. 403–404 and William E. Griffith, "The November 1960 Moscow Meeting: A Preliminary Reconstruction," Walter Laqueur and Leopold Labedz, eds., *Polycentrism*. New York: Praeger, 1962, pp. 107–126.

[25] Sh. Sanakoyev, "The Socialist Community and Mankind's Progress," *International Affairs*, No. 3, 1962, pp. 6–12.

[26] Harry Schwartz, *Russia Enters the 1960's*. Philadelphia: Lippincott, 1962, p. 33.

[27] *Ibid.*, p. 120.

[28] *Pravda*, December 13, 1962.

[29] V. Kudryavtsev, "Problems of Afro-Asian Solidarity," *International Affairs*, No. 5, 1963, p. 52.

[30] "Whence the Differences?" Editorial in the Peking *Jenmin Jih Pao*, February 26, 1963.

[31] *Ibid.*

[32] *Peking Review*, No. 51, 1962, p. 9.
[33] *Peking Review*, No. 1, 1963, p. 12.
[34] *Peking Review*, No. 2, 1963, p. 8.
[35] *Peking Review*, Nos. 10 and 11, 1963, p. 61.
[36] *Ibid.*, p. 36.
[37] *Ibid.*, pp. 56–57.

CHAPTER X

[1] *New York Times*, June 11, 1963.
[2] *New York Times*, July 5, 1963.
[3] The text of the Soviet statement is in the *New York Times*, July 15, 1963.
[4] *Peking Review*, No. 30, 1963, pp. 28–29.
[5] *Izvestiya*, August 25, 1963.
[6] *Jenmin Jih Pao* editorial as quoted by New China News Agency dispatch from Peking, August 22, 1963.
[7] New China News Agency dispatch from Peking, August 7, 1963.
[8] *Kommunist*, No. 11, 1963, pp. 3–36 *passim*.
[9] New China News Agency dispatch from Peking, July 31, 1963.
[10] *Pravda* and *Izvestiya*, August 4, 1963.
[11] These quotations are taken from the text of the Chinese statement printed in *Peking Review*, No. 33, 1963.
[12] *Pravda*, August 21, 1963.
[13] *New York Times*, September 1, 1963.
[14] *Ibid.*, October 14, 1963.
[15] *Ibid.*, October 27, 1963.
[16] *Ibid.*, November 2, 1963.
[17] Taken from the full English text in *New York Times*, September 14, 1963.
[18] New China News Agency dispatch from Peking dated September 13, 1963.
[19] New China News Agency dispatch from Peking dated October 21, 1963.
[20] *Peking Review*, October 11, 1963, p. 14.
[21] *Jenmin Jih Pao*, October 31, 1963.
[22] *Kommunist*, No. 15, 1963, pp. 13–47 *passim*.
[23] *Pravda*, September 22, 1963.
[24] *Kazakhstanskaya Pravda*, September 29, 1963.

CHAPTER XI

[1] *New York Times*, September 1, 1900.
[2] *Peking Review*, No. 30, 1963, p. 7.

Appendix

RUSSIAN-CHINESE TRADE IN SELECTED YEARS, 1697–1962

Year	Russian Exports to China	Russian Imports from China
	(in millions of dollars*)	
1697	.11	.11
1729	.17	.17
1761	.58	.92
1800	4.88	4.88
1850	8.3	8.7
1893	3.6	29.0
1900	5.8	40.0
1910	17.6	68.7
1913†	25.1	65.9
1923/24	4.1	9.7
1930	24.8	21.3
1940‡	9.8	19.3
1944	.6	31.4
1948§	124.6	90.3
1949§	198.9	143.2
1950	388.2	191.3
1951	476.3	331.9
1952	550.2	413.7
1953	705.5	474.7
1954	759.3	578.3
1955	748.3	643.5
1956	733.0	764.2
1957	544.1	738.1
1958	634.0	881.3
1959	954.6	1100.3
1960	816.3	847.3
1961	367.0	550.9
1962	233.2	515.8

SOURCES: 1697–1955—M. I. Sladkovsky, *Ocherki Ekonomicheskikh Otnosheni SSSR s Kitaem*, pp. 359–60. 1956–1962—*Vneshnyaya Torgovlya SSSR* for corresponding years.

* Converted into dollars of present gold content taking account of the gold content of the ruble in different periods.

† Trade with Outer Mongolia not included in data for 1913 and later years.

‡ Does not include Soviet credit deliveries to China.

§ Includes trade with both Nationalist-controlled and Communist-controlled areas.

Index

Aigun, Treaty of, 52–3, 194
Albania, 13, 180, 187–8, 191, 217
Albazin, 29, 34–6
Alexander II, Tsar, 71
Alexeyev, Gen. Eugen, 71–8
Alexeyev-Tseng agreement, 73–5
Alma-Ata, 126, 147, 153
Altyn Khan, 27–8, 39
Amur River and region, 22, 28–36, 42–5, 50–2, 65–73, 158, 163, 235
Anglo-Japanese Treaty (1902), 75–6
Argun River, 22, 36, 41
Arshinsky, Danilo, 31

Baikov, Fyedor I., 30
Bakunin, Mikhail, 50
Bandung Conference, 154
Barga, 86, 90; Barguts, 90
Barmine, Alexander, 118
Bashkirs, 209
Berdyayev, Nikolai, 19
Beria, Lavrenti P., 12, 152
Bernstein, Eduard, 176
Bezobrazov, A. M., 71, 76–8
Blagoveshchensk, 73, 235
Blok, Aleksander, 25
Borodin, Michael, 92, 106–8
Boxer Rebellion, 70–3, 230; indemnity, 93–4, 100
Breckinridge, Clifton, 62
Bucharest congress (1960), 180–1
Buddhism, Buddhists, 15–6, 84, 90
Bulganin, Nikolai, 153, 155
Bur, Treaty of, 41
Burma, 16, 239

Camp David, 172, 174
Canton, 43, 46, 47, 53, 103, 108, 109, 120, 125, 142

Cassini, Count, 77
Castro, Fidel, 189, 200
Catherine the Great, 19, 27, 45
Changchun, 140
Changkufeng Hill, 124
Chang Tso-lin, 99, 100, 109
Chekiang, 120
Chen Tu-hsiu, 103
Chen Yi, 143, 182
Chiang Kai-shek, 92, 101, 106–11, 114, 119–28, 131–3, 145, 174
Chin Shu-jen, 117
Chinese Changchun Railroad, 134, 139, 140, 146, 149, 154
Chinese Communist letter of June 14, 1963, 202–10; replies, 211–27
Chinese Eastern Railroad, 67–8, 82–3, 93–9, 100, 106, 109–14, 132, 134
Chinese Peoples Republic, creation of, 142
Chinese Revolution (1912), 82–91
Chinese soviets, 119–20
Chita, 147
Chou En-lai, 13–4, 123, 151–2, 158–9, 168, 182, 186, 187
Christianity, 14, 15, 16, 32
Chu Tzu-chi, 221
Chungking, 125, 126, 130, 137
COMECON (Council for Mutual Economic Aid), 151, 207
Cominform (Communist Information Bureau), 151, 187
Comintern (Communist International), 119, 122, 128, 130
Communes, Chinese people's, 167–8, 222–3
Confucius, 16, 103
Crimean War, 52, 56
Cuba, 188, 190, 213, 220, 236

Dairen, 67–8, 79, 132, 134, 140, 146–7, 153
Daurs, 29
De Gaulle, Charles, 12, 225
Djety-shaar, Emirate of, 58–60
Djilas, Milovan, 137
Dogmatism, dogmatists, 176–8, 180, 191, 205–8
Dostoevsky, Fyedor, 26
Dzungars (Western Mongols), 40–2

Eisenhower, Dwight D., 166, 171–8
Engels, Friedrich, 92, 180
Extraterritoriality, 53–5, 100

Feng Kuei-fen, 17–8
Feng Yu-hsiang, 99
Formosa, 43, 65
Fukien, 68, 120

Gantimur, 31–4
Genghis Khan, 23, 84
Gerbillion, Father, 35
Ghandi, Mme. Indira, 219
Golovin, Fyedor A., 35
Golovkin, Count Y. A., 49
Gomulka, Wladyslaw, 159
"Great leap forward," 167–8, 222

Han people, 16, 23
Hankow, 108
Hanyang, 108
Harbin, 68, 83, 110, 140
Harriman, Edward H., 81
Harriman, W. Averell, 81, 136
Hay, John, 68, 71, 76–7
Himalayas, 189, 191
Ho Chi-minh, 152
Hong Kong, 191, 194
Hoxha, Enver, 188
Hsu Shu-tseng, Gen., 95
Humphrey, Sen. Hubert, 169
"Hundred flowers," 161
Hungarian Revolution (1956), 159

Ides, Izbrand, 38
Ignatiev, Gen. Nikolai, 53–4
Ili Valley, 58, 195; Treaty, 194
India, 172, 189, 191, 219
Irkutsk, 49, 86, 147
Irtysh River, 57
Ivan the Terrible, 24, 26

Joffe, Adolf, 99, 105
Juikin, 120

Kalgan, 28, 55
Kalmyks, 43, 56
Kamchatka, 48–9, 51–2, 56
Kang-Hsi, Emperor, 39, 40
Kang Sheng, 175
Kao Kang, 142
Karakhan, Leo, 99, 100; Declarations, 93–5, 99, 111
Kashgar, 54–9
Kazakhs, 55, 116
Kennedy, John F., 12, 189, 202–3, 236, 237, 240
Kerensky, Alexander, 94, 101
Khabarov, Yerofei P., 29
Khabarovsk Protocol (1929), 111
Khrushchev, Nikita S., 12, 13, 21, 152–8, 161 ff.
Khutukhtu (Urga), 85, 90, 95
Kiaochow, 67–8
Kirghiz, 56, 116
Kirin, 67, 140
Kolchak, Adm. Alexander, 93–5
Korea, 16, 63–4, 69–81; Korean War, 147–52, 155
Kowtow, 16, 30, 33
Kozlov, Frol R., 171, 172, 201
Kuldja, 55, 57, 59, 60, 61
Kuomintang, 98, 101, 104–28, 131, 137, 176; 1927 massacres, 108
Kuropatkin, Gen. Alexei, 61, 70–8
Kuusinen, Otto V., 178, 186
Kyakhta, 53, 55, 57, 88, 96; Treaty of, 41, 44, 84; details of trade, 44–8

Lake Baikal, 28, 35
Lake Bor Nor, 115
Lamsdorff, Count Vladimir, 70–7
Lanchow, 57, 126, 153
Langa, Lorents, 40–2
Lenin, Vladimir I., 12, 92, 97, 101–2, 151, 177–8, 180, 205, 216, 236
Li Hung-chang, 62–75, 83
Li Ta-chao, 103
Liaotung Peninsula, 65–79
Linevich, Gen., 72
Litvinov, Maxim, 114
Liu Shao-chi, 151, 158
Livadia, Treaty of, 60–1
Lobanov-Rostovsky, Prince A., 70
Long March, 120–1
Lumumba, Patrice, 220
Lung Yun, 148
Lushan meeting (1959), 172–3

Ma Chung-ying, Gen., 117–8
Ma Hu-shan, Gen., 124
Macao, 43, 191, 194
Maimachen, 47
Malenkov, Georgi, 12, 151–4
Manchukuo, creation of, 113–5
Manchuria, 22–3, 46, 65–7, 70, 73–8, 81–4, 91, 93, 99, 100, 109–14, 138–40
Mao Tse-tung, 12, 14, 15, 103, 119–28, 136–7; after 1949, 143 ff.
Maring, 103–5
Marx, Karl, 92, 103, 180
Matsu, 166
Matsumura, Kendzo, 222
Matsuoka, Yosuke, 127
Mif, Pavel, 119
Mikoyan, Anastas, 153, 158, 170
Mohammedanism, 15; Mohammedans, 60
Molotov, Vyacheslav, 133, 136, 152, 154, 161, 163, 186
Mongolia, 27–9, 37–42, 56; Outer, 22–3, 45, 81, 84–97, 99, 100, 109, 112–6, 127, 147
Mongolian National Bank, 88
Mongolian revolt (1911), 86, 96
Moshi conference (1963), 192, 199, 215
Moslems, 14, 16, 23, 56, 58, 116–7
Mukden, 78, 79, 81, 100, 112, 140
Muraviev, Nikolai, 49–52, 56

NATO powers, 211
Nagy, Imre, 12
Nanking, 108, 123, 142; Treaty of, 194
Napoleon, 19, 46, 49
Nehru, Jawaharlal, 189
Nepal, 239
Nerchinsk, 34, 35, 37, 52; Treaty of, 36–9, 51, 56
Nevelskoy, Capt. Gennadi, 51
Newchwang, 76
Nicholas I, Tsar, 49
Nicholas II, Tsar, 65, 66, 69, 71
Ningpo, 53
Nishi-Rosen Protocol (1898), 69
Nomonhan, 124
Nuclear test ban treaty, 12, 210, 223, 237

Ochab, Edward, 158

Okhotsk, 52
Open Door doctrine (U.S.), 68
Opium War, 49

Paikes, Alexander, 97, 99
Pakistan, 239
Pauley, Edwin W., 139
Peking, Treaty of, 54, 55, 58, 194
Peng Chen, Gen., 34
Peng Chen, 180
Pereira, Father, 35
Peter the Great, 19, 35, 37–43
Plehve, Vyacheslav, 76, 79
Port Arthur, 65–79, 132, 134, 140, 146, 149, 153, 235
Portsmouth, Treaty of. *See* Russo-Japanese Treaty of 1905.
Posyet Bay, 124
Poyarkov, Vasily, 28
Putyatin, Adm. Evfimi, 52, 54

Quemoy, 166

Racism, Chinese, 192, 199, 215–16, 220, 222, 237
Radek, Karl, 103
Raguzinsky, Count Savva V., 41
Revisionism, revisionists, 174–6, 194–6, 209; Yugoslav, 165–6, 176
Roosevelt, Franklin D., 131, 132, 201
Roy, M. N., 102, 108
Russian-Korean Bank, 69
Russo-Chinese Bank, 66–76
Russo-Chinese Declaration (1913), 87
Russo-Chinese Treaty (1902), 76
Russo-Japanese War of 1904–5, 76–9, 113, 132; Treaties—1905, 79, 80; 1907, 81; 1910, 81; 1912, 81; 1916, 81
Russo-Mongolian Treaty (1912), 87

St. Petersburg, Treaty of, 61
Sakhalin, 48, 50, 51, 56, 79, 132
San-go-tu, Prince, 35–6
Satyukov, Pavel, 186
Selenginsk, 40, 45
Semipalatinsk, 57, 116
Seoul, 63, 69
Shanghai, 53, 103, 108, 123
Shanhaikwan Pass, 140
Sheng Shih-tsai, Gen., 117–8, 124–5, 130–1, 141, 147
Shensi Province, 121
Shimonoseki conference, 65